Also by Gregg Olsen and Rebecca Morris
*If I Can't Have You: Susan Powell, Her Mysterious
Disappearance, and the Murder of Her Children*

Also by Gregg Olsen
NONFICTION
A Twisted Faith
The Deep Dark
Starvation Heights
Mockingbird (Cruel Deception)
If Loving You Is Wrong
Abandoned Prayers
Bitter Almonds
The Confessions of an American Black Widow

FICTION
Now That She's Gone
The Girl in the Woods
The Girl on the Run
Shocking True Story
Fear Collector
The Bone Box
Betrayal
Envy
Closer than Blood
Victim Six
Heart of Ice
A Cold Dark Place
A Wicked Snow

Also by Rebecca Morris
*Ted and Ann: The Mystery of a Missing Child and Her
Neighbor Ted Bundy*
*Bad Apples: Inside the Teacher/Student Sex Scandal
Epidemic*

A Killing in Amish Country

Sex, Betrayal, and a
Cold-Blooded Murder

Gregg Olsen and Rebecca Morris

St. Martin's Paperbacks

A KILLING IN AMISH COUNTRY

Copyright © 2016 by Gregg Olsen and Rebecca Morris. Foreword copyright © 2016 by Linda Castillo. Afterword copyright © 2016 by Karen M. Johnson-Weiner.

All rights reserved.

For information address St. Martin's Press, 175 Fifth Avenue, New York, NY 10010.

ISBN: 978-1-250-11870-7

Our books may be purchased in bulk for promotional, educational, or business use. Please contact your local bookseller or the Macmillan Corporate and Premium Sales Department at 1-800-221-7945, extension 5442, or by e-mail at MacmillanSpecialMarkets@macmillan.com.

Printed in the United States of America

St. Martin's Press hardcover edition / July 2016
St. Martin's Paperbacks edition / April 2017

St. Martin's Paperbacks are published by St. Martin's Press, 175 Fifth Avenue, New York, NY 10010.

10 9 8 7 6 5 4 3 2 1

For Barbara Weaver:
Remembered by her children,
forsaken by her husband

He who commits adultery lacks sense;
He who does it destroys himself.
—Proverbs 6:32

Contents

Dramatis Personae

The authors have elected to use pseudonyms for some in the narrative. They are indicated in *italics* here.

Candy Denton, one of Eli's girlfriends
Jamie Wood, cell mate of Barb Raber

FRIENDS & ACQUAINTANCES

Steve Chupp, fishing friend of Eli's
Mark Weaver, friend of Eli's
David Weaver, Barb Raber's former lover
Cora Anderson, contact of David Weaver, who offered to
    find a hit man
Ruby Hofstetter, childhood friend of Barbara Weaver

THE LAW

Michael Maxwell, Wayne County Sheriff's Office detective
John Chuhi, Wayne County Sheriff's Office detective
Joe Mullet, Holmes County Sheriff's Office deputy
Edna Boyle, Wayne County assistant district attorney
John Leonard, Barb Raber's defense attorney
Andy Hyde, Eli Weaver's attorney
Robert Brown, Wayne County Court of Common Pleas
    judge

Foreword

by Linda Castillo

GREGG OLSEN IS a master of true crime and one of the most respected writers of our time. I've had the pleasure of reading many of his books, two of which are true crime set among the Amish: *Abandoned Prayers* and this one (with Rebecca Morris), *A Killing in Amish Country.*

Amish society is deeply religious. For centuries, the culture has changed little and remains virtually untouched by outside influences. Most of us couldn't imagine living without cell phones and cars and all of the conveniences modern life offers. Yet the Amish continue to flourish without any of those things. No electricity. No telephones. No gasoline powered vehicles. The contrast of old versus new is profound.

One of the things that makes the Amish so fascinating is the fact that it is a closed society. Their church districts are tightly knit. Most children speak Pennsylvania Dutch before they speak English. Neighbors truly know their neighbors. Amish communities are connected in ways that mainstream America is not.

There's no doubt the Amish make good neighbors. They're good custodians of the land. Barn raisings are not an invention of Hollywood; they are part of Amish life. When tragedy strikes a neighbor—even if that neighbor is "English"—the Amish are the first in line to help in any way they can. Their lives revolve around family, worship, clean living, and hard work.

But no cultural group can always be so neatly categorized; no group is immune to the human weaknesses, faults, and frailties that affect all of us. As the authors so deftly underscore in *A Killing in Amish Country*, sometimes those all-too-human shortcomings manifest into something darker: The complete lack of a conscience. Lust. Narcissism. And a capacity for violence.

With *A Killing in Amish Country*, Gregg and Rebecca have written the stunning account of what happens when the dark side of human nature collides with the gentle and religious world of the Amish. Their research, not only on the legal and police procedural aspects of the crimes, but the details of Amish life most of us never see, is spot on and makes for an intense, educational, and addictive read.

1

Thunderclap

Where did my friend, love, trustworthy husband go to?
He hates me to the core.

—BARBARA WEAVER, IN A LETTER TO HER COUNSELOR
ABOUT THE DEEP DIVIDE IN HER MARRIAGE.

A pleasant stillness is one of the hallmarks of most June nights in Apple Creek, Ohio. No incessant chatter coming from the television. No buzzing of fluorescent lights. None of the loud voices that come from people who have had too much to drink and something to prove. Nothing wafts over the hilly terrain but the softness of warm air circulating around the plain white farmhouses, barns, and outbuildings that dot much of Wayne and Holmes Counties, where most of America's Amish people live.

From the outside, things are picture-perfect. Boys and men in light-blue shirts and suspender-supported trousers; girls and women in an array of dark purples, blues, and greens with paper-thin bonnets covering long hair pinned up on the back of their heads. Houses with no power lines. Dirt driveways rutted with buggy tracks.

That veneer of undeniable charm and quaintness belies reality. During the late-night hours of June 1, 2009, the quiet of the milieu ebbed when the clouds opened and it began to rain, then, drop after drop, the wind kicked up. There was thunder, too. The weather brought a kind of restlessness across the community. Some of the children in Eli and Barbara Weaver's house left their upstairs bedrooms and made their way downstairs to sleep away from the noise of the storm and closer to the master bedroom on the main floor.

With the light of a gas lantern casting long shadows over the room, Barbara, a pretty young mother with dark-blond hair, rocked her youngest, Lizzie. There was nothing more important to Barbara and her sister Fannie Troyer than their children. Barbara had five, and Fannie had four, all under the age of nine.

On this evening, there was a blended group sleeping at the Weavers'. Four of Barbara's children, Harley, Sarah, Joseph, and Lizzie Weaver, and their cousins Susie and Mary Troyer, were winding down after a day of play. Barbara encouraged them to speak in hushed tones so as not wake the ones that were beginning to get drowsy in Barbara's bed. The cousins had come to the Weavers', and Barbara's son Jacob had stayed at her sister's house, after a birthday party for nine-year old Harley at the Troyers' the night before.

Susie settled on the sofa and Harley found a cozy spot on the recliner that was his father's main place of refuge when he was home and not working at the family's hunting and fishing supply business, Maysville Outfitters. Except Eli Weaver was rarely home, and he didn't consider it a sanctuary. None of the children would recall seeing much, if anything, of the Amish man in recent days. Which wasn't new. He was almost never home for meals—an important time in Amish family life—and he didn't like his children hanging out at his store. At least twice in their young lives he had disappeared for weeks or months at a time.

At some point in the early morning of June 2, Eli came home and carried Mary, Sarah, and Joseph upstairs. He had just a couple of hours to get some sleep before he left on a fishing trip to Lake Erie.

After little Lizzie cried out from her room on the main floor, Susie left the living room and slept upstairs for the rest of the night. That left just Harley on the other side of his parents' bedroom wall.

With the gaslights off and the wind rolling across the farmhouse, Harley listened as the shower ran in the bathroom down the hallway. Soon after, slumber overtook him. Only once during the night did he stir. A thunderclap, he thought, woke him. But he turned over and fell back to sleep.

Later, the boy would play that noise over and over in his head, trying to pinpoint just what it was that he'd heard.

And what or who had made the sound.

AROUND 8:00 A.M., the house stirred to life. It was late. Barbara Weaver liked to get up early and write in her journal. But when the girls in the upstairs bedroom awoke, the house was silent. As the oldest girl, Susie got up and started to help with the children—a role she enjoyed. But Mary wanted breakfast and Lizzie was crying, and it was a bit too much for Susie to handle.

Then Susie heard the younger children shrieking. Still in her nightclothes, she followed the sobbing down the hall to her Aunt Barbara's room.

When she pushed open the bedroom door, Susie knew

something was very wrong. Her sister, Mary, and her cousins Sarah and Joseph were clutching at the comforter. Barbara Weaver was still, her bedding splattered with red.

Blood?

Susie hurried out of the bedroom and found Harley.

In the Pennsylvania Dutch dialect spoken by the Amish, she cried out to get his attention. Harley hurried into his parents' bedroom. It was as though the house were alive by then, breathing in, sucking all of the children into that one room. They surrounded the bed. They cried out. They screamed.

Something's wrong!

With a trembling hand, the boy touched his mother's leg. It was cool.

Something's very wrong!

Susie thought it was possible that Barbara had been sick and maybe thrown up some blood. The color red was imprinted on the minds of the young people looking on and wondering what had happened.

Why isn't she answering? Why isn't Mama moving?

Harley, who had been around guns all his life—his father had a shop that sold them—knew what had happened. Their mother had been shot. He was almost certain of it. Even so, the boy wracked his brain. It didn't quite compute. He hadn't heard any gunfire.

Just a thunderclap in the storm.

IN THE CHAOS of that moment, the children tugged at their mother. One of them tried to open her eyes. They called out for her to wake up, but her eyes looked into nothingness. Her lips were tinged a strange hue. Someone pulled back the comforter, revealing an ugly hole in their mother's chest.

Harley extricated himself from the room and the confused and frightened children. He dressed as fast as his arms could move. There was no phone in the house. No way to call for an ambulance. Though he was sure his mother was dead, a tremendous urgency fueled each step as he ran across the road to the home of Linda and Firman Yoder. He needed help. They all needed help.

Something terrible has happened to our mother!

On that June day, things began to change in Amish country. Quiet nights, a distancing from modern technology, a promise to stay close as a family and a community—all of what makes up the Amish way of life—would unravel like the frayed edges of a treasured quilt. And like torn fabric, things never could be completely mended. The damage would always be visible.

2

The House

*He wants me to be the submissive little wife and
I want to be, but what's right counts more.*
—Barbara Weaver, on the expectations
she felt as an Amish wife

The half-eaten birthday cake was gone. It had sat forlornly on the kitchen counter for days. The bloody comforter with a bullet hole had been removed, too. Later, twelve jurors and two alternates would see photographs of the house as it was the day thirty-year-old Barbara Weaver, devout Amish wife and mother of five, was murdered in cold blood. Now it was just a nearly empty structure, the scene of a heinous crime. Little was left of what had made the house a home.

On Thursday, September 17, 2009, three months and fifteen days after Barbara Weaver was killed with a .410 gauge shotgun to the chest, jury members walked through the two-story house on Harrison Road, in Apple Creek Township, in Wayne County, Ohio. Wayne County and its neighbor Holmes County are home to the majority of the sixty thousand Amish in Ohio.

There were no Amish on the jury. Because they believe in forgiveness and not judging others, the Amish have long been excused from jury duty. Ohio made it official in 2004, adopting a law excusing the Amish from jury duty for religious reasons.

Unlike the homes of jury members, the house did not have electricity. The Weavers used propane to heat water, operate a stove, and light the home, shop, and barns. A refrigerator with the electrical parts removed and a new chunk of ice every week kept perishables chilled.

There was no telephone and no SUV parked in the driveway. The Amish have rules—many unwritten but adopted over the years—called the Ordnung (the German word for "order"), guidelines for life and the use of conveniences the majority of Americans take for granted. The Ordnung isn't static; it can change and has changed, in some groups more than in others. Andy Weaver Amish—the order that the Weavers were members of—is much slower to adapt than some other Amish groups. Though some of the Ordnung goes back as far as the 1800s, new inventions and innovations have led to modifications. Some things haven't changed. The Amish make a distinction between ownership and use. In the 1920s the Amish set rules concerning modern life that stand today: they may ride in a motor vehicle but not drive one, and they may use a telephone but not have one in the house. After all, no one would visit if they could phone instead.

The Amish are not Luddites who find technology frightening. They just believe it's important to adhere to the old ways. When a new invention or new technology arrives on the scene, the Amish are concerned not only with how it will affect their lives, but also with how it will affect their children and grandchildren, too. They believe the focus in America is on the individual. *Their* focus is on church first, then family. Not too long ago, most Americans lived like the Amish. They farmed, and they knew their neighbors. It's America that's changed, the Amish say, not them.

Judge Robert J. Brown, who accompanied the jury for the fifteen-minute drive from the courthouse in Wooster to the Weaver house, instructed the jury not to talk about what they saw and not to read media coverage. He called the house "the alleged crime scene" and told them not to form any opinions yet. Rob, as his friends called the judge, was in his late fifties, good-looking with a handsome face, close-cropped hair, and blue eyes. He had spent his life in the area, growing up just two counties north. He had been an assistant prosecutor for three years and a trial judge for more than twenty. He hadn't seen many crimes involving the Amish—there had been only two reported murders among the Amish in America in more than 250 years.

Neither of the two people charged with the murder accompanied the judge and jury to the house. The attorney for the killer didn't want the jury to get a "mental image" of his client at the scene.

The prosecutor, however, was there. Edna Boyle, Wayne County assistant district attorney, wife, mother of two young children, and former municipal court judge, would seek justice for Barbara Weaver.

The jury was overwhelmingly made up of women thanks to Boyle, who knew a group of females would be sympathetic to the victim, a young mother. They were shown key areas of the house, including the basement, where an open cash box with a large amount of money had been found, a sign that the killer, who entered through a nearby unlocked door, wasn't there to rob. They also saw the living room; the upstairs bedrooms and main-floor nursery where the younger Weaver children slept; and the kitchen, where the cake had sat since a family birthday party for Harley two days before the murder. The killer had also ignored more cash for the taking on a kitchen counter.

There was no evidence that the crime was random, the result of a break-in. Someone had walked in with a shotgun, aimed, and fired once at the sleeping woman.

The house was not empty. There was a sofa and a recliner in the living room, as well as an adult-sized pair of boots in the living room, as if their owner had thought, " 'We'll be right back,' " Boyle said.

The master bedroom, where Barbara Weaver was found, was at the end of a hall on the first floor. The jury would hear that Barbara was wearing a plain, homemade light-blue nightgown, purple underwear, and a white head covering pinned to the top of her head when one shot smashed through the right side of her chest, sending pellets to her heart. They would learn that it was the children who had pushed open the bedroom door the morning of June 2 and tried to wake their mother.

The jury saw Maysville Outfitters, a fishing and hunting shop run by Barbara's husband, Eli, twenty-nine, on property adjacent to the home. Inside were essentials needed by hunters and fishermen, including shotguns, ammunition, rain jackets, and fishing gear.

There was a shanty near the store that looked like an outhouse but housed a telephone. The structures are a common sight—the Amish share phones to conduct farm business or reach family members in other communities. There was also a portable toilet outside the store. The jurors saw two sheds and the barn where Eli stored feed. The prosecution would tell them it had been the scene of trysts between Eli and one of his lovers.

Some members of the jury may have been inside an Amish home before. Although they live different lives, the

Amish and the English (what the Amish call the non-Amish) live among one another and do business with each other. For 250 years the Amish had farmed Wayne County, Ohio. Until the middle of the twentieth century, all Amish farmed. Today, only one-quarter do. Nonfarmwork pays better than farming, and since the 1970s, farmland has been scarcer. Cornfields have been turned into Walmarts.

More and more Amish have turned to nonfarming occupations to support their families. While many do get jobs working for non-Amish business owners, where Pennsylvania Dutch–speaking Amish employees rub shoulders with English coworkers building gazebos and storage sheds, others have become entrepreneurs and moved into a variety of nonagricultural enterprises.

The Amish are worried about the move away from farming. As one bishop said, "The lunch pail is the greatest threat to our way of life."

The English, in turn, sometimes work for the Amish. It's common for the Amish to hire an English man or woman to drive them long distances or to places where it is not practical to take a horse and buggy. Eli Weaver regularly hired an English woman to drive him on business and pleasure trips.

Now that they had seen the house where Barbara Weaver was murdered, the jury would hear one question repeatedly: Who would kill a young wife and mother with her children sleeping nearby?

3

Sisters

This isn't the end of it. When Satan gets hold of
a person, he isn't going to let go easily.
—A SKEPTICAL BARBARA WEAVER TO A NEIGHBOR,
ON ELI'S RETURN HOME AFTER LIVING AS ENGLISH

Few people knew as much about the Weaver marriage as
Fannie Troyer did. Barbara's sister would be invaluable in
the early days of the investigation. She was at the murder
scene minutes after her sister's body was found.

Fannie and Barbara Miller grew up near Orrville, Ohio,
a town of about eight thousand and home since 1897 to
the J.M. Smucker Company, maker of jams, jellies, and ice
cream toppings. ("With a name like Smucker's, it has to be
good!") The sisters—Fannie was the big sister—and their
two brothers grew up members of the Andy Weaver Amish.
The conservative Amish group adheres to beliefs about
driving, hair length, men's facial hair (mustaches are forbidden), and electricity. The differences between Amish sects
can be mindboggling. The Swartzentruber Amish—the
most conservative Amish—paint their barns red, believing

white is too flashy. The Andy Weaver group falls between the ultraconservative Swartzentruber Amish and the more progressive Old Order Amish.

Locally, members of Andy Weaver are known as Dan Gmay (pronounced *Gamay*), literally "Dan Church." After the split from the Old Order in 1952, led by Andy Weaver, all the ministers in one district had the first name of Dan, and the nickname took and has continued.

There have been ugly, bitter church schisms in Wayne and Holmes Counties, usually over issues of how the different sects view excommunication, education, and the use of barns and modern-day conveniences.

The Amish first settled in Pennsylvania in the early 1700s after fleeing persecution in Switzerland over their beliefs as Anabaptists, Christians who believe in adult baptism, separation of church and state, and nonviolence. In Europe, the Amish had alienated both Catholics and Protestants with their views on adult baptism. Until the middle of the twentieth century, the Amish attended public schools in America. But when school consolidation began, with the pressure to bus students to large public schools and a growing emphasis on extracurricular activities that cut into the time young people could be with family, the Amish established their own schools.

Barbara and Fannie attended an Amish school through eighth grade, then left—as most Amish do—to help with housework and farm chores and prepare for their most important roles: wife and mother. More education, the Amish fear, could lead to the demise of the church.

Amish children have been called "the most cheerfully obedient" of children. There's a strong work ethic, with boys helping their fathers with the farm and girls helping their mothers in the kitchen. Families sit down and eat meals together.

There are no television or video games to distract young

people or their parents, but it's not unusual for Amish youth today to have cell phones, or for boys to own a truck.

Barbara wasn't one to test boundaries, though she could have when she was a teenager. During Rumspringa—defined as a period of "running around"—life for Amish teenagers is a gray area. They're becoming more independent and forming friendships with peers away from their family. Because they are not yet baptized, they are not technically under the church's Ordnung. This period may last from age sixteen until a young adult is in his or her mid-twenties and decides to either become baptized into the church and accept the Ordnung or leave the Amish faith. Many, like Barbara, don't stray too far from their parents' teachings, but some formerly cheerfully obedient children test their newfound freedom by going to parties, trying alcohol or drugs, watching races at the Wayne County Speedway, wearing nontraditional clothing, or driving a car. Most youth do eventually choose to remain with the Amish Church, but an estimated 10 to 15 percent leave, maybe because they want to have a car or conveniences or pursue an education, are drawn to more charismatic churches, or are gay or lesbian. No one knows what percentage eventually return.

There was never any doubt that Barbara would remain Amish. She spent her Rumspringa years at slumber parties with her friends, eating pizza and reading romance novels featuring Amish girls. Barbara's friend Ruby Mast (now Hofstetter) was a big reader and would share her books. They read the House of Winslow series by Gilbert Morris, which traces a fictional family from their arrival on the *Mayflower* to the 1940s. They also passed back and forth Baby-Sitters Club and Sweet Valley High books, and Christian romances by Lori Wick.

"Barbara was very friendly, supernice, not shy, but kind of laid-back," Ruby said.

Ruby's mother, Ella Kay Mast, remembers the girls staying up all night, giggling, playing Rook, and, in the winter, sledding and ice-skating. "Barbara was like a daughter to me."

The girls lost touch when Ruby's mother divorced her father. Ruby and her mother left the Amish life. "I was kind of shunned. Her parents would not have encouraged her to stay friends with me. They would be afraid I would be a bad influence," said Ruby, now married and the mother of two sons. She occasionally ran into Barbara where most Amish and formerly Amish meet—at Walmart. Ruby never met Eli.

Twenty million tourists visit Amish communities each year, largely thanks to the 1985 movie *Witness* and the long, sultry looks exchanged between a Philadelphia cop played by Harrison Ford and the Amish widow, played by Kelly McGillis, whose farm he hides on. Tours selling nostalgia—a reminder of when life was simpler in America—stop at Amish-owned produce stands and stores offering handmade quilts.

The simple life, or what tourists think Amish life is like, appeals to stressed-out visitors who fantasize about living a slower life. They see the peaceful farmland, clusters of white houses, windmills that power pumps for well water, families walking together, boys with suspenders and straw hats, girls in long dresses and bonnets, and buggies. Tour-bus drivers routinely ask their customers how many of them wish they lived without TVs, cell phones, and other daily distractions. Everyone raises their hands, then they return to checking their cell phones.

The Amish arrived in Ohio in 1809, about a hundred years after settling Pennsylvania, and the largest Amish population in the world now straddles two counties in Ohio.

Holmes County, to the south of Wayne County, is more

scenic, with rolling hills and cute stores for tourists who wander through towns named Charm, Sugarcreek, and Mount Hope. Wayne County is flatter, less woodsy, and not as tidy or prosperous-looking. There are more Swartzentrubers, the most conservative of the Amish, in Wayne County, and their houses are not the source of pride they are for other Amish. There's a stark look to them and they lack the well-kept yards and landscaping seen at other Amish homes. In place of flowers, there are overgrown grass, weeds, and muddy driveways.

The northern, non-Amish end of Wayne County has more crime, too.

There is less tourism in Wayne County, but what there is, is important. The biggest tourist draw is Lehman's Hardware in Kidron. Lehman's is 32,000 square feet spread out in four pre–Civil War buildings and sells the trappings of the simple life—woodstoves, butter churns, oil lamps, and tools—to the Amish and non-Amish. They also sell to aid workers or missionaries going to third-world countries, and to movie studios and TV producers who need authentic props.

In addition to being the base of Smucker's, Wayne County was the home of Rubbermaid, founded in 1920 originally to manufacture toy balloons. A dustpan changed everything in 1933, and since then the company has been making trash cans, laundry baskets, food storage containers, and hundreds of other items for the home. It moved its headquarters to Atlanta in 2003.

One of the largest employers of the Amish is Pioneer Equipment, which manufactures horse-drawn carts and accoutrements and ships all over the world. Nowhere is there a more iconic image—a horse and buggy sharing the road with SUVs—than in Amish Country.

The Amish don't take or pose for photographs (though tourists do take photos from a distance), so there are no pictures of Barbara Weaver, but a childhood friend of Barbara's remembers her as sweet, with a round face and hazel eyes, friendly and warm and "very approachable." She was "devoted" and "happy where she was." Like other Amish women, Barbara had probably never had her long hair trimmed. She looked slender, but her autopsy described her as a sturdy five feet eight and 172 pounds.

Barbara had known Eli Weaver since they were children. He was outspoken but likable, and began to spend more time with Barbara when they were eighteen or nineteen. Barbara wanted what she saw other happy Amish women had: a mature, responsible husband and father who would provide for his family. At the time, Eli seemed to fit the bill.

Eli was also a member of the Andy Weaver group. Eli's father and one of his brothers were ministers and would trade off preaching with other men. In the days after Barbara's murder, Eli's mother and father were overheard by a neighbor saying that they couldn't imagine who had done this terrible thing to Eli. And his wife, of course.

A friend remembers that Eli's parents were quick to take his side when he was young. He could sweet-talk himself out of trouble, a talent that came in handy when he became a husband. Trouble for young Eli may have meant he had a radio or a camera, or English clothing, or drank alcohol or visited a movie theater. The Amish call it "getting into things." Those were common "getting into things" activities, all frowned upon by Amish parents and the Amish Church.

Barbara and Eli courted for a year, attending Sunday evening "singings," where single Amish youth from a wide area gather for supper and an evening of singing and socializing. The young couple spent many hours on buggy rides, talking together as the horse trotted its way through the gently rolling countryside. They married in 1999. Their wedding day was traditional: a long day beginning with a religious service and the exchange of vows at a neighbor's house and then everyone making their way to the home of the bride, where female relatives, close neighbors, and friends had been busy preparing two feasts for the guests. Like all Amish brides, Barbara wore a homemade royal-blue dress with a snowy-white starched cape and apron fastened over her dress with straight-pins. For the last time that morning, Barbara wore her black satin Kapp, worn by single girls for formal occasions. After the wedding ceremony, she exchanged it for a white Kapp. Like all Amish grooms, Eli wore a homemade dark suit and white shirt. After the wedding, Eli allowed his beard to grow out, the sign of a married man.

It used to be that Amish girls weren't told about sex before their wedding day. Now there's more discussion, and the Amish have publications that help parents discuss sex with their teens. As a friend of Eli's, himself the father of two Amish teenagers, said, "Growing up around farm animals, most children figure it out rather young and, I know from experience, ask questions."

Amish marriages follow traditional gender roles. The husband farms or works elsewhere to support his family, and the wife maintains the house, raises the children, and respects her husband. "You honor God by honoring your spouse," is a frequent saying. The Ordnung speaks of wives submitting to their husbands as the head of the home, but it also instructs couples to be kind to each other and make decisions as partners.

Many Amish couples share the load—the husband is the head of the home, but most Amish women have an equal say in most matters. Amish women are likely to drive buggies during the week, especially if their husband works away from home. And they are often in charge of the yard work. Divorce is considered a sin and is forbidden.

An Amish elder estimates that the divorce rate among Amish is probably .001 percent.

Yet after ten years of marriage, Barbara found herself thinking of divorce. She hadn't known before she married him that Eli had deep streaks of immaturity and selfishness, was obsessed with sex, and saw himself as something of a "ladies' man". After his Rumspringa, Eli had been torn between the life he *could* lead and the life he *would* lead as an Amish man. But ultimately, he opted to stay in the community, and was baptized at twenty-one.

If only he had left then.

Barbara gave birth to five children in seven years. Her life as a mother was fulfilling. Her marriage was not.

Fannie said that Eli wouldn't give Barbara enough money to feed and care for the children and that she had no access to their bank account. It wasn't about a lack of money—Eli and Maysville Outfitters were doing fine. It was about control.

Barbara had found unpaid bills around the house. She brought them to Eli's attention, but he didn't seem to care. She was stunned to find that he owed a local printing shop—which was demanding its money—$9,000 for help printing and mailing a fishing magazine to his customers.

When it was her turn to bake pies for gmay, or church, Eli wouldn't give her the money to buy the ingredients.

"Failing to produce pies that the church people were expecting to eat after lunch humiliated her," an Amish friend said. "It was very upsetting to her. That poor woman."

Eli's absences, his neglecting to feed and care for his wife and children, and his physically shoving and grabbing Barbara—witnessed by their children—add up to domestic violence. But as one Amish leader said, if Barbara had reported Eli's conduct to the bishop, she would have been asked: "What did you do that your husband would treat you like this?"

Eli was gone a lot overnight—presumably on hunting or fishing trips, though Barbara suspected otherwise. Barbara had told her sister that Eli wanted oral sex, something Barbara didn't want any part of. Fannie later told investigators that she believed Eli had "become forceful" with Barbara when he wanted sex. She said Eli didn't harm the children but didn't want to be a father.

In 2006, after several years of marriage, Barbara was lonely and discouraged about Eli, and she wanted to be closer to her sister. Eli had left the family to live with an English woman, so Barbara and the children packed up, left where they were living—on property next to Eli's parents in Millersburg—and moved about fifteen miles north. Now Barbara and the children were just three miles from Fannie's home in Apple Creek Township, a small pocket of Ohio just south of Wooster, the seat of Wayne County. A map of Wayne County's sixteen rural townships looks like a quilt—with Apple Creek, Salt Creek, Sugarcreek, Chester, and other small communities of a few thousand making up the perfectly drawn squares.

Barbara and Eli were still somewhat dependent on his parents. After Eli returned to the family, his father bought a house and a nearby shop, and they rented from him. Still, Barbara thought the home and business could be a new start for her and Eli.

A friend of Eli's said most Amish in the area were of two minds about his move home. They rejoiced that his family would be reunited, but they didn't want him as a neighbor.

This may have been about the time that Barbara asked Fannie if she could take her five children while she "sorted things out" with Eli. Although Fannie had her own family, and the sisters' father and brother were living with her, she told Barbara a definitive yes.

But Barbara and Eli never did take time to focus on their marriage.

Eli began running Maysville Outfitters soon after his return. And with customers coming in from outside the Amish community, he had even more contact with the English. Someone had given him a cell phone, and he was able to indulge in what became an obsession with Internet chat rooms. With a few numbers punched into his cell phone, he could meet a woman who, unlike his wife, would participate in any kind of sex he wanted.

IT WAS COMMON for the cousins, Barbara's five children and Fannie's four (soon to be five), to spend time at each other's homes. The sisters saw each other at least twice a week. The Amish keep their aging parents at home, and when their mother was dying in 2008, Fannie cared for her. Barbara relieved Fannie of caregiving duties a few times each week.

On Sunday, May 31, 2009, the entire Weaver family—even Eli—went to the Troyers' to celebrate Harley's birthday. Barbara took dinner and a store-bought birthday cake. At the end of the evening, Fannie's two daughters, Susie and Mary, went home with their aunt and uncle. Barbara's son Jacob stayed at the Troyers' to spend time with his cousin John, who was also seven.

Earlier that day, dutiful wife that she was, Barbara had told her children to go play outside, opened her arms to her wayward husband, and made love with Eli.

The two sisters didn't have contact on Monday. But on Tuesday morning, June 2, Fannie set out in a buggy with the children. They were headed to the Weaver house to spend the day. They stopped at a bulk food store to buy some items for lunch. That's when they saw an ambulance rush by, siren blaring. Fannie had a bad feeling.

"As I turned into the driveway, a neighbor lady stopped me and said that they had found Barbara dead in her bed that morning and that they thought someone had shot her," Fannie said. "And my first thought was, 'Where are the children? Where is Eli?'"

She pulled the buggy into the barn on a nearby farm and a man took her horse. She learned that the children had been taken to a neighbor's house and she went to join them. She did not enter the Weaver house to see her sister's body.

Later that day, and for weeks to come, investigators questioned Fannie about the Weaver marriage. She told them that Eli had been unfaithful more than once and that Barbara thought he was having another affair.

"She was a dear, sweet sister with a strong faith in God. Her life was not easy, but she made the best of her situation," she said. "He was never willing to go for counseling and lived a very fast-paced life with his shop, hunting, and fishing. He is not a man at peace with God."

Fannie also told detectives that Eli may not have been physically abusive to her sister beyond shoving and grabbing—although he could be rough during sex—but he was verbally abusive. "All of his problems were her fault. And I know he wanted her to do sexual things that were against her beliefs."

The morning of June 2 was filled with confusion and chaos. As detectives and the coroner arrived, Fannie tried to protect the Weaver children and her own.

Within a day of the murder, she told detectives that she thought Eli had killed her sister. There were the affairs. There was his use of a cell phone, sometimes in secret, sometimes not. Fannie mentioned his friendship with a neighbor who sometimes worked in his store. She thought it was unusual that the woman, without her husband, had gone fishing with Eli and some other men. And there was another woman they needed to know about, Eli's driver, a woman named Barb Raber.

There were letters, Fannie told detectives. Barbara Weaver had seen a counselor and had corresponded with him after she had moved away from Millersburg. She also kept a diary. Her own words might hold clues to her murder.

4

The Letters

I asked him why he feels so bitter towards me.
"I don't know."
—Barbara Weaver, on her struggle
to improve her marriage

Barbara Weaver's life was unraveling and she knew it. Every second of her day was consumed with the grief she felt about her marriage. Eli had hurt her deeply before. He'd left her. He'd gone to live in the world outside of the community. Whenever Eli vanished from her life, Barbara knew what he was doing. He was doing things with other women. When he'd come back, he'd beg for forgiveness. He'd tell her that he'd never hurt her again. And then, just as he'd always done before, he would betray her and he'd chide, cajole, and even try to intimidate her into performing sex acts that she would never do.

The list of Eli's transgressions was a long and varied one. He told each of his lovers that she was the only one. A few believed him. Some he had sex with. Some, however, were merely fantasy lovers suited to sexually explicit texting and phone sex. A few only held hands or kissed. Barbara probably wasn't aware of all of them, although she had found love letters written to him.

Everyone in the community knew of Barbara's heartache, but few could fathom the depths of her despair. While she wasn't stoic, Barbara was private in her pain. She didn't confide in many about the specifics of her husband's swinging-door betrayals. It was embarrassing, ugly. She had children to think about, and no matter what their father tried to do to her—no matter how many tears she shed when she cried herself asleep without him—she respected his position and God's law that called her to submit to him.

Barbara loved to sit at her kitchen table early in the morning, pen in hand, lined notebook pages in front of her, after Eli had left for work and while the children were still asleep. She wrote to the person she hoped would help her understand her husband and save her marriage: Duane Troyer, her counselor at Hoffnung Heim, a Christian counseling practice with a focus on the Amish and Mennonite communities. Her marriage was not what she had hoped for or expected, she wrote. Her husband violated the most sacred beliefs of the Andy Weaver Amish.

Eli was angry when he learned she was getting counseling, so, as a sign of good faith, she stopped. But she continued to write to her counselor and sometimes telephoned him from her parents' house.

Reaching out to a counselor had not been easy for Barbara. The Amish believe in modesty and humility and frown on talking about themselves. Twice Eli had left his wife and children to live among the English. Now, Barbara wrote, she thought he was straying again.

She began each letter with the same salutation:
Greetings in the name of our Lord.

Although Eli had been forgiven by his community, Barbara knew he had not changed his ways.

I feel sure (almost) that he is having an affair.

She was referring to the time when her husband was caught having sex with one of his girlfriends in his store. He couldn't talk or charm his way out of that. He had repented to the bishop and to Barbara. She wanted to believe he would change, but she never knew when Eli was telling the truth.

Sometimes I already know the truth, other times I find out the truth later. I ask him why he feels so bitter towards me. "I don't know." I said I wished he would be honest with me. I'd like to know where he would like me to improve. It makes me feel better to try and tell him how I feel, but it's so one-sided.

When Eli left the second time for the English life he craved, he purchased a pickup, shaved off his beard, and began wearing English clothes. But a few months later, when Eli did what he always did—changed his mind—he went through the motions of repenting and returned to Barbara. She felt Eli used her.

I feel like our intimate life is on hold and has been for so long that without counseling for us both how can I ever heal, knowing his past adultery? I feel sometimes like all he wants is "his relief".

Duane Troyer knew that one of the issues in Barbara and Eli's marriage was Eli's desire for a kind of intimacy his wife wasn't comfortable with. Eli blamed her for his affairs because she didn't fulfill his desires for oral sex and English women did.

Barbara confided to the counselor:

I know oral sex is wrong—yet if he asks me to kiss, etc. him there, that's all wrong too? I'm embarrassed to ask, yet I need guidelines and I don't know where to turn.

For her part, Barbara longed for another kind of intimacy, one Eli withheld. She wanted the closeness of an embrace.

Whenever there was the smallest of reasons, Eli would find a way to hurt his wife with hateful words. Everything was her fault. During one of their arguments about their marriage, Eli boasted that he could have fifty girlfriends if he wanted. While many men would deny their dalliances with other women, Eli threw them in Barbara's face. At times he made her feel unworthy. Other times he made her feel lucky that she had him for herself. Whatever he could say or do to swing the results in his favor, Eli would do it.

The counselor asked the troubled Amish wife if she was afraid of her husband. Had he threatened her?

No, I don't think so, she wrote back. *But he hates me.*

She even described a conversation the two had shared about her death. She was hoping to shock Eli into being kinder to her.

I told him leave. Once I die you won't have to put up with me. He says "Once I do you can get another man." I said "I don't want another man!" I asked him, "If I'd die, would you actually cry?" He answered, "Oh yes." I don't believe he would because I'm so far from what he wants.

Her friends and family said Barbara didn't seem afraid of Eli. She told one friend that she wasn't afraid of Eli— only of his girlfriends.

In the autumn of 2006, Barbara wrote in her journal that she had learned she was pregnant. It was only a couple of months since Eli had lived with an English woman. There's no mention in Barbara's letters of any happiness over expecting a fifth child. But Barbara wanted Eli to hold off before telling certain friends.

He promised he would but then told them anyway.

It was as if he was proud of having made his wife pregnant. The pregnancy was a gift from God. He never bragged about his other baby—a daughter he had with one of his lovers, the ultimate betrayal that Barbara knew nothing about.

* * *

OVER THE YEARS of their seesawing marital life, Barbara documented how her husband continued to come and go as he pleased. She kept a log of when Eli came home, how long he stayed, if he had supper with the family, and his excuses for leaving again—which ranged from taking his dogs to the vet, to hunting rabbits, to going to dog shows, to fishing, to the vague excuse of "meeting someone".

> *Monday—gone after supper awhile*
> *Tuesday—gone to 8:30. Dog to vet, a few hours'*
>   *drive.*
> *Wednesday—gone 8–8:30*
> *Thursday—gone to 10*
> *Saturday—gone on hunt overnight*
> *Sunday—not home till 4 p.m. Told me he'd be home*
>   *by noon.*
> *Wednesday—left 3:30 a.m. Home from work. Goes*
>   *rabbiting until 9, 9:30 p.m. Not home for supper.*
> *Thursday—home 4:30. Says "I'm meeting someone*
>   *in Coshocton to get my new dog hauler for truck"*
>   *and flies out door. Not home for supper.*
> *Friday—home 11 a.m. To bank. Lunch 11:45. Goes*
>   *at 12:30 for Indiana. Takes 3 others along, his*
>   *truck. Are gone 2 nights.*

She made other notes in a diary she hid in the house:
Fri. eve. He is going to bulk [food store]. I ask if he'd take 2 oldest along, they need fresh air, outa house. Eli— "No, it'll get dark." I said, "They'd be okay about that." Eli—"Well, do you have any idea how full the store's gonna be?" And I said "Okay, they don't need to go along." Eli— "I can see you don't agree with me! When was the last time you agreed! You don't!" Slams door and leaves. Boys yell

out from living room, "Is Dad mad?" I said, "Yes, I don't know why he gets so mad. You shouldn't."

In addition to writing about his emotional distance and forcing her into doing sexual things she didn't want to do, Barbara also documented Eli's financial withholding. She knew his store made money and didn't understand why he wouldn't provide for his family and made her beg.

Another issue is . . . what is my place when we need money for groceries, etc. . . . he has the business in his name, therefore I cannot write out checks, and we have no personal checking.

Barbara confided some things to her sister, Fannie, but she hoped the counselor, with more worldly experience than her sister, could help her.

Could you please send me some answers? But send them to my sister's address as Eli would be upset if it came here—as you know.

Do I simply accept these issues, even as God plays no part in his life? Or rather means nothing to him?

Barbara's last letter for help was postmarked May 15. Duane Troyer wrote back, but he never heard from Barbara again.

Time had run out.

5

Fishing

This is now Friday and I need to send the boys to the store today, but Eli forgot to lay out money for me and he went to Lake Erie at 3:30 a.m. to fish walleye (has two more times booked for June).

—BARBARA WEAVER, IN A LETTER TO HER COUNSELOR
A FEW DAYS BEFORE HER MURDER

It was time to go fishing for walleye on Lake Erie and that meant a very early start. At 3:15 a.m. on June 2, Steve Chupp pulled up in his Dodge Caravan at the pristine white house to pick up Eli Weaver. David Yoder, also in the van, went up to the house and knocked on the door.

No answer.

Yoder stood there confused for a moment.

Where was Eli?

Steve joined him and they moved around to the back of the house, knocking on several doors.

No answer.

No Eli.

Steve made his way to the door off the back deck, which

was close to Eli and Barbara's bedroom. Finally, a light came on and what seemed like a very long time—five or ten minutes—later, Eli appeared. He offered some feeble excuse, so ineffectual that later no one could remember just why he'd kept them waiting. A moment later, they made a quick stop at his store, then continued down the road to pick up a couple more fishermen. Eli slid into the front seat, next to Steve.

As Steve drove, he watched Eli out of the corner of his eye. Eli was very intent on his phone. Preoccupied, even. En route, the group stopped at a gas station in Wooster for snacks and beverages for the trip. After that, they went for breakfast at Vansons, a family-style restaurant on SR 20 in Monroeville.

"That's a lot of food you've ordered!" Steve said as two piled-up-high plates were set in front of Eli.

But while he had ordered so much food, Eli barely ate. And he—and his cell phone—went into the men's room a couple of times during the meal.

"Did you notice how much Eli ordered?" Steve asked the others as they looked at his uneaten food.

"He's kind of acting strange, don't you think?" one of the other men said.

Not one of the group disagreed. He *was* acting strange.

The long drive in the dark in Steve's Dodge Caravan was mostly a quiet one. The group of Amish and Mennonite men en route to a morning of fishing on Lake Erie talked a little and slept on the way. In the front seat next to driver Steve, Eli Weaver pulled his jacket close to hide his cell phone.

"What are you looking at, the radar?" Steve asked.

Eli rolled his shoulder a little and grunted.

Steve ignored his passenger's indifference. They'd known each other for only a few months—they were thinking of doing some business together—but he had heard all about Eli's questionable character. And the truth was, he was mostly making a joke when he asked if Eli was checking to see if the storm that had hit the area that morning would affect their fishing on the lake.

In fact, Steve had encouraged Eli to get a cell phone. Steve ran an auction business, an extremely successful one, Steve Chupp Auctions. Eli was running a business, wasn't he? He would need a phone. Eli admitted that he already had one, but that Steve couldn't have the number unless he promised only to text.

"No calls," Eli said.

As formerly Amish himself, now Mennonite, Steve understood. Phones were forbidden, and answering a text could be done quietly and in secret.

Although Eli's store was small, Steve thought he could get him involved in trade shows and the auction side of things.

Eli could have done worse than to take the business advice of Steve Chupp. A handsome man by anyone's standards, with thick, dark hair, he had shaved his beard when he left the Amish and began living as Mennonite. A graduate of the Reppert School of Auctioneering in Indiana—which offers the two-week equivalent of an MBA in auctioneering—Steve is a licensed auctioneer in five states, including Ohio. He auctions furniture, trees and shrubs, tools, farm equipment, real estate, and hundreds of other items. One of his most lucrative days was when he sold a whitetail deer for nearly half a million dollars. One of the smartest and most elusive of big game animals, whitetail deer are known for large racks, or antlers. Size matters. Although a good number of people in Amish Country think deer bred to have abnormally big racks are "freaks," there is money to be made in artificial insemination.

The men reached Lake Erie at about 6:00 a.m. and met up with Dan and Tami Murphy, the owners of Knot Lost

Charters. The men had paid $100 each to go out with the Murphys on their thirty-foot charter.

As they set out, Eli continued to call attention to himself in strange ways.

At one point, Eli asked the others if they'd seen his tackle box.

"You got it right there in your hand!" one of them said and everyone laughed.

They had fished for only a couple of hours when Steve's phone rang. It was Firman Yoder. It was bad news. Firman needed to speak to Eli. Steve handed the phone to him.

6

The Knock

One Sunday morning, Harley asked, "Dad, we didn't pray yet." Eli said, "We can later." So I helped him pray.
—Barbara Weaver, noting in her diary that Eli frequently ignored his children

My mom's dead." They were the first words Linda Yoder heard when she answered a knock at her door and opened it. It was Harley Weaver.

"My mom's dead."

Harley told Linda that his cousin Susie Troyer had gone into his parents' bedroom. She couldn't wake Barbara. She ran to get Harley, and he couldn't wake his mother either. He could see blood on her nightie. He touched her leg but quickly withdrew his hand. Her leg was cold.

As Harley stood at Linda's door, she hurriedly put on her shoes and walked with him the short distance to the Weaver house. It appeared to be just a normal June day. A few clouds. Temperatures in the upper sixties. There would be a trace of rain later.

It was anything but a typical day.

Linda and Firman Yoder were the closest neighbors, geographically, to the Weaver house. Their home was one half of the building Eli's shop was in. In other ways, the Yoders were not close to the Weavers at all. Eli embarrassed them. English women hung around his store, and the Yoders knew he neglected his wife and children. Firman was reluctant to admit he was friends with Eli.

Linda sometimes worked for Eli in the store. She had worked the day before when he had left at 1:00 p.m. to go fishing. His friend "the taxi lady" had driven Eli, David Yoder, and Mark Weaver to Berlin Reservoir and back. Linda would be working again today because Steve had picked up Eli and some other men early to fish at Lake Erie.

As Linda approached the house, she saw that some of the Weaver children were outside and some were in the kitchen. Linda entered the house through a door off the deck and walked down the hallway leading to the back of the first floor. The bedroom door was closed and she called out Barbara's name. When there was no answer, she opened the door and stepped into the room. The first thing she noticed was that Barbara's lips were blue. As she moved closer to the bed and said Barbara's name again, she saw blood on the comforter. Linda pulled it back and saw Barbara's bloody chest. She replaced the blanket and ran to a neighbor's for help. She didn't stop to knock but rushed inside, finding Katie Petersheim at her sewing machine.

"I told her, 'Barbara is not responding and I wish I never would've pulled the blanket back,'" Linda said. Katie ran to get another neighbor, Amanda Troyer, while Linda rushed to call for help.

Firman started to gather the children. Sarah, who was about to turn six, had been running around repeatedly asking, "Mom, where are you?" Harley was overheard saying, "If this was Dad, then he's had it!" Firman took them to his house and stayed with them while Linda waited for the ambulance and sheriff's deputies. Another neighbor, a Mennonite, said her first instinct when she saw the commotion was that Eli had harmed Barbara. *He's really done her in now*, she thought.

The ambulance, the one Fannie Troyer had seen rush by, arrived at the house.

Phillip Chupp, assistant fire chief and a paramedic for the Fredericksburg Fire Department, asked Linda what the problem was. She didn't speak but just led him into the house and pointed to the bedroom door. Chupp saw a "late twenties female lying partially on her right side . . . with blue lips . . . and an ashen pale color." He checked for a pulse and couldn't find one. He saw that a bullet hole had blasted through the bedcovers, leaving a black edge. He gently pulled down Barbara's nightgown a few inches and found what looked like a gunshot wound to the right side of her chest. He thought she was dead but used a heart monitor to confirm she was, then immediately called the sheriff's office. She was pronounced dead at 9:30 a.m., but determining when she died was going to be complicated.

Wayne County Sheriff's Office deputy Thomas Holmes was the first patrol officer on the scene. He joined Chupp in the bedroom. After Sergeant Ryan Koster arrived, he and Holmes cleared out everyone, including the paramedics, then walked through the entire house from the basement to the children's bedrooms upstairs. They secured the house, phoned for detectives and the coroner's office, and began to take witness statements.

Linda told them that the last time she had seen Barbara Weaver—before she saw her in her bloody bed—was at eight o'clock the night before, when Linda turned the sign on Eli's store to "Closed." As she looked across the yard, she saw Barbara on her porch. She did not hear gunfire during the night.

Firman told the sheriff's deputies that he had arrived home from his job at a mill around 11:00 p.m. Monday. He'd glanced at the Weaver house and thought it unusual that the lights were on so late. He'd assumed Eli was getting ready for his fishing trip the next day.

When Detectives Michael Maxwell and John Chuhi arrived at the house, the sheriff's deputies were taking statements, paramedics were still on the scene, and neighbors of the Weavers were clustered outside. Sergeant Koster briefed Maxwell and took him inside the home. Coroner's assistant Luke Reynolds arrived and joined Maxwell in the bedroom.

The only photographs ever taken of Barbara Weaver were in death. With her dark-blond hair pulled back, and freckles, she resembled the fresh-faced Amish teenagers depicted on the romance novels she liked to read.

She was beautiful.

Reynolds gently pulled back the white blanket and opened Barbara's nightgown so that Maxwell could photograph the wound near her right breast. Maxwell also took photos of her hands, arms, and legs; of the bullet hole in the comforter; and from the doorway where he thought the assailant had stood. Maxwell moved to other areas of the house, photographing the kitchen, the living room, the children's rooms upstairs, the money on the kitchen counter, and the open cash box in the basement, with twenties, tens, fives, and ones neatly segregated, plus change. There was also a shotgun that was disassembled and a pellet rifle.

It was the home of a young family, except neater and simpler. Harley's mostly homemade birthday cards were taped to a wall in the hallway. Crayon drawings of birds were stuck on the refrigerator. Instead of a television, video games, and computers, there was a grandfather clock, candles on a doily, and a wall hanging that read: "Under His wings you will find refuge." Psalm 9:14. A white family

Bible had a prominent place on a hutch. Picture frames held poems or pretty artwork, not photographs. A wood plaque, with two hearts joined and Eli's and Barbara's names and the date of their wedding, was displayed. In the living room, there was a blue plush sofa and recliner, and blue curtains.

Upstairs, the boys' room had an outdoors theme. Antlers hung above a window, and two paint-by-numbers paintings, of a horse and a wolf, were framed. A set of the first five Laura Ingalls Wilder books, including *Farmer Boy*, stood on a dresser with a Native American dream catcher. A small backpack lay on the floor, a teddy bear and a toy tractor nearby. The girls' room had a pink teddy bear and a crib. A pink item of clothing had been left on the floor. An extra bedroom had a few playthings, including a child-sized table and chairs, ready for a tea party. A poster of Disney's *Bambi*, the kind that might have been included with a book or DVD, was on the wall above the tiny furniture. Barbara had sponge painted the walls light pink.

The master bedroom looked like one in a million other homes, with a maple four-poster bed, dresser, and bedside table, probably made for Barbara and Eli at the time of their marriage. In the closet, a few of Barbara's modest calf-length dresses, all in dark hues of brown, green, gray, or black, hung next to a few men's white shirts. On the bedside table were two windup clocks, a candle, and a lamp.

The kitchen table and chairs were also maple pieces. Children's books were on the table, and several pairs of children's shoes were piled in a corner. About a quarter of a white cake with white frosting sat in a clear plastic grocery-store container. One lonely blue flower was all the decoration remaining on the cake.

The detectives didn't know it, but the house—which the Weavers rented—was unusual for members of the Andy

Weaver Amish. The house had conveniences, like natural gas lighting installed in the ceilings and patterned linoleum, that were typical among Old Order Amish but forbidden to Andy Weaver Amish. At one time Eli had expressed interest in joining the Old Order—he wanted fewer rules—but his family and ministers discouraged him from doing what the Amish call "jumping the fence," drifting to another Amish group.

The basement was bare, except for a washtub and a clothesline. There was a coal- or wood-burning stove. A few toys were scattered about, including one Rollerblade. Two boy-sized straw hats hung by a door.

The front of the two-story house had a three-quarter porch with baskets of flowering plants hanging above it. There were two doors into the basement, one on the front, or north, side of the house and one on the west. The home had well-maintained grass, trees, and shrubs. In a side yard there was a tricycle and a small trampoline. Barbara was probably responsible for the trim lawn and plantings.

Detective Maxwell prepared evidence to take back to the sheriff's department, including the comforter and Barbara's blue nightgown, the covering on her head, and her purple panties, which were removed from her body. They were sad reminders of a young woman who was a good Amish wife and mother yet liked a few pretty things.

Maxwell took photos of the exterior of the ten-year-old, 1,798-square-foot single-family home. Most Amish homes and many barns are painted white, as this one was. He looked around the property and saw two sheds, the barn, and the aluminum building that housed Eli's store. In front of the store was the phone shanty, the portable toilet, a barbecue grill, and a duck blind. To one side was a paved area with a basketball hoop.

Inside the store there were fishing poles and tackle for sale, a few rifles, and rain jackets. A cabinet housed rifles and several trophies Eli had won in beagle competitions. On the wall by the cash register was a cartoon of a man with his head in a bucket crying, "Help!" Above the illustration it said: "Of all the things I've lost . . . I miss my mind the most."

The Weaver house was, like others nearby, set on just a couple of acres—too little land to farm. Other homes, one with a man-made pond and another with grain storage tanks, buggies, and the occasional wagon used for hauling, were to the east.

During a search of Eli's outbuildings, Maxwell found a small-caliber rifle and a large-gauge shotgun—one too small and the other too large to make the wound that killed Barbara Weaver. But while searching Eli's business, the detective found two .410 gauge shotguns—exactly the size they thought could have caused the wound—one behind shelving and one in a closet. One shell was missing from a box of shot shells that still had a sales tag on it. Detectives took the shotguns and opened box of shells as evidence.

As harsh as it might seem, detectives knew it was crucial to interview the children as soon as possible. After taking dozens of photographs, Maxwell sat with a representative of Children Services while she interviewed the children. Detectives learned that something—maybe a storm—had scared the children the night before and both Harley and his cousin Susie had moved downstairs to the living room. Later, Susie had gone back upstairs. They said they never heard an intruder in the house.

As deputies searched the house and the outbuildings, and the children and neighbors were questioned, everyone at the scene asked the same question. Where was Eli?

Firman knew. He went to the phone shanty, and called Steve, and identified himself. He said he had bad news and needed to speak to Eli.

7

Waiting

*There's been no true repentance expressed since a year
ago when he got caught.*
—BARBARA WEAVER, WRITING TO HER COUNSELOR THAT
ELI WAS UP TO HIS OLD TRICKS

It was curious. Eli didn't want to talk to Firman Yoder.

"I told him he needs to come home, that his wife is un-responsive, and that we had called the ambulance," Fir-man said. "And then he said, 'Here, I'll hand the phone over to somebody else.'" And he did. Firman found him-self delivering the grim news to the driver for the day. Fir-man told Steve that Eli's wife was dead. Steve said they'd be home as soon as possible.

While the investigation continued and everyone waited for Eli, one of the sheriff's deputies interviewed the Weav-ers' neighbor Amanda Troyer. She had visited with Barbara the night before. Eli was gone, so she sat and chatted with Barbara for about an hour while the children played outside. Amanda's description of Eli was one they would hear re-peatedly.

"Never home. He didn't seem comfortable at home. He wasn't truthful to Barbara. She said, 'I feel there is an affair going on; it's just a matter of time,'" Amanda told detectives. "He'd be out so long that if she asked where he was, he said he was choring. But he didn't have many chores. Never took the boys along, didn't suit [him] or [there] wasn't room."

Amanda was familiar with how Eli exerted his control over Barbara by withholding money for food and ignoring the children. Two years earlier, family and friends had given Barbara six thousand dollars to help her and the children move and get settled after Eli had left. When Eli returned home, he took the checkbook and her money.

Despite not having found a weapon in the bedroom, detectives asked Amanda if Barbara Weaver had seemed suicidal. "Never. She'd get the blues but [was] never suicidal." She also said she had seen no signs of domestic violence and knew of no one who would want to harm Barbara.

The only person to ever voice concern was Barbara's mother, Emma Miller. "She had been fearful for some time that someday Eli might do something to Barbara," a family friend said. Barbara's mother died of cancer in 2008. She wouldn't be there to see her worst fears realized.

THE MURDER OF Barbara Weaver on June 2, 2009, provides a clear example of how the Amish and English coexist. Short of murder, Amish bishops almost always punish members from within the community. Rarely do the English step into Amish country.

Each Amish congregation—made up of twenty-five to thirty-five families—is led by a bishop, two ministers, and one deacon (all men), who are chosen from the congregation by the drawing of lots. They receive no formal theological training. Only married men who are members of the local church district are eligible.

Twice a year bishops meet to clarify the Ordnung, the unwritten set of rules and regulations that guide everyday Amish life. Then members vote to accept the Ordnung and affirm their agreement to live according to it. The rules govern hairstyle, dress, style of buggy, use of electricity, and divorce. The rules of the Ordnung can differ among groups of Amish. In some groups, Rollerblades are okay but bicycles are forbidden; others have adopted the bicycle. Some Amish permit flip-flops; others stick with more traditional footwear. Most forbid bright colors, such as pink, yellow, and orange, but some Amish women now wear red.

Unwritten but taken for granted is that the Amish do not have sex outside of marriage. Bishops and ministers decide if a member who has sinned or committed some other infraction is placed under a Bann and then shunned by church members. The Andy Weaver Amish practice strict shunning; it is why they split from the Old Order Amish in 1952.

Shunning may take the form of eating separately, not doing business with a person, not accepting gifts or rides from a shunned individual, and generally excluding him or her from community activities. It's a kind of tough love, a way of getting a deviant person to change his or her behavior and reaffirm his or her commitment to the church. Offenders can return if they repent.

Some families will set a place at the dining table for a shunned family member, a symbolic gesture. But if the individual continues to flout church rules, the bishop will move to excommunicate him or her. The place setting disappears.

In Eli's group, the Andy Weaver Amish, family and

friends may still keep in contact with the Banned member, but they can't eat at the same table or travel with him. Family can give the Banned member food, lodging, or transportation, but they can't accept it in return.

If a young person decides after Rumspringa to leave the community, he or she is discouraged from returning to see his or her family.

Eli Weaver had left his family and community twice to live like the English. Twice he had repented—or claimed to—and had been forgiven. His bishop, ministers, and deacon had experience with members who bent the rules. They did not have experience with murder.

The murder of Barbara Weaver was the first in an Amish community for the paramedics and sheriff's deputies called to the house on Harrison Road in Apple Creek. Crimes are rare among the Amish. Sheriff's deputies have more experience at the scene of an accident between buggies and automobiles than they do at the scene of a murder. Because the population and services in the townships are sparse, it took three counties to investigate the case.

Wayne County's coroner, Dr. Amy Jolliff, arrived at the murder scene to determine the cause and time of death. Summit County's chief medical examiner, Dr. Lisa Kohler, conducted the autopsy. Wayne County Children Services would be involved in the welfare of the Weaver children. Deputy Joe Mullet with the Holmes County Sheriff's Office, whose first language was a German dialect called Schwäbish, was loaned to Wayne County to translate recordings of phone calls made from jail. Pennsylvania Dutch—or simply Dutch, the shorthand all use—is the "mother tongue" for most Amish.

Like others in rural Ohio, Dr. Jolliff wore several hats. Coroner since 2005, she was a longtime family practice physician with additional training in forensic medicine.

She arrived at the house at 11:30 a.m. and entered the bedroom. First she took a good look at the room to see if anything seemed out of place. Then she carefully lifted the layers of blanket and nightgown off of Barbara Weaver so she could see her skin. She studied the bullet hole and found bruising on Barbara Weaver's hands and legs, possibly unrelated to the shooting.

Dr. Jolliff looked for stippling—the pattern that gunpowder and gunshot residue leave that determines the distance from gun to victim. Barbara's body was placed in a body bag and taken to Summit County for the autopsy. Time of death, which is required for a death certificate, is a tricky issue. It's determined at the crime scene and is based on blood pooling in tissue or skin, as well as body temperature. The coroner issues two reports, the first before an autopsy, the second after. The autopsy does not help determine the time of death. Dr. Jolliff estimated the time of death as 2:00 a.m., with a window of midnight to 5:00 a.m. The cause of death was a gunshot wound to the chest, and the death was ruled a homicide.

Detective Chuhi took eleven items from the coroner to be kept as evidence, including nail clippings, hair samples, fingerprints, DNA evidence, and shot pellets.

In all the interviews the deputies conducted that day and for days to come, they would ask this question: What motive could anyone have to harm Barbara Weaver?

Her friends and family were hesitant to speak. Linda Yoder told them she was afraid to answer the question. "I asked her who she was afraid of," Deputy Holmes wrote in his report. "She stated her [Barbara's] husband. She said, 'I'm not saying he did anything, but in the past their marriage hasn't been the greatest.'" The Yoders had reason to fear Eli.

Sheriff Thomas Maurer issued a statement saying that

the killing of Barbara Weaver was an apparent homicide and the investigation would receive highest priority.

He added that it was especially disturbing because six young children were in the house at the time of the murder.

8

The News

If I tell you the truth, I feel sure (almost) that he's having an affair, on the phone if not some other way. Am I too suspicious?
—BARBARA WEAVER, ON HER FEELING THAT ELI HAD
RETURNED TO HIS BAD HABITS

As Mark Weaver worked at his welding job, he thought of how he would rather be fishing. He liked his work—mostly welding cylinders and parts for Amish businesses—but some of the best fishing on Lake Erie was in June.

Mark (no relation to Eli) was in his late thirties, the father of four young children. He and his wife, Elsie, had met Barbara Weaver and her children when Eli first left his family and Barbara and her children rented a house nearby. Mark met Eli as he came and went from the English life he was living then. When Eli moved home again and repented and was forgiven, he, Barbara, and the children moved across the road to the house with the adjoining store. Eli and Mark started hunting and fishing together.

Friends describe Mark as stocky, very friendly, and a helpful kind of person. At one time he had a welding shop at his home and would fix things for free for neighbors. For generations his Old Order family had farmed Wayne County. That was then, and this was now. His father had left farming thirty years earlier, and while they still lived on the homestead, Mark worked for an Amish company that converted electric equipment to hydraulic so Amish businesses could use it.

This time the day before, he had been fishing on Berlin Reservoir with Eli and some others. Barb Raber, a Mennonite woman who often provided taxi service for Eli, had driven them. Barb was a good ten years older than Eli, married and the mother of three, and not nearly as pretty as Eli's wife. But she had some kind of hold over Eli. He had once worked for Barb's husband, Ed, in construction. Mark couldn't help but notice that Eli and Barb seemed to seek out every opportunity to be alone.

Although Mark had been along on other hunting and fishing trips with both Barb and Eli, he was one of the few in Eli's circle who didn't know that Eli had resumed his affair with the taxi lady. Maybe because Eli knew Mark took the Amish life and faith seriously. Their children played together and their wives were good friends.

There was a lot Mark didn't know about Eli—but he sure knew when two people acted peculiar.

"Eli and Barb were talking about something serious," he recalled sometime later. "They were whispering. They acted sneaky. As if they had something to hide."

It was routine for Barb to drive the group to the fishing spot of the day, leave for several hours, and return to take them home. That's exactly what she did on June 1. Barb hooked up David Yoder's boat and trailer to her Ford Explorer and drove the Amish men to Berlin Reservoir, an eighteen-mile-long paradise for walleye and bass fishing, powerboating, water-skiing, sailing, Jet Skiing, and wind-surfing.

Eli took his place in the front seat next to Barb. Mark, David Yoder, and David's son, Norman, sat in the back. When the fishing party stopped for a bite to eat, and when they unloaded and loaded the boat at the public dock, Eli and Barb took the opportunity to huddle and talk in low voices.

"It was as if they couldn't wait to be alone," Mark said. He had never seen his friend Eli so nervous.

"He was very wired up, very on the go, talking a lot, extra uptight," Mark said. "Something was on his mind."

The weather was perfect, but clouds began to roll in by early evening. It started to rain on the drive home. It was late, about 11:00 p.m., by the time Barb dropped Mark and Eli at their homes. Eli had only a few hours before he was to be picked up to go fishing with Steve Chupp and some others. Mark had planned to go, but he'd had to cancel.

Mark was lost in his work when his sister-in-law phoned. She lived near Eli's house and could see the ambulance and sheriff's department cars lining the road. She told Mark she'd just learned that Barbara Weaver had been found dead.

"I can't believe it," he told her. "I had planned to go to Lake Erie, but something came up."

Mark immediately phoned Steve.

"I just wanted to know if you've heard the news," he said.

Steve had. He told Mark that Firman Yoder had called to say that Barbara was unresponsive. Mark was more candid than the Weavers' neighbor.

"She's dead," Mark said. "We don't know why for sure."

Eli wouldn't speak to Firman, but now he grabbed Steve's phone and fired questions at Mark.

"How is Barbara?" Eli asked, seeming frantic. "What hospital is she at? What happened?"

Mark gave Eli the bad news. "She's not at a hospital, Eli. She died." He said there were rumors she had been shot.

"Oh, no!" Eli cried. Mark heard him repeat the words over and over. Eli collapsed, going down on his knees, and crying out that it couldn't be so.

Steve, who was right beside Eli, knew Eli *sounded* as if he was crying, but he saw no tears.

Steve took the phone back.

"You have to come back," Mark told him.

"We're on our way," Steve said.

The Murphys immediately headed the boat for shore. When they reached the dock, someone suggested that they pause to say a prayer.

They formed a small circle and prayed for Barbara and Eli.

Eli's hands were shaking.

Back in the Dodge Caravan, Steve connected with a friend at the Apple Creek Fire Department.

"He said, 'Prepare for the worst. There's been no radio talk,'" not a good sign when an ambulance has been sent to the scene.

Eli told Steve to drive faster.

The next phone call came from Detective John Chuhi.

"Where are you, and exactly where is Eli?" the detective asked Steve.

"We're on our way back to Maysville," Steve said. "Eli is right here."

"Your next stop is the Justice Center in Wooster," the detective said. "Do not stop—anywhere."

"Okay," he said. "Okay. Got it."

The Dodge Caravan was a gas-guzzler and Steve

needed to fuel up. He pulled into a gas station in Ashland. Eli jumped out and disappeared toward the men's room. Steve glanced over and saw Eli texting.

A few minutes later they were on their way.

By the time they reached the Justice Center, the men had agreed that the kind thing to do would be to go in with Eli—not just drop him off to face the news alone.

"We're here to support Eli," Steve told Detective Chuhi, while their friend and fishing pal followed the detective down the hallway for an interview. Steve and the others sat waiting, unsure of what exactly they were waiting for. Would Eli rejoin them and would they take him home?

While they waited, Mark called again with the news that the deputies on the scene were saying Barbara had been murdered.

"We put our heads together," Steve said later. "Red flags went up. We knew Eli was a possible suspect."

Detective Chuhi approached the group, alone.

"This is a homicide," Chuhi said. "This is a murder and it is under investigation."

He asked Steve to stay, but the others could leave. As for Eli, he wouldn't be going anywhere for a few hours.

9

Temptation

I feel sometimes like all he wants is "his relief."
—BARBARA WEAVER, ON ELI'S INSATIABLE NEED
FOR SEXUAL GRATIFICATION

Detectives were anxious to talk to the husband of the murdered woman. Only a few hours had passed since they were called to the murder scene and got an earful about Eli's double life. It sure sounded like a motive.

When Eli's fishing buddies brought Eli to the sheriff's office, Detective John Chuhi and Lieutenant Kurt Garrison ushered him into an office and read him his Miranda rights. They weren't too impressed with Eli. This shaggy-haired, unkempt, long-bearded man thought he was God's gift to women? More important, he seemed oddly apathetic when they told him his wife was dead. Detective Chuhi wrote the following in his report:

It should be noted during the interview with Eli Weaver that he was found to show very little emotion for someone who learned about losing their wife

that morning. When confronted with involvement or
knowledge of his wife's death, he stated a number
of times he understood why we would believe he was
involved. Eli also displayed weak denials and had
a "casual" attitude during the interview.

They had Eli walk through the timeline of the last two
days. On Monday he had left to go fishing at Berlin Reservoir sometime between 2:30 p.m. and 3:00 p.m., and
returned between 11:00 p.m. and 11:30 p.m. Barb Raber
had driven him and his friend Mark. When he returned
home, Eli did some chores, including feeding deer and putting a horse in a stall. He spoke to his wife, who was in
bed, then he showered and went to sleep. He overslept and
was awakened by Steve Chupp and David Yoder at about
3:15 a.m. Eli told Chuhi and Garrison that none of the
children were awake when he left. He exited the house
through the west side basement door and didn't remember
if he locked it.

The detective asked if he and Barbara had argued that
morning. No. What was she wearing? A blue nightgown.
Had the couple engaged in sexual conduct before he left?
No. When was the last time they did have sex? Sunday
afternoon.

He told them his last conversation with Barbara was as
he was dressing. She got out of bed to help him find some
clothes. She asked if he had caught any fish Monday and
if they'd had fun. The last time he saw his wife she was
walking or standing near the bedroom. Harley, Susie, and
Lizzie were sleeping on the main floor. Not one to kiss his
wife or children good-bye, he simply went down the stairs
to the basement and left through the west door.

The detective asked about the state of his marriage. "It's
fair, and [we are] working to get it better."

Eli's version of his life and the day's events swung between creative and outright untruthful. He told them that, yes, Firman Yoder had telephoned him on the boat to say they should return home and said only that Barbara was "unresponsive." Eli said there was another call, from Mark Weaver, telling him Barbara had died of an aneurysm.

Then they asked about his extramarital affairs. He admitted to having had an affair with a woman named Cherie Lindstrom. He claimed to have confessed the affair to Barbara—only because he had been caught with Cherie—and as far as he knew, his wife had forgiven him. With prompting, he admitted to one other liaison—with Barb Raber, his driver. When he had returned to his family and repented, the bishops had warned him not to see Barb. He did anyway. They had sex several times in January at his house. Were there other affairs? the detectives asked. Eli said no. Did he have any knowledge of or involvement in the death of his wife? No.

Eli agreed to take a polygraph the next day. What would the result be? he was asked.

"Truthful," he said.

TELLING THE TRUTH—and temptation—were problems for Eli. While the Ordnung guides the Amish in everyday life, forbidding the use of electricity and owning a car or a television, there's another guide for the Amish. Rules of a Godly Life is composed of forty-seven proverbs intended to help the Amish center their daily life on God through their everyday thoughts, words, and deeds. One of those proverbs is Matthew 7:12:

When you are tempted by others or by your own impulse, to do harm to a fellowman, pause to consider how you would feel if others did so to you. Do nothing to others that you would not wish them to do to you.

For those more familiar with the Ten Commandments than with the Rules of a Godly Life, Eli had broken just about all of them.

The world around Eli was changing. Running a business, he was exposed to the facts of life—modern life, that is—and the lures not only unavailable to the Amish, but banned, including phones, the Internet, cars, and extramarital sex. He could have turned to his faith, to his community, and to his wife for support when he felt weak. Other Amish do. Instead, he gave in to his temptations. As detectives were beginning to learn, Eli had coveted a lot more than just his neighbor's wife. And now his own wife was dead.

While one of the other detectives stayed with Eli, Detective Chuhi pulled Steve into a room to talk with him.

Steve said he had arrived at Eli's house just after 3:00 a.m., but Eli wasn't up. It took Chupp and another member of the fishing party, David Yoder, both pounding on a door of the house to wake him. Finally a light went on and a few minutes later Eli came outside. They made a stop at Eli's store to get a fishing license for one of the men, and then the group set off.

Chupp told detectives that Eli acted strange all morning. They stopped for breakfast and Eli ordered a large meal but barely touched it. At some point, he disappeared into the men's room for a long time. It was almost as if he was making a secret phone call. Later in the morning, Steve saw Eli searching for his tackle box when all the while it was in his hand. And Eli—who had fishing-trip requirements down to a science—had forgotten to bring a reel for one of the people on the charter. To sum it up, he was distracted.

They'd arrived at Knot Lost Charters on Lake Erie's Western Basin, about eighty miles north of Wooster, at about 6:00 a.m. The usual eight-hour-long fishing trip was interrupted by the mid-morning phone call from Firman Yoder.

Oddest of all, Chupp thought, was that on the drive back, when he told Eli that the police had called and they were to go directly to the Justice Center, Eli didn't question why.

Steve was thanked and sent on his way. He stopped by Eli's house to drop off the jacket and tackle box left in his vehicle.

The detectives drove Eli to his house. He briefly saw his children. He gave permission for another search of his house, the outbuildings, the barn, and the store. Eli had his hands tested for gun residue, and agreed to give his clothes to detectives for lab testing.

The detectives wanted to take his clothes into evidence but didn't want him entering the house. One of the deputies went in and got him a change of clothing and they went to the barn for Eli to strip. Although Eli had worn more contemporary clothes when he lived among the English, he was dressed in traditional Amish garb now. Detectives took every stitch he was wearing, from head to toe, including a blue jacket, blue pants, a blue vest, a white shirt, tan work shoes, men's underwear, white socks, and a gray sweatshirt. They photographed what Eli had taken on the fishing trip, including a red and white tackle box, two fishing rods, and a plastic bag with a can of pizza-flavored Pringles potato chips, bags of peanuts, other snacks, and a bottle of water. They confiscated the tackle box and a second jacket.

With his children at their aunt and uncle's, the detectives

drove Eli to his parents' home in Millersburg. They said
they would pick him up the next day to take him to Rich-
field, in Summit County, to take a polygraph.

In the meantime, was there a phone number they could
reach him at? Apparently not. Eli said he didn't have a
phone.

They soon learned different.

Someone tipped off the detectives and gave them Eli's
cell phone number. Maxwell quickly contacted Verizon
Wireless to request a preservation notice, which saves the
texts sent to and from a phone. Then he met with assistant
DA Edna Boyle to get a search warrant to send Verizon.
Without those texts, two people might have gotten away
with murder.

MARK WEAVER WAS too upset to stay at work. His phone
had rung dozens of times since he first got word that Barbara Weaver was dead. He had to get home to Elsie and
the children. When he arrived, he joined his family in
watching the parade of law enforcement vehicles from his
brother-in-law's house near Eli's.

Mark's phone continued to buzz with friends calling,
sharing what they knew and asking what Mark knew. Almost everyone had heard the news. An Amish woman had
been killed in her bed as she slept.

Among the calls Mark received were decidedly peculiar ones from Barb Raber.

"She was asking questions she shouldn't have known
to ask, like 'Are they blaming Eli? Was it a shooting? Do
they have any other suspects?' "

Mark spoke to her once—and then quit answering her
calls and texts.

That evening, Mark and his father sat on the porch talking about the horrible death of their friend and neighbor.

Mark wasn't suspicious of Eli. He wasn't even home when it happened. He had been fishing. But he told his father about Barb Raber's calls and texts.

"It's strange, Dad," he said. "She is asking all these questions, as if she knows something we don't know. Like 'Are the police looking at Eli? Do they have other suspects?' It's just odd. I quit answering her calls," Mark said.

"Let me hear some of the messages," his father said.

Mark played a couple of the phone messages and showed him the texts. As they were going through the calls, Mark's phone rang.

"It's her!" Mark said. "It's Barb Raber."

"Answer it," his father said, "and put her on speakerphone."

Mark activated the speaker function on his phone.

"Hi, Mark. It's Barb again. I was wondering what you have heard. Where is Eli? Did the police talk to him?"

"Barb, I don't know anything."

But she was persistent.

"Do they think Eli killed her? Are they looking for someone else?"

"There's nothing new. I've got to go."

After they hung up, father and son discussed the call. Barb had gone off the deep end. Nothing she said made sense. Mark knew he could depend on his father for advice.

And he got it.

"That lady is guilty," his father said, "and you had better let someone know!"

THE AMISH HOTLINE was burning up.

Word of mouth was always the preferred way of communicating. But cell phone towers were busy pinging, too.

Like Mark, Steve was getting lots of calls. He stopped

answering the ones from Eli. The messages were always the same: "Steve, this is Eli—call me. I need to talk to you. I've got to talk to you!"

Finally, Steve got a call from a number he didn't recognize. It was Eli. Eli had a new phone number.

"I've got to ask you—when you woke me up, did you see her, my wife, when you woke me up?"

"No, I didn't hear her or see her," Steve said.

Pause.

Click.

Eli had hung up.

The day after the murder, Steve and the other members of the fishing group—except Eli—met up to go to breakfast. Eli's fishing buddies didn't know they could still be surprised by Eli. But on their way to breakfast they passed a Ford Explorer; it was Barb Raber driving Eli *somewhere*.

The men gathered at the Wagon Wheel to eat and talk. One had invited a pastor to join them.

"The pastor wanted us to open up. He led a prayer. He wanted us to talk about how we felt," Mark said later. They were still in shock and had more questions than answers. But most of them were beginning to think that Eli was up to something. Mark knew what the pastor was thinking. He was thinking that Eli had pulled the wool over their eyes, that he had deceived them.

Despite their growing doubts, they decided that the right thing to do was to pay their respects to Eli's family and Barbara's family. Eli, his parents, his siblings, Barbara's family, and an Amish minister had gathered at a neighbor's house to accept condolences.

In all, there were about forty people in the house. The men clustered in the living room, the women in the kitchen. There were children playing, including Eli's.

"We shook hands and I put an arm around Eli's shoulder," Mark said. "He cried and I cried."

"No one knew what to say," Steve said. The men expressed their condolences, and left after about half an hour.

10

The Taxi Lady

*When he called me he didn't seem upset. Not at all.
Like it was normal conversation. "Somebody shot my
wife." He was at his dad's and he'd call me later.*
—Cherie Lindstrom, one of Eli's girlfriends, on receiving
a phone call from Eli

Am I a suspect?" the woman on the other end of the line asked. Detective Chuhi told Barb Raber he didn't think so, but he did want to meet with her to talk about Eli Weaver. It was the day after the murder. He had already heard a lot about Eli's good friend, known to many in the Amish community as the woman who never seemed to be far from Eli, but he wanted to talk in person. They agreed to meet in the parking lot at the medical center north of Millersburg, where Barb, her husband Ed, and their three sons lived.

If Eli looked younger than his twenty-nine years, with the face of a teenage boy framed by his chopped hair and long beard, Barb looked older than her age, thirty-nine. She had a small frame, shoulder-length brown hair beginning to gray, and oversized glasses. Her hangdog look aged her. Occasionally, with her hair in a ponytail, she looked like the young woman she once was.

She told her life story to Chuhi, how she was adopted when she was six months old and was New Order Amish until the age of twenty-two. She and Ed had started attending a Mennonite church and stayed on after their children were born. Now she identified herself as Conservative Mennonite.

Leaving the Amish to become Mennonite is not unusual. Sometimes the lure is a similar faith but a more modern lifestyle without all the restrictions. Mennonites are Christians descended from sixteenth-century Anabaptists, as are the Amish, but are not separated from the modern world like the Amish. Mennonites believe they are more spiritual than the Amish, and have a greater focus on scripture and sharing their faith. Old Order Amish might have a glass of wine with dinner. Some Mennonites drink a little wine. It all depends on the individual church and its rules. Some Mennonites drive horse-drawn buggies and dress similarly to the Amish. But some love their cars and cell phones and wear T-shirts with their skirts, and even shorts.

THERE WAS A lot Barb didn't tell the detective. The story of her life was one wrought with tragedy. The smell of desperation clung to her wherever she went. The Amish knew her for two things—she was the lady taxi driver and she was the girl that came from the Sugarcreek family that had endured the devastating and mysterious loss of all their young sons.

Like most Amish couples, Katie and Menno Miller, Barb's parents, wanted children—as many as possible. For some, having a large number of children is a necessity.

Milking, farming, and household chores take the effort of many hands when there are no gas- or electric-powered appliances or equipment to do the job. Exactly nine months after they married, Katie checked into Union Hospital in Dover and on February 16, 1959, Michael Allen Miller was born. He weighed seven pounds, seven ounces. His parents called him Mickie.

Outwardly, the Millers seemed overjoyed with God's gift of a little boy. But that joy was muted. Katie told people that she thought something might be wrong with the baby—though the doctors at the hospital had said he was perfectly healthy. In time, the young mother became fixated, obsessed with the possibility that something would go wrong. Was it a premonition, she wondered, or was she preparing herself for a worst-case scenario? She saw something wrong, something that others couldn't see. She wondered if her boy was developmentally disabled.

Ten years later she wrote about the experience for the readers of an Amish magazine, *Family Life*:

> How such fathers and mothers must feel! What if it should happen to us—to Menno and to me and little Michael? I did not want to think about it, but I just couldn't shake the thought from my mind. It was as if someone were telling me I was to have such children. "Oh, no!" I said to myself. "Not me." Sometimes I would walk to his baby bed when he was sound asleep and look at him and whisper to myself, "Oh, what would I do if he was retarded?" But, no, the doctor said everything is all right.

As the weeks and months flew by, it was apparent to Katie that something was terribly wrong with her baby. At five months, Michael was unable to hold his head up. When she tried to get him to respond to her with a toy or the sweet words of a mother, he didn't react.

Beside themselves with worry, the Millers sought the help of a doctor, who told them Michael was just "slow." Another blamed the boy's diet for his below-average development. Finally, a chiropractor conceded that Katie's worst fear had been correct. The boy was "mentally retarded."

She wrote in *Family Life*:

> *Retarded! Mentally retarded, oh no, not that! No, not my baby. I tried to make myself believe something could help him.*

At seven months, Michael became violently ill with spinal meningitis. He survived but was forever sickly and "very nervous." He had bouts of endless crying. He'd pull hair from his head, and he'd hit his head against the crib until he bled. And now there was a consensus that he was intellectually disabled.

"It was sad," a friend of the Millers' recalled. "They were heartbroken."

And yet life went on. Michael had special needs—and always would—but he'd be loved just as any child would be. The next year, the couple was blessed with a second son, Timothy Ray. When he was three weeks old, joy over the newborn shifted to worry. Timmie was an exceedingly fussy baby, crying and spitting up all the time. No matter what Katie did, she was unable to calm him. She worried that he, too, might have physical or mental deficiencies.

And she was right a second time. Doctors did X-rays at the hospital and examined him very carefully. The prognosis was not good. He, like his brother, was developmentally disabled.

To go through that trial once was a very heavy burden. A second time was more than many could take. Amish friends of the Millers did what they could to help, baby-sitting to relieve the parents once in a while, bringing over meals, and even helping with doctor bills. They encouraged the parents to bring the children to church.

The circle of love and attention around the Millers was of some comfort, but it could only do so much to ease the pain that permeated their Sugarcreek farm. They were desperate for a solution, and when they read about a clinic in Denver that "cured" developmentally challenged children, they accepted money from the members of their order and got on a train for a long trip with two sick children. Once at the clinic, the Millers were instructed to leave the boys for three months of treatment. And while it broke their hearts, they did and went back to Ohio empty-handed.

When they eventually returned to Denver, Timmie had flourished, but Mickie had lost weight and looked "white as a sheet."

They were advised to continue in Ohio with a chiropractor, a medical practitioner favored by the Amish. For a while they did, but when there was no progress, they ended all treatments.

Breakthroughs in genetic testing were a decade and a half away. Still, many doctors knew a little about inherited problems and chromosomal abnormalities. Katie and Menno could have been warned about having other children and the probability of a genetic problem they were passing on.

They weren't.

On August 2, 1961, Katie gave birth to a third little boy, Rudy Jay. Doctors said they couldn't see anything wrong, but by now her fears were her constant friends. The baby was fussy and colicky, then at six weeks, his body was swollen. Doctors said it was "something serious." He was taken to a hospital in Columbus.

"Your baby has a very serious disease," a doctor told them, though he was unable to diagnose the infant. Genetic testing had not progressed to that point. "I'm afraid we cannot help your baby. The disease may be fatal, but we'll do all we can."

Several weeks later, Katie's prayers—that her child's suffering would end—were answered.

God did send an angel to gather little Rudy into the fold. Loneliness crept over us and we prayed for added grace and strength. Life never seemed quite the same as before, but God gave us courage to bear it.

Timothy and Michael were sick a lot, prone to pneumonia. Certain foods didn't agree with either little boy, so their parents were careful about their diets.

As he neared three years of age, Michael began to experience swelling on the tops of his feet and around his eyes.

There was no help for him for he had the same sickness little Rudy had. Again we prayed, Please, God, if it is Thy will, come and take Mickie from his suffering.

Mickie died when he was five years old.

"They loved all those boys so much," a longtime friend said. "We went to a lot of viewings and funerals."

Not long after, Timmie began to get weaker. The Millers took him to Johns Hopkins in Baltimore in October 1964. For the first time, they sought an explanation more than treatment. The specialists were puzzled. All the symptoms seemed to point to PKU, or phenylketonuria, a condition in which the body can't break down an amino acid called phenylalanine. Without treatment, phenylalanine builds up in the blood and causes health problems, including seizures, intellectual disabilities, skin rashes, and swelling. PKU is inherited.

However, Katie understood the doctors at Johns Hopkins to say that they had tested for PKU, but that the boys didn't have it. Her sons, they explained, had a "new" sickness.

"We're going to work on it," one doctor reportedly told her, "and in years to come we may be able to help such children. We do not even have a name for this rare disease yet."

Still, no one told the family how to cope—or to stop having children in the hopes that one would be normal.

"They always thought the next child would be healthy," a family friend said.

In August 1965 a fourth boy, Matthew, was born. Within weeks, he was having convulsions. One doctor said Matthew was not developmentally disabled. One said he was.

Timmie's condition was worsening. The Millers did not hospitalize him but cared for him at home.

Rudy died in 1961. He was six weeks old.
Michael died in 1964. He was five years old.
Timothy died in 1967. He was seven.
Matthew died in 1969. He was four.

Today, Katie and Menno's sons would have newborn screening that likely would find a rare genetic condition called an inborn error of metabolism. They would immediately be fed a low-protein diet and, depending on the specific diagnosis, could be candidates for a liver transplant. They likely would not have cognitive impairment, they would not die at such a young age, and they would live a close to normal life span.

No FARM IN Sugarcreek knew as much sadness as had the one owned by the Millers. The dark pall of the little boys' tragic deaths hung over the farm like the blackness that comes before a thunderstorm. Four boys gone.

Katie and Menno Miller adopted a baby girl shortly before Matthew's death.

During the next few years, they would adopt two more. Barbara, or Barbarann as she is listed in Amish records, was the middle one. Her adoptive mother made a lovely home, though the specter of a family tragedy hung over the household in the way that unimaginable family tragedies sometimes do. Her father, kind but strict, worked in a brickyard and was a New Order Amish bishop.

By all accounts, the oldest girl was an answer to the Millers' prayers. She appeared to be the healthy, caring child they had always wanted. But something was "off" with the other two from the start. The youngest got into scrapes and disobeyed her parents. The greater problem was the middle daughter's lying.

"Barb lied; her stories just didn't make sense," a family friend said. "She exaggerated. She fibbed. And her mother knew she lied and didn't know what to do about it. It was a big problem."

A family friend witnessed the three girls grow up in the shadow of the boys who had died.

"I don't know how it affected the girls," she said. "I think it had to; Katie and Menno knew they couldn't have their own children. They had loved those four who died. Maybe the girls could never quite make up for what had been lost."

Katie and Menno Miller still live in Sugarcreek and their farm remains a place where those who know them pass by, remembering the tragedies that visited the couple there.

And yet the focus is no longer on the little boys and the four small tombstones that mark their graves. Their tragedy has expanded to include the fact that of the three adopted girls, only one—Edna, the oldest, and presumably the most stable—has led an untroubled life.

Now Barb, the middle daughter, was being questioned about a murder. The Millers stood by Barb. They'd always been true believers in the power of prayer—no matter what God handed them.

Although New Order Amish are less restrictive than Andy Weaver or Old Amish, the order didn't allow Barb any of the freedom she craved, and as soon as she could, she left home. During the more than fifteen years since she'd left the Amish, Barb had built a new life—marriage with Ed Raber, membership in the Conservative Mennonite church, and three sons whom she loved but tended to neglect. And despite all that, Barb still felt trapped. To fill whatever hole was inside her broken spirit, she engaged in several extramarital affairs with local Amish men.

"If she'd had any confidence in herself or her ability to be more than just a vessel for some man's pleasure, she might have made different choices," a sympathetic friend said many years later.

Beyond the sex and the skulking around the community, there was also the matter of her house in Millersburg. It was the home of a woman who was overwhelmed, depressed, anxious, and utterly compulsive. The two-story brick house on Township Road 310 was years beyond messy or cluttered. Those who visited left shaking their heads and wondering how Ed or the children could find anything at all. Stacks of stuff—toys, computers, piles of clothes that would never see an iron—filled every available space.

"If that woman's home life had been a cable TV show, it would have been something along the lines of *Amish Hoarders*," said a friend familiar with the conditions inside the house. Her relationship with Eli was like the state of her trashed house—completely out of control.

It wouldn't have been difficult for Detective Chuhi to learn anything about Barb Raber's situation and what had turned her from wife and mother to lover and possible murder suspect.

All he had to do was ask someone.

"The Amish are the biggest gossips and rumormongers on the planet," said one of the women who was involved with Eli. "They know everything about everyone."

But the detective wasn't interested in understanding Barb. His job was to bring whomever was guilty of murder to justice. It didn't matter one bit to anyone that the woman had come undone long before Eli Weaver coaxed her into the back of a barn for sex.

MOST OFTEN THE weakest is culled from the litter. Occasionally, however, the weakest inspires pity. Amish children sometimes beg for the safety of the runt in a litter of piglets, but their fathers seldom listen. It's a waste of time and effort. Resources must be devoted to the ones that will bring a profit at the Kidron auction.

Barb Raber was the weak, the vulnerable. She was the perfect target for Eli Weaver's bidding. In that way, she had real value.

Times when they sat in her Explorer, Eli pushed Barb for the solution he needed. He wanted his wife gone. He wanted to be free to live a life that he desired—not one encumbered by the rules of the Amish or a wife who would not submit to his needs.

"I want her dead," Eli repeated.

Barb was at the ready. She loved Eli. She knew that while circumstances would prevent her from leaving her husband and boys, getting rid of Eli's wife would make her trysts with Eli less of an issue. She could come over and give him oral sex at his house. Maybe in his bedroom. Maybe more often.

Definitely without his wife around.

As she stared out the window of the Explorer, she ran down a list of ways she and Eli could kill his wife. Living on a farm as she had, she knew that poisons were readily available. Nothing was worse than having a crop decimated by insects. Tempo, for example, was an insecticide used by veterinarians to get rid of insects around barns, horse stables, and livestock. Golden Malrin was another insecticide beloved by farmers and ranchers for its deadly effect on raccoons. Some farmers mixed it with peanut butter, milk, or grape soda.

The same thing could be done to Barbara Weaver.

And yet poison had its risks. While Eli thought that killing his wife with poison could be a solution, it was possible that she'd die slowly. He was in a hurry to get on with his life.

"Maybe you could blow up the house?" Eli suggested.

Barb Raber blinked. "What about your kids?" she asked.

Eli appeared to shrug it off. "The kids will go to heaven because they're innocent."

Barb nodded. When she thought about it for a moment, his answer made complete sense.

Eli asked her to do more research.

"What do you have in mind?" Barb asked.

"We could try other poisons."

"I could go on the computer and see how much it would take," she said.

"Do that."

And that's what she did. She searched. And searched. And searched.

For more than a year, Eli had floated the idea of getting rid of his wife to a few of the women he met online.

He told them he wasn't happy in his marriage and admitted he wanted more freedom.

He never mentioned his five children and where they fit into his dream of a life of various lovers and no wife.

Later, Eli would admit talking to a number of women about getting their help in killing his wife. But it was Barb Raber, he said, who "bit."

Eli Weaver had given Barb Raber plenty of suggestions on how to get rid of his wife. Poisons. Blowing up the house. Shooting her at home. Of all of the potential ways of giving Barbara Weaver a one-way ticket to heaven, shooting seemed the most efficient option. Blowing up the house would be too messy and costly, poison too inefficient. Shooting was clean and quick.

Eli told Barb that he'd be leaving early one morning for a fishing trip.

Barb had a surprisingly pragmatic side to her personality. She wanted to know how she was going to get into his house.

"I'll leave the basement door unlocked," Eli told her. "Go up to the bedroom and get it done."

Late that night while her husband, Ed, was asleep on the couch, Barb took her shotgun to the car and drove the half hour to the Weaver house. Over and over she told herself that she could do what Eli had begged her to do. It wouldn't take but a moment. She could get in that basement, go up the stairs, tiptoe down the hallway to the master bedroom. Eli's wife would be asleep. Barb Raber would never even have to look into Barbara Weaver's eyes. In a flash it would be over.

Halfway there, Barb eased up on the gas and hit the brakes, stopping her Explorer. Something was off. The timing wasn't right.

*   *   *

AS THE DETECTIVE continued to interview Barb in the parking lot of the medical center, she told him how she had met Eli many years before when he worked with her husband. Since then she had become Eli's driver, taking him fishing, hunting, and to business appointments. Their sexual relationship, she confessed to Chuhi, stretched back several years. They had become close—"very close"—when Eli left his family and the Amish community. Barb, who was Amish half her life and even baptized Amish, felt she understood Eli in ways no one else did.

"They pushed him away and I was there for him through the hard times," she said. Despite her own marriage and children, Barb always had time for Eli. She owned shotguns and a muzzle loader and sometimes went on overnight hunting trips with him. Barb had killed two deer the year before, and one so far in 2009. She liked to make a present of venison to family members.

As opposed to Eli, who told detectives they'd had sex only in January 2009, Barb explained that their *last* sexual encounter had been that May. She didn't know if Eli's wife knew about the affair. Barb knew of one other woman Eli had had an affair with, but she didn't know her name.

Chuhi asked her about the Weaver marriage. Barb said she knew they had disagreements, but that they usually worked things out and seemed to be happy. "He loved her and the kids," she said. Did Eli ever talk about getting rid of his wife? Well, there were times Eli seemed frustrated, but any comments made about doing away with his wife were said in a joking manner. She knew nothing about Barbara Weaver's murder.

As for her own marriage, she said her husband Ed suspected something was going on with Eli. He wished Barb would quit driving him around all the time. Members of Barb's Mennonite congregation didn't know the details—even the Amish say Mennonites are not as gossip prone as they are—but they knew that Ed and Barb were getting church counseling.

All those times Barb was with Eli, did he talk about leaving his wife? "He talked about leaving not because of his wife but because of the way the Amish reacted," she wrote in her statement. Eli knew that although he had been accepted back into the Amish community, the bishop had his eye on him. She said she had learned of Barbara Weaver's death Tuesday morning like everyone else. The detective didn't ask her how she had heard about the murder. And then she said something surprising. Detective Chuhi asked her if she had talked with Eli since his wife was found murdered. Not only had they talked, they had met up at the house, but only for a few minutes. She went out of her way to point out that they had not been alone.

INTERVIEWS AND PHONE records would show that Barb Raber had been busy the day of the murder. Sobbing, she had telephoned one of her sisters to tell her that Barbara Weaver had been murdered. She had texted Eli's friend Tabitha Milton, interrupting a session in a tanning bed, to give her the same news.

At 2:46 p.m. Barb had texted Eli:

Whatever you do don't give them your cell phone, please.

Later, he had received another text from Barb, saying she planned to change their phone numbers so their calls and messages couldn't be traced. Also on her list of tasks was to ask a friend and former lover, David Weaver, to make a call to the telephone in Eli's shanty. He was told to leave a specific message.

11

The Children

On Wed. I asked if it's possible for the boys to walk to neighborhood bulk food store, as I'm to bake pies for gmay [church] and need things . . . so he mockingly said, "Well, the boys have feet to walk." He never gave me the money to send them. I didn't ask again.

—BARBARA WEAVER, ON HER HUSBAND'S
CONTROLLING NATURE

The woman introduced herself to the boy. "Hi, Harley. Ich bin LaVina." She asked if he was comfortable speaking in English. He said he was.

Harley Weaver's first language was Pennsylvania Dutch, so LaVina Miller Weaver was on hand to translate if Harley didn't understand questions asked of him. The interview was conducted by Natasha Siebert from Wayne County Children Services and Detective Maxwell.

"What does it mean to tell the truth?" Harley was asked.

"To tell the truth is not to lie," he said.

All of the Weaver children knew what had happened. They had seen their mother's body and screamed when they couldn't wake her. Two-year-old Lizzie sensed a loss she didn't know how to put into words. Harley, the oldest, had touched his mother and felt her coldness. He was present for the chaos that followed the arrival of the ambulance, the sheriff's deputies, and the detectives.

His mother had been murdered two days after his ninth birthday.

At least the children were now in a place that was familiar and where they felt safe, at the home of their aunt and uncle, Fannie and Cristy Troyer.

During the interview, Harley seemed dazed and said he couldn't remember the hours before finding his mother. With gentle coaching, the memories returned, but Harley remained emotionless the entire time he spoke with the adults.

It had been storming that night. He and his cousin Susie were frightened so they had gone downstairs to sleep. Susie took the sofa and Harley took the recliner. For a time, some of the other children were in Barbara's room. Harley remembered seeing his mother holding Lizzie for a while in a rocking chair and later putting her in her crib in the nursery near the master bedroom.

Harley was asked when he had last seen his father. He said Eli had gone to the birthday party for Harley at the Troyers' on Sunday. He knew his father had slept at home Sunday and Monday nights and got up early Tuesday to go fishing. But he had not actually seen his father since Sunday. They had to ask, so they did—had his parents argued much? Had his father ever hurt his mother? Harley said no.

Harley was asked about weapons in the house. He said he knew there were various guns around, both in the house and in his father's store.

The boy thought it was about 11:00 p.m. Monday when he heard the shower running. Then Harley fell asleep and didn't hear anything until morning.

Susie woke him at eight o'clock saying the children wanted breakfast and Lizzie was crying. When Susie heard Mary and Sarah crying in their mom's room, she went in to wake Barbara, and found her dead. Susie told Harley and he hurried to his mother's room.

"There was blood right here," he said, pointing to his own chest. By the time he touched his mother's cold leg, all of the older children were also in the bedroom, crying. He dressed quickly and ran to the Yoders'. He told the interviewers that he didn't think Linda believed him when he said his mother was dead.

Susie thought Barbara had thrown up blood. Harley thought she had been shot.

Detective Mitchell had Harley draw a floorplan of the house to get a better idea of where the children had slept. They noted that the recliner Harley was in was near a wall. His parents' bedroom was on the other side.

Miller Weaver told him in Dutch that what had happened was not his fault and that it was all right to be sad.

Sarah, six, required the translator's help more than her brother had. Standing next to Miller Weaver with the woman's arm around her waist for comfort, Sarah said she had slept upstairs but was scared because of the storm. She and two of the other children had gone downstairs. Sarah remembered falling asleep in her mother's room, but someone had carried her upstairs later. She didn't know who.

She described going to her mother's room in the morning and knowing she had died. "Her eyes were closed and her lips were yellow," she said. Later, she would tell Fannie, "We tried to open Mom's eyes, but we couldn't."

Like Harley, Sarah had not heard any disturbance in the house during the night. She couldn't recall if she had seen her father on Monday.

"Did your parents do things together?" she was asked.

No. Did she spend time with her father? She would occasionally go to his store. She had never witnessed her parents fighting. She knew there were guns in the store, but she didn't think there were guns in the house.

Did the girl know how her mother had died? "No," she said. As she had with Harley, Miller Weaver told her in Dutch that her mother's death was not Sarah's fault, and that it was all right to cry. The girl had sweated so much during the interview that Miller Weaver's arm was damp.

They spoke with Susie Troyer next. By now she had overheard someone say that her aunt had been shot. The girl became emotional and Miller Weaver comforted her in Dutch. Susie talked about going home with her aunt and uncle after Harley's birthday party Sunday night. She hadn't seen Eli since then. She had moved from the living room back upstairs when she heard Lizzie crying "Mama, Mama" from her crib.

In the morning Susie was awake and playing with the children. Mary and Sarah had gone into Barbara's room and Susie heard them crying. The girls were standing near Barbara's head. Susie felt her aunt's feet and they were cold. She pointed to her own chest and described the blood she saw on Barbara.

The adults asked her how she knew Barbara was dead. She said she had touched her grandmother when she died and knew what a cold body meant. She didn't know of any arguments between her aunt and uncle, but one night her aunt had slept at their house. She didn't know why. It was unusual.

From Susie the adults learned that Harley had told her he had heard a "crash, bang, boom" in the night. Was it thunder or a gunshot?

Susie's sister Mary, four and a half, was able to relate how she and Sarah had become scared during the storm and climbed into bed with Barbara and Joseph. Later, she had been carried upstairs, maybe by Eli. When she awoke in the morning, she and her cousin Sarah chatted, making plans for the day. They went downstairs and Sarah said she needed her glasses—she thought she had left them in Barbara's bed. That's when Mary, Sarah, and Joseph found Barbara. Mary demonstrated how the blood covered the front of her aunt's nightgown. How did the girl know Barbara was dead? "She looked yuck," she said.

Sarah finally found her glasses on a kitchen counter.

Next was Joseph Weaver, also four and a half. He spoke and understood only Pennsylvania Dutch. He remembered being frightened by the storm the night before and going to his mother's bed. He believed his mother had carried him upstairs after he fell asleep but agreed that it could have been his father. He was with his sister and cousin when they found Barbara dead. He saw blood on his mother's arm and her nightgown. He did not hear a shot during the night.

It was clear from talking with Joseph that Eli's children were lonely for him. Joseph's experiences with his father weren't about fishing trips or other outings. His only memory of spending time with his father was in the living room. He said he liked it when his dad held him—but he didn't like it when he tickled him under his arms. Harley said his father had taken him fishing just once.

Joseph's memories of his mother were much fuller. He liked it when she read to him. In fact, he said he liked everything about his mom. He liked that if the children did something wrong, their mother calmly talked with them and told them not to do it again.

When asked if he'd seen his parents fight, he remembered a time when his father dumped water on his mother. He thought it might have been for fun, but he wasn't sure.

Jacob Weaver, seven, had stayed with his aunt and uncle from Sunday evening to Tuesday. He was in the buggy with his aunt Fannie when they saw the ambulance race by and followed it to the Weaver house. Harley told Jacob that someone had shot their mother and she was dead.

Jacob couldn't remember the last time he'd seen his father. He liked both his parents, and he liked it when his dad played games with him. He didn't like it when his mother made him eat foods he didn't like. He also remembered the water-throwing incident. He didn't know if his parents had been angry or playing. He had seen his father hurt his mother, and using Miller Weaver's shoulder, he demonstrated how he had seen his father grab his mother by the shoulders. He said they fought "about what they needed or wanted to get."

Jacob said that he knew his father sometimes hurt his mother because he would hear his mother say "ouch." He said Eli had hurt him by spanking him too hard.

Children Services had made arrangements for the children to stay with the Troyers. Fannie was worried—she was convinced Eli had killed her sister. What if Eli showed up at her house? She was told to call the agency immediately if he did.

For now, the children were together.

12

The Women

*I really wanted to cuddle last night but I fell asleep
before you came home. I guess I was hoping you would
wake me and want to fool around. But you didn't!
I worry I don't turn you on enough. I realize
my body needs lots of work.*

—SHELLEY CASEY, ON KEEPING ELI, HER LOVER, FROM STRAYING

He called himself Amish Stud online. Whether Eli Weaver
had an attack of conscience or experienced a fleeting
moment of common sense, he later changed his screen
name to Amish Guy.

He wasn't shy. His subject line read:

Who wants 2 do an Amish guy!

And in his online profile he wrote:

*Love hunting, fishing, anything outdoors. I want friends
and if u have what it takes u can b my friend.*

Plenty of women wanted to be his friend. It was obvious what he was looking for and it wasn't dinner and long
walks on the beach. It didn't hurt that his photo showed a
young, fit man, from the neck to his briefs, with muscled

arms and toned abs. Even men thought he was good-looking—when he wasn't in one of his disheveled phases. "He was quite handsome," a friend said. "But he seemed to act like he knew it and was proud of it."

He had 141 "friends" with names such as 2_much_ass, 69smileygirl, blackbarbiefisheye143, lovemeasiam, naughty-littlesexysexslave, and tweetybirdfan on his page on MocoSpace, a free mobile phone social network.

But before he became the Amish Stud, there was Shelley. He met her the old-fashioned way.

Eli had left his wife and children and was living among the English. Shelley Casey met him at a beagle hunt—rabbits are the prey—in May 2006.

Detectives wanted to talk with her. They were interested in just how far back Eli's motive for murder went.

She agreed to talk to Detective Chuhi one morning after she got off work. They met up at an exit off I-76 in Mahoning County.

Shelley told him that when she met Eli, he was dressed in blue jeans and a T-shirt, was clean shaven, and had short hair. He said he had recently left his Amish community. A week or two later he texted her. They began going to other beagle hunts and hanging out. When their relationship became sexual, he moved in and lived with her and her parents during the spring and summer of 2006.

The depth of Shelley's feelings for Eli are clear in letters and notes she wrote to him. There were problems—in the beginning he didn't have work; he appeared to have a brief pang of guilt about not seeing his children. Her letters show that she was more invested in the relationship than he was.

Sometimes I think you are worried it won't work out. Honey, I am going nowhere. I love you. I want to be with you. I have never been happier. I thank God every day for bringing you into my life. I am the luckiest woman alive.

Eli had told Shelley that his parents—Andy Weaver Amish—didn't approve of his choices. Regardless of the discord between Barbara and Eli, Shelley encouraged Eli to see his children.

I just think like I said you got to go visit them at least one afternoon a week.

Staying away to me makes it even worse. But that is up to you.

Around the end of June he returned to Barbara and the children. He stayed just two weeks, then went back to Shelley, who wrote about his return.

You showed me that you do love me, like I love you. And honey, you tried. You went there and you spent a week of boredom and being miserable.

I would follow you to the ends of the earth. . . . I would go back with you if I could and give everything I have up. Something was always missing in my life and now I know that it was you.

Shelley seemed ecstatic and confident that they were building a life together.

I wish you knew what kind of job you were gonna get so I can move my schedule to match yours. I just want to be with you . . . you are the greatest thing in my life. You are what I asked God for.

Eli found a job, working for a trucker.

Eli, good luck with your new job. I am so proud of you. I know you will do very well.

By August, when he left Shelley for good, his wife and children had moved to Apple Creek, so that's where he went. Barbara Weaver found the incriminating letters from Shelley among his things after he returned.

Shelley told detectives she'd never heard Eli wish his wife dead. But sometime in May 2009, nearly three years after he had come and gone from her life, he contacted her. He texted, saying he wanted to see her. She said no.

It was about the time Eli was going through the Rolodex in his mind, looking for someone to kill his wife.

BARB RABER FONDLED the bottle of pills before handing them over to Eli. He'd promised her the moon if she'd help him with the murder of his wife. He was anxious. Out of sorts. Barb gave him the pills she had acquired. Then she went home to wait. She expected a text would come telling her that everything was just as Eli wanted. His wife would be gone and Barb would be rewarded with his attention. His devotion.

As the inhabitants of the big white house on Harrison Road settled down for the evening, Eli dissolved all of the pills in a glass of Sierra Mist soda. He set the glass on the kitchen counter. A trap. A snare. Barbara saw the soda and smiled. She loved Sierra Mist. How thoughtful of Eli to leave it out for her.

Thoughtful indeed.

Barbara took a sip, made a face, and spit it out into the sink.

She turned to him. His face gave away that there was something wrong.

"What was in this, Eli?"

The wheels in his brain spun. He needed an answer. "Sleeping pills. I was going to kill myself," he said.

Barbara started to cry. She retreated to the bedroom and he followed.

She searched for words as she'd done countless times. There seemed no reaching him. His purported angst and depression were endless. She assumed it was caused by his yo-yoing between the Amish and English worlds.

"Eli," she said, "what will it take for you to change your ways? To give yourself under the church?"

He stayed mute, but she went on and made him an

offer that later some would wonder if Eli had seen as an invitation.

"I'd give my life if I knew it would keep your soul from hell," she said.

The incident gave Barbara a sense of dread. She told a friend that she was suspicious of the drink that Eli had "just happened" to let her taste. Barbara didn't say she thought Eli was trying to poison her. Saying something like that aloud even to a trusted friend would be giving voice to something so horrible, so ungodly, that she doubted she could carry on as if nothing had happened.

Barbara was concerned. Scared.

Turns out she had every reason to be.

Eli continued to wrestle with his demons. Later, he wrote to a family member:

My heart was still bitter and by then I should have learned my lesson, but I didn't and a couple days later I was really down and in my mind everybody was working against me.

That's when his plan went to the next level.

TABITHA MILTON NEEDED a diversion. She was single, the mother of three, and dog tired from her job at an Ohio frozen-food company.

Tabitha was in her thirties with long hair that was black and straight—thanks to the intervention of hair dye and a flatiron that had been her go-to styling routine since she was fifteen. Her arms were inked with the story of the loves and heartaches of her life. Though she was tough when she had to be, she was known for her joyful spirit. When she laughed, her gray-green eyes would widen to take in the joy of whoever was with her. She was energetic and blessed with the kind of personality that drew people in.

She was a beautiful young woman, but being beautiful

hadn't made her life an easy one. She struggled with relationships like so many of her friends. Men seemed to come and go. The only constant was her children, whom she loved more than anything. Men? Take 'em or leave 'em. It hurt to be close to them. It was also lonely without them.

Until Eli Weaver showed up, that is. He came with the promise of friendship and maybe something more. He'd never hurt her.

Or so she thought.

In 2009. she logged on to Lavalife—"Where Singles Click"—and scrolled through the photos and profiles of men looking for the same thing she was: friendship, maybe more. One profile in particular caught her eye. It featured a bearded man with the distinctive cut of the Amish. He didn't say he was Amish. Tabitha didn't ask. But, like other Ohio women, she was curious about the Amish. The two flirted for a while and engaged in sexting.

"Are you Amish?" she asked.

"Yes, I am."

"You're not supposed to have a cell phone, are you?"

"No. But I do. I keep it in the barn and charge it there too."

He didn't say that he was married, and she didn't ask. He told her about how he had a sports supply store and wondered if she was tech savvy enough to help build him a website.

"Sure," she said.

A short time later she drove down to Apple Creek to meet him face-to-face. And yes, he was Amish. He admitted that he was married, too.

Tabitha was lonely and looking for love, but she was not about to get involved with a married man. Especially an Amish one.

"You could get divorced," she said.

"No. I can't. The Amish won't allow it," he said.

"If you wanted to, you could."

"I'd lose everything. My house. My business."

She told him that he could start over.

He looked at her and shook his head. "I can't. I have no education. I can't do it."

Tabitha said she could help him get his GED.

Eli Weaver brightened a little at the prospect.

"It was like there was a little bit of hope," she said later.

TABITHA KNEW HER way around a computer. She told Eli that one pathway out of his bad marriage was to learn how to use technology for his business. He could create an e-commerce site to sell items that could easily be shipped—bows and arrows, for example.

He kept telling her that he wasn't smart enough, that he couldn't manage all that. Would she show him how? Would she be his teacher?

"All I know is Amish," he said. "Farming and hunting, that kind of work."

"You can do more," she said, cheerleading a bit.

She liked Eli so much. Feelings stirred. Not romantic, but a kind of deep friendship that made her want to do more for him.

Later, after so much had happened, Tabitha looked back on those early days of friendship.

"I think he was a lot smarter than he said he was. He caught on too quick," she said.

Every now and then when Tabitha and Eli spent time together, the subject would veer to sex. He'd tell her about an Amish girl he'd been having sex with. Or a Mennonite girl who worked at an Amish restaurant. He'd complain that his wife didn't give him the kind of sexual attention that he wanted.

"I've never gone down on a woman," he told Tabitha one afternoon.

It was the kind of statement that Eli would make every now and then. It didn't shock her. They were best friends and he was looking for someone who could help him.

"What about with your wife?" she asked.

"She won't let me."

"Oh," she said.

"Yeah," he told her. "What does it take for a woman to have an orgasm?"

"Different things," she answered, not sure what else to say. She wondered if the Amish didn't talk about those things. If they didn't have any framework for understanding the way sex works. She figured they didn't learn about it in school. She felt sorry for Eli, but she did her best to answer. They were only friends, so there absolutely was not going to be any show-and-tell.

TABITHA WAS IN a world of hurt. She been laid off from her factory job, had no source of income, and had a family to feed. When she told Eli the bad news, he comforted her, telling her not to worry. He'd help out. He also told her that for all her talk about how he should transform his life through education, she should, too.

Eli gave Tabitha the laptop he'd purchased for the Web site, and told her to get off her butt and start taking classes. When her bank account was close to zero and she was late on her Saturn payment, it was Eli who gave her cash to stay current.

"He really was my best friend," she said later. "Maybe the best friend I'd ever had. He was there for us. He'd come over and we'd have pizza with the kids. Watch TV. He was just an all-around great guy. When my mom could no longer care for her beagle, Eli took the dog in. He was always so helpful to us."

13

Amish Stud

*He used to tell me about all the rumors and dumb
stuff the Amish did. We'd laugh and carry on about it.*
—ONE OF ELI'S GIRLFRIENDS, CHERIE LINDSTROM,
ON ELI'S DISLIKE OF THE AMISH

The Rolodex in Eli's brain had many names in it.

Eli first went online in 2006, soon after returning to his
wife and children. It was three years before he would meet
Tabitha. Some women he met for sex. One relationship
went farther than he planned. The police learned from an
Amish friend of Eli's that he had fathered a child with one
of his girlfriends.

After receiving a tip from one of Eli's friends about how
to find her, Deputy Alex Abel interviewed Misty Stevens
in his unmarked patrol car in front of her parents' house.
Misty and her young daughter lived with her parents.

Misty's relationship with Eli began with a text message
from someone she didn't recognize, the equivalent of a
wrong number. But she responded and they stayed in touch.

At first, Eli didn't tell Misty that he was married and

had children. And she didn't ask. It wasn't until after two months of texting that she asked if he had children and if he had been married. He finally told her the truth. Yes, he was married. Yes, he had children—four at that time (soon to be five). She continued the relationship anyway.

Misty began seeing Eli "romantically." She would pick him up at the store or his house early, at 3:30 or 4:00 a.m., so Barbara would think he had gone fishing or hunting. Then they would go to a motel and out to eat. One time she went out of town with him to a gun show.

Eli told her he wasn't happy with his marriage and that he wasn't receiving the love and attention that he deserved and liked. He told her that should his wife "happen" to pass away, he would leave the Amish community and be with her.

In November, about two months after the sexual part of their friendship began, she learned she was pregnant. "Pretty much after that we were no longer romantically involved," she told detectives. Misty knew he wasn't going to leave his family. He kept giving her excuses about having to sell the store and move. So she said she didn't want to see him anymore. "I pretty much told him I couldn't be with someone who was married."

Misty gave birth to a girl in July 2008. Eli never saw the child, but each month he sent a check for $350, written on the store's bank account, to Misty. The week of Barbara Weaver's murder, Misty received and cashed what would be the last check.

WHEN WAYNE COUNTY detective Michael Maxwell and lieutenant Kurt Garrison showed up at Tabitha's place a couple of days after the shooting, they pressed her hard for whatever it was that they thought she knew. The three sat outside at her picnic table.

They were insistent, but Tabitha was no wallflower. She pushed right back.

"Fuck," she said, "I don't know anything."

She could see the detectives switch tactics and try to win her over, by disclosing a few details and watching her reaction.

"The Weavers' home was invaded and Mrs. Weaver was murdered. Eli was out fishing," Detective Chuhi said.

She pushed back again.

"Like I said, I don't know a thing about it."

There was a lot she didn't tell the detectives. As he did with many other women, Eli confided in Tabitha. "He never said he hated his wife, just hated his marriage to her," Tabitha said later. "Said he needs to get out. He was very unhappy . . . she was mean to him."

At least a dozen times, Tabitha heard Eli talk about killing his wife, but she never took him seriously. Eli would say things like, "I could just choke her—she yells at me all the time" and "What could I use to poison her? I wish she would just go away. We should do it together. Could you get rid of her?"

Not long after the two officers left, Tabitha finally heard from the one person she knew would tell her what had happened.

Eli phoned.

"Tabitha," he said, "I'm so sorry. Someone killed my wife! My children found her!"

Tabitha's head started spinning.

She told him how the detectives had come over. She knew they were insinuating that Eli had been involved and she knew him far better than they did. He was not the kind of man who would kill his wife. Certainly, he was unhappy. Unhappy doesn't mean murderous.

"I'm not working with these guys," she told him. "I know you didn't do this."

After Tabitha hung up, she sat down and collected her-self. Her mind raced to a conversation she and Eli had had about a month prior. They were at her grandmother's house, just kicking back talking. The subject turned to his wife once more. Eli talked about how hateful and mean she was.

"She hates me," he said. "She never lies in bed with me. She's turned everyone in church against me."

As Tabitha saw it, Barbara Weaver was the "meanest" Amish woman who ever walked the earth. She practi-cally abused her husband by doing everything she could to hurt him.

The conversation took a turn when he asked Tabitha how to poison someone.

"You're smart," Eli said, carefully weighing her re-sponse. "Help me figure this out."

The question caught her completely off guard. She wasn't sure what he was really getting at.

"You can use rat poison to poison rats. I don't know anything about poisoning people."

"What about putting it in Barbara's Tang? She likes to drink it every night before bed. Would it kill her?"

"I don't know," Tabitha said.

"Make her sick?" he asked.

She looked at him, measuring where he was coming from, then they laughed it off.

Eli and Tabitha texted several times a day. Finally, there were so many conversations about his unhappy marriage that she began to ignore him—at least when he was rant-ing about his wife.

"I love Eli as a friend. He's been great to me. However, I only loved him as a friend. I think he loved me more than that," she told detectives.

Eli appears to have been a better friend than he was a husband. When Tabitha's phone broke and she needed a new one, and a computer too, he got them for her. They belonged to Barb Raber, but he didn't think that mattered. Tabitha became the third "family member" on Barb's Verizon Friends & Family plan. Eli let Tabitha assume he was paying for the use of the phone. He wasn't. Good old Barb was.

Tabitha had never met her cell phone benefactor, Barb Raber, but they texted. It was Barb who told Tabitha that Eli's wife had been "shot in the heart." Barb said she'd heard that's what the autopsy showed.

Barb had phoned her at the tanning salon to tell her of the murder.

Tabitha was beside herself when Barb said Eli's wife was dead.

"Tell me what the hell's going on," she pleaded. "This is a joke, right? It's not real."

Barb coolly said, "No, it's real."

"What happened?"

"Someone broke into Eli and Barbara's house and shot his wife with a .410 gauge shotgun."

The number .410 stuck in Tabitha's head.

After the murder, Tabitha texted her friend Brian about Eli.

> We joke about it, you know. People say things like "I'm going to kill her, blah, blah," But I never took him serious.

Later, she wrote:

> I guess he wasn't joking. He said he wanted her dead and wanted me. How could he . . . put something like this on me and hurt his five kids.

In a follow-up interview, Detective Chuhi and Lieutenant Garrison asked Tabitha the million-dollar question. Did she think Eli had killed his wife?

"In my heart, no. In my gut, yes."
She was blunter in a text to Brian.

Eli killed his wife and I knew about it. I just never thought
he meant it.

WHILE TABITHA THOUGHT she was Eli Weaver's best friend, another woman in another small Ohio town was hearing the same tune sung by the Amish Stud. And like Tabitha, Candy Denton had been pressed into service because she could help Eli with his Web site.

In time, Eli and Candy traded photos. At first they were somewhat demure. His face. His smile. Over time the images veered to the sexual, including photographs of his penis. She drove out to Sugarcreek and the two of them shared an intimate moment talking at a local park.

He said her loved her and wished that he was no longer Amish so they could be together.

His wife was cold. She refused to sleep with him. Barbara even hurt him physically.

"He told me about her clawing him," Candy later told detectives.

Candy's heart went out to Eli. He played on her sympathies, telling her that he'd been abused as a child. He told her he was lonely. He offered to pay for Candy and her son to move to a better apartment. Eli was good at making women feel that they could heal him, make him happy.

Eli told his girlfriends he couldn't get divorced. It is almost unheard of among the Amish, but it was an option for Eli. If he had put the energy he spent plotting Barbara's death into improving his marriage—or leaving it—his wife and children would have obviously been better for it. He would have been shunned and placed under a Bann and forced to leave the community. But he didn't *want* to be

Amish. He didn't care what his neighbors and bishop thought of him. If Eli had left and sought a divorce, it would have affected Barbara's future more than his. She would not have been allowed to remarry because it would have been considered adultery. But for whatever reason, Eli didn't seem to see it this way. For him, the only way out was if his wife was gone.

14

Dancing in the Rain

He can look into my eyes and lie.
—BARBARA WEAVER, ON HER HUSBAND'S
CONTINUING DECEPTIONS

MocoSpace was very good to Eli. He made lots of new friends and exchanged nude photos with some. He met Cherie Lindstrom online in April 2008 and they eventually met in person at Eli's store.

Cherie was like a lot of young people whose lives hadn't gone exactly as they'd planned. In her twenties, she was working at a job and trying to care for her daughter. Alone. Sure, family members were helpful. She also had a decent place to raise her child in Canton, about half an hour away from Amish Country. Things could have been much, much worse. Once her daughter was in bed, though, the evenings passed slowly. She logged on to MocoSpace to chat and—if she was lucky enough—maybe meet someone.

The name on her screen intrigued her.

Amish Stud.

This can't be real, she thought, as she typed out a

message. She'd always been intrigued by the Amish. Curious about them. Her great-grandfather had been a livestock dealer and she'd been around the Amish when she rode along as he made sales. She thought of them in that romanticized way many people do.

"They were from an innocent culture," she said long after the relationship ended. "It appealed to me. I never thought that I'd meet an Amish guy online. They don't even have phones."

This one did.

Over the next few weeks, Eli and Cherie exchanged text messages. Eli hid in the basement late at night to text. When they finally talked on the phone, they talked about hunting and fishing and how much they both loved the outdoors.

"We'd laugh and carry on," she said years later. "I liked him. His personality was fun. He was always telling me the dumb stuff the other Amish did and how the rumors were flying. Everyone had something to say about everyone else."

When she thought about it later, she wondered what they'd been saying about her and her visits to Eli's shop.

"Probably wasn't good," she said.

He told Cherie that the world of the Amish was nothing like she thought it was. Eli complained about his family and the ironfisted rule held over him by his older brother, a minister in the church.

"Eli told me he hated his brother. Hated the Amish. They expected him to be socially acceptable in their culture, but he wasn't. He couldn't be."

When they first met in person, it was as friends only. She brought her daughter along and Eli gave her a fishing pole.

Eventually it turned to romance, then sex.

"He tried to teach me Dutch. He joked. I knew he was

married, but he wasn't happy. He told me how he'd left the Amish before and he was thinking about doing it again. I didn't expect to, but I fell for him. I cared about him. I never thought he was capable of anything like murder."

THE FIRST PLACE they had sex was Eli's store. When Eli couldn't get away from the ball and chain that was his life among the Amish, they had no choice but to make do.

During those encounters, Eli would lock the door and they'd duck down behind the counter.

One day he forgot to lock the door.

Cherie heard the door open and saw a man stop and back away. She watched him leave.

"Eli, there was a man here," she said. "He was Amish. He *saw* us."

"Don't worry about it," he said.

The man went right to the bishop, who later chastised Eli but provided no further punishment.

The affair was exciting because it was forbidden. Initially, Cherie and Eli traded nude photos on MocoSpace. It was a diversion for the young mother dealing with lonely nights. While Eli was a good-looking guy, it wasn't until they met that she was won over by his eyes.

"His soft, gentle eyes," she remembered. "And I normally hate brown eyes."

She found herself falling for him. It was a relationship built on sex and promises. On her day off from work, Cherie would pick up Eli at his house or store and they would spend the whole day together at her house having sex. They each told the other they were in love. Cherie fulfilled Eli's craving for oral sex—something he complained his wife refused to do. He satisfied her, too. They would talk for hours, about her childhood, her daughter, and—increasingly—Eli's problems.

All of a sudden Eli began wanting more of her: more time, more attention, more of her listening to his complaints. It began to feel uncomfortable. Even dark. It went way beyond what Cherie had signed up for when she contacted the Amish Stud.

Eli was always making plans—plans for a life without his wife and children. Cherie wasn't exactly sure how she fit into things, but he kept asking her to be there for him when he left. He asked her to help find him a job so he could start over. She knew he had those little kids at home and it made her sick inside.

Yet he always managed to spin things around so that whatever it was that he wanted was the righteous thing.

"He was capable of making me feel guilty," Cherie said. "I knew I was his out. I feel bad about that now, but at the time I didn't see he was playing on sympathy to get what he wanted."

She remembered Eli as very childlike—or very good at playing the part. When Cherie would pick him up for a drive out of Amish Country, Eli would beg for her to take him to McDonald's.

"It was funny. Weird. He was always excited to go to McDonald's. If it was morning, he'd want an Egg McMuffin and coffee and if it was lunchtime, he'd want a Quarter Pounder with cheese and a coffee. It was always such a big deal to him. He had a kind of playful arrogance about him. He was so naïve, but he was just playing the part."

Cherie would come down from Canton to sit in Eli's shop at a little table next to the door. Mostly they'd be there chatting between customers. Some days were very slow and they had more idle time than what conversation could fill. In addition to the Amish man who reported them to the bishop, one of Eli's children had also entered the shop at an inconvenient moment, and they'd had to quickly get themselves together.

One time Eli's wife came in to hand her husband some coffee while Cherie was sitting at the little table by the door.

"That's my wife," Eli said to Cherie.

Cherie felt a pang of guilt, but Eli had made it so very clear that his wife was cold to him and that his needs weren't being met. It was easy to forget that there was a wife and mother of five kids in the mix.

Barbara had been marginalized so much that Cherie was unable to recall anything specific about her.

If love is blind, it can also be selfish.

"I can't even picture her in my mind," Cherie said later. "All those Amish women look alike."

It's hard to say exactly how Eli moved from flirting, to sex, to asking a woman if she would kill his wife, but he did. Often.

Two months after they met, Eli started talking about leaving his marriage. That got old, and although they continued their sexual relationship, Cherie encouraged him to remain committed to his wife and children.

But he could be oh so charming.

IT WAS THE plot of a romance novel. One full of clichés. They were from two worlds—Amish and English. They were in love. There were obstacles. And like the frenzied reader of a sexy novel, Cherie Lindstrom could not stop herself.

There was even the day they danced in the rain.

Cherie and her Amish lover both liked the outdoors. She would drive them to the Wilderness Center, a nature preserve near Wilmot. They would walk the ten miles of hiking trails, passing by old-growth forest, prairie, and lakes and ponds. It wasn't about the nature, of course; it was all about finding a place to be alone, a place to have sex.

During one of their walks, the skies opened and it began raining. She begged him to dance with her. He resisted, saying he didn't know how to dance, but Cherie could be persuasive and he finally gave in.

"It was romantic," she said later. "It was perfect. Walking, holding hands, ducking raindrops."

While she loved the Eli Weaver who was passionate but also "giggly" and "goofy," she pulled back when he turned moody.

They had known each other long enough, about a year, that he could no longer hide his fallback behavior, which was manipulation.

"I'm going to leave my family. I really am," he told her on the walk.

"Sure, Eli," she said. "You always say that."

He stared at her with those brown eyes she'd grown to love.

"No," he said. "I really mean it."

Cherie was unsure.

"You need to stay and fix things with your wife, and be there for your kids," she said.

She had told him that before. Now she was insistent. But his whining was getting on her nerves. He didn't catch on.

"I'm bored," he said. "I don't like the control the church has over me. I want out. I want a different job."

That was a sore spot with Cherie. She'd tried to help him out by connecting him with other job prospects.

"Eli, I opened a door for you," she said. "You said you wanted to work at one of the big outdoor stores. You wanted to work with archery equipment. I called some stores for you, I told them about you. You were supposed to go in for interviews and you didn't!"

"Well . . . " Eli knew there was no way to defend himself.

"I said, 'Here's the phone number of the store. I'll even drive you,' but you never followed up."

Eli shrugged.

She called Eli out.

"You want me to feel sorry for you," she said, letting him have it. "You say, 'I'm bored, I'm under my brother's thumb in the church.' I don't have time to feel sorry for you, Eli. Deal with this. This is the life you chose when you were baptized. Why did you get baptized in the first place if you didn't want to be Amish?"

Eli looked down at the ground. "It was expected of me."

Cherie, who'd done all that she could to make something of herself, grew angry. "There are a million things expected of me, too. That's the way life is."

She'd reached her breaking point. Cherie knew it and Eli knew it. They didn't talk for a couple of weeks. It had happened before. Then one of them would call or text a smiley face and they would make contact again, meet for sex, then reach another impasse.

"He was trying to get me to rescue him," Cherie said later.

But I'm the princess, she thought. *Someone is supposed to rescue me.*

Cherie chose to see less of Eli.

"HIS WIFE WAS murdered!" Cherie couldn't believe her ears. She asked the friend who worked at a mill with the Amish to repeat what he was saying as she slumped into a chair in her Canton area home.

"They found Eli's wife dead this morning!" he told her.

"What are you talking about?" she asked.

"There's a rumor going around that someone shot her!" Cherie started to cry. She lost it completely.

She thought back to a photo Eli had sent her just two weeks before. It was a photograph of the chair that she sat in when she was at Maysville Outfitters.

"Something's missing here," he wrote. "You."

She hadn't seen him for a while so after getting his note she dialed his number and good old Eli had her laughing and missing him all over again. He also played the sympathy card again, telling her that his wife was colder than ever.

"If you see her in a parking lot, run her over," he said.

"Are you serious?" she asked, feeling a slight chill at his request.

"Just kidding," he said after a beat of silence.

Reeling from the news that Barbara Weaver was dead, Cherie dropped everything and went to her cousin's house three doors down. The cousin had a relative who was a lawyer. Cherie called the lawyer. He told her to call the sheriff.

She did.

She also called her father and when the two of them arrived at the offices of the Wayne County Sheriff, Cherie was composed but shaking inside. When the detectives told her that Eli had mentioned her name to them as a potential suspect, she crumbled.

She started sobbing.

"Really?" she asked.

"I know where I was," she said. "I didn't have anything to do with it."

They asked her for the names of the people she'd been with the night of the murder and she provided them. Phone numbers, too.

The detectives asked her to make a controlled phone call to Eli in their presence. She called his cell and got a recording saying the number had been changed. The detectives sat her down at a computer in the sheriff's office.

She no longer had a MocoSpace account, but she created a new one and sent a message to Eli asking him to call her.

"He will call me back," she said.

But he didn't. She waited. The detectives waited. Nothing. An hour later, they gave her a small recorder and some audio equipment so she could capture everything he said if and when he called back.

Fifteen minutes later, just outside of Dalton, her phone rang. She pushed the Record button and answered. Eli was "real nonchalant" when he spoke. "Somebody shot my wife," he said.

"What?" she asked, pretending to be surprised.

"I can't talk right now," he said. "I'm at my dad's. I'll call you later."

She immediately dialed the detectives and told them of the call.

"He sounded so cold. He didn't seem upset," she said. "It was like a normal conversation. 'Somebody shot my wife.'"

She was so done with him.

AT HER HOME in a village in Holmes County, Tabitha Milton was struggling with something only she knew. It niggled at her. It was a scab that kept falling off. Tabitha couldn't shake the thought from her brain. Barb Raber had said something to her that she hadn't heard on the news. It was during the first phone call.

She was specific about the weapon used to kill Eli's wife.

"Someone broke into Eli and Barbara's house and shot his wife with a .410 gauge shotgun."

It was something only the killer or killers could have known.

15

Friends

*Your dad and probably whole family says something is
wrong with you. Well they are sorta right. You are too
full of life to be controlled. You doing what makes you
happy isn't wrong.*

—SHELLEY CASEY, THE WOMAN HE DATED IN 2006,
ASSESSING ELI AND OFFERING HERSELF TO HIM

The work of sifting through Eli's life—and the lives of
others who might be suspects in the murder of his wife—was
well under way. Barbara Weaver's death wasn't suicide—
there was no firearm by the bed. It wasn't burglary—there
was cash sitting out in at least two places in the house.
Someone had wanted to murder the thirty-year-old Amish
wife and mother of five.

Detectives interviewed friends, neighbors, family, and
the ever-growing number of women Eli had known. Who
was this guy?

Not everyone disliked Eli. He had charisma; he could
be entertaining and even polite. A Mennonite woman who
was also a taxi driver (not Barb Raber) said he was always

"a perfect gentleman" when he came to her door looking for a ride. "He was so apologetic for interrupting me when he saw I was in my pajamas," Betty Stolfus said. "I assured him that it was no problem." One time when Barbara Weaver was caring for her handicapped uncle, Eli carried the man gently down the steps and placed him in Betty's van for the ride home.

Later, Betty spoke of the irony. "I have to wonder in retrospect how he could show compassion for a handicapped person and have none for his wife," she said.

Tips were coming in to the sheriff's office. Word had gotten around that someone in Barbara's family didn't want people to talk to the police. But the Amish proceeded to talk and talk—to each other and to their English and Mennonite friends.

A few called the sheriff's office. They wanted detectives to know that a man had been overheard at a gas station talking about a "hit list" of people he intended to kill; that Barb Raber never reined in her foul mouth or sexual overtones even when others were present; that Eli was a womanizer; that one of Eli's girlfriends was an exotic dancer. The staff of a pizza parlor in the nearby town of Kidron called to say Eli was "sly," and either committed the murder or was involved. There were other leads phoned in: Eli physically abused his wife; Eli liked drugs, alcohol, and pornography; Barbara Weaver had been seen through a window of her house the night before she was murdered, pacing the floor. And there was information they already knew: that the dead woman had been seeing a counselor and that Eli had fathered a baby with a girlfriend.

Ed Raber—not Barb's husband but another Ed Raber, the one whose route emptying Porta-Potties took him to Eli's store—said that Eli had asked him, "Why don't you kill my wife, my bitch for me?" Then, he said, Eli laughed and said he was kidding. Eli wasn't kidding when he told Ed that if it weren't for his children, no way would he be married.

Several people told investigators about the day, almost exactly one year before the murder, Eli was caught in his store with "an English lady in his arms"—and he wasn't selling her fishing tackle. A witness went to Eli's bishop, who confronted him. At first Eli denied it, but he finally admitted the public indiscretion and even claimed he had been praying he would be caught and had made peace with God.

Barbara's counselor, Duane Troyer, shared with investigators some of what Barbara had confided over the previous three years. Her first appointment at Hoffnung Heim, the Christian counseling practice, was in April 2006. Barbara and Eli were living in Millersburg in a house on his parents' property. She saw Troyer every other week for several months. It was probably the worst time for Barbara and her children. During that time, Eli left his family, living as English with Shelley, driving a pickup, wearing English clothes, and even shaving off his beard, occasionally returning home for brief stays.

When Barbara and the children moved to Apple Creek Township, Eli said he'd live with her again if she moved back to his parents', but she refused. Duane Troyer tried to reach out to Eli and offered to speak with him, too, but Eli would never take his calls.

Troyer summarized the Weaver marriage this way: they had "very serious marital problems."

No one knew why Eli finally left Shelley and went home to Barbara and the children in Apple Creek. He blabbed about a lot of things to his friends, but he didn't talk about that.

Neighbors learned that Eli had moved back. One

woman told Barbara she was glad her husband was home. Barbara answered that Satan still had a hold on Eli.

Betty Stolfus drove Eli to a local sporting goods store so he could talk with people about how to set up his own store. She waited for a few hours. A few weeks later, Eli opened Maysville Outfitters. He may have moved home to his family, but he remained an absent husband and father.

Except for Eli, there was a lot of joy in Barbara's life. The taxi driver remembers one time driving Barbara to Fannie's. Barbara and her sister laughed a lot when they realized they had both made a Jell-O cake. "Barbara just seemed so happy at that time that I would never have suspected all the heartache she was holding inside," Betty said. "I also can hear so clearly in my mind Barbara saying in a bright, cheerful voice, 'Okay, kidders, let's go!' whenever I would take her and the children somewhere."

According to Betty, Barbara's way of quieting or comforting her children was to pull them close and show her love. Eli's way was to give them a candy bar or a snack from his store. He didn't like them bothering him. On the rare evenings he was home, he didn't sit down with his family for dinner. Barbara would prepare a plate of food for him and Harley would take it to him in the shop.

Eli had another getaway. He would ask Betty to take him to a high hill south of Fredericksburg, west of Maysville, in the evening. He said he wanted to be alone to watch for deer. At least that's what he said he was doing. Betty would pick him up later.

Eli seemed polite—but odd. One day he took the children to Barbara's sister's house, but he forgot the baby. So Barbara asked Betty when she returned to take the baby and she did. "It made me wonder how he could forget his own child," Betty said.

For a time Eli raised dogs to sell. A neighbor remembers

the caged dogs howling late at night. She also recalls lighting sparklers in her yard after dark and how much Eli's children loved playing with the sparklers.

In January 2007 Eli was reinstated in the church, but life didn't get better for Barbara. Eli was still away a lot—"with an English taxi driver," Barbara told Duane Troyer. And Barbara suspected there were other women.

The detectives heard back from Tabitha. She was remembering more details that might be important. Not only had Barb Raber called her the afternoon of the murder to tell her about it, she'd also contacted Tabitha two days after the murder, on June 4.

Tabitha told her she had been questioned by the police. Barb seemed distracted, nervous, and denied mentioning Barbara Weaver's autopsy and cause of death to Tabitha during their earlier conversation.

"She told me she had to go, and called me right back from a different number. She said she had to call me from that number from now on and was short and said goodbye quick."

Tabitha also told John Chuhi about a text Eli had sent her two months before the murder. He wanted to find someone who would kill his wife in the early morning, maybe when she was outside doing laundry.

"I said something like 'Are you serious?' and we joked about it," she said. Eli also talked about putting rat poison in his wife's Tang. He wanted Tabitha to research it.

"I never did," she said.

16

The Go-To Attorney for Wayward Amish

*He told me $300 is the limit for groceries each month,
and that sounded okay, but by the time you get coffee,
Pampers, milk, and eggs, etc. once a week there's barely
enough. I've asked him to please get the groceries but
he doesn't have time.*

—BARBARA WEAVER, ON HER ABSENT HUSBAND'S
CONTROLLING NATURE

It was early Wednesday morning, two days after Barbara's body was found, when lawyer Andy Hyde pulled into the driveway of Eli's father's house. Hyde looked over the scene. It was a checklist for what visitors expect to see in Amish country. Immaculate white house. Pristine limestone walkway and driveway. White aluminum and steel barn that reflected brightly in the sunshine. Buggy tracks toward the barn.

The reason Hyde was there was diametrically opposed to the scene.

A call from an English friend of Eli's had sounded the alarm that an Amish man, Eli Weaver, needed an attorney.

"His wife just got killed," Gary Schrock had explained to Hyde.

Hyde—all lanky six feet, six inches of him—watched a man hitch up a team of horses, then lead it right past Hyde and his prospective client without a word or a glance.

Eli leaned toward the lawyer and mumbled, "Don't pay any attention to him."

The man who passed by without a word to anyone was Eli's father.

"He walked right by us without saying anything," Hyde later said, still trying to come to grips with the cold slight. "I put out my hand to shake his," he said. "He didn't acknowledge me. No handshake, no invitation to come into the house."

Eli was staying at his parents' house east of Millersburg. His parents were not happy he was there. They were even less happy that Eli had hired a lawyer. It was a very non-Amish thing to do.

With his long hair and even longer beard, Andy Hyde could easily be mistaken for Amish.

He isn't. His appearance is less about looking at home around the Amish than it is about his hobby: reenacting battles of the French and Indian War on historic battlefields in Ohio. Hyde describes himself as an "Amish family lawyer" and has been involved in controversial crimes in the Amish community before and since the murder of Barbara Weaver.

When he met Eli, Hyde was forty-three years old and the father of four children. He couldn't stop thinking about Eli's children, who were now without a mother.

Hyde, Eli, and Gary stood in the driveway and talked. Wayne County Sheriff's Office detectives were due any minute to pick up Eli and take him for a polygraph test.

Andy thought Eli was strange—especially for a husband who had just lost his wife.

"He was happy to see me," he recalled. "But he was sending off very weird signals for an Amish guy. Usually when you're talking to a suspect, they really listen and focus on you. Their lives are in your hands. But Eli was not focused. It was clear his mind was somewhere else."

When Eli's phone rang, he didn't say a word before answering. Instead he walked off, then squatted on the driveway and turned his body away from Hyde.

"Here's a man whose life you're there to save and taking a phone call is more important," Hyde recalled. "Anyone else would have said, 'I'm talking to my attorney; let me call you back.' Not Eli."

When Eli finished talking, he turned back to his lawyer. They began to talk about the day of the murder.

"He said he had been fishing up at Lake Erie and that his wife had been seen by someone after he left that morning."

Hyde learned later that Eli had lied. No one had seen his wife the morning of the murder.

He tried to prepare Eli for the scrutiny that was to come.

"I told him, 'They're looking at you. Ninety-nine percent of the time they'll look at the husband as a suspect. Understand they're going to look at you.'"

Eli didn't ask many questions about the case but focused on the costs associated with his defense if he should be arrested.

"I told him it would cost a lot of money for me to represent him," the lawyer said later, "and he said 'fine.'"

About a half hour later, Detective John Chuhi and Lieutenant Kurt Garrison drove up to the property. Hyde and the detectives were on friendly terms. Holmes and Wayne Counties were rural and crime rates were low. Lawyers and deputies were busy, but not so busy that they didn't know who everyone was. Hyde told them he was representing Eli and needed time to talk to him.

"Eli will take a polygraph," he said, "just not right now."

A moment later, Chuhi and Garrison shook hands with the lawyer and drove away.

Standing outside in the morning sunlight while the blue sky stretched as far as they could see, Hyde talked privately with Eli for a few more minutes. The attorney known by many as "the go-to attorney for wayward Amish" was once more surprised by Eli's attitude. He didn't ask questions. He didn't ask about what would happen next. Eli Weaver didn't seem overly concerned with the investigation.

Or that his wife had been murdered.

Later when he replayed that first meeting with his client in his head, Hyde conjured images of a circus performer trying to keep objects upright, to keep them from falling.

"He was spinning plates on sticks," he recalled.

Though Eli didn't know it at the time, some were already shattering on the ground.

MARK WEAVER WAS having a tough time. He was a loyal husband and father. A hard worker. A good friend and a good neighbor. He asked himself over and over how it was possible that his friend was somehow involved in a murder.

Steve Chupp knew Mark had a lot of questions. He did, too. When he had an appointment to meet with Detective Chuhi, Steve asked Mark to come, too.

The trio met over Cokes at Wendy's in Dover.

"I don't usually do this," the detective said, "but I wanted you to have a clear picture of what we know and what we think happened."

Mark and Steve listened as Chuhi laid out what he believed connected Eli to the murder.

"Eli had a friend of his call an attorney right away," he went on. "Some people would do that, but it's not usually the first thing a grieving husband does. We know you, Steve, had trouble waking him up to go fishing. We know he had left his wife twice. He was meeting women online and having affairs."

Some of this was news. Mark and Steve didn't know the extent of Eli's affairs or that he'd advertised himself online as Amish Stud.

But the biggest shock was yet to come.

"I'm going to tell you something I shouldn't tell you," the detective said. "We also know that Eli talked to people about poisoning his wife or killing her in an explosion. He was trying to find someone to kill his wife."

The two men sat there speechless. It was worse than they thought.

Chuhi told the men that he hoped to get Eli's phone records—if Eli had a phone. Mark had some welcome news for the detective. He shoved his Coke to one side.

"Detective, I have Eli's phone number," Mark said. "And I have another phone number for you—Barb Raber's. And I have phone messages from her. You need to look at her. She and Eli were talking about something Monday. She is asking way too many questions about the murder."

Mark played Barb's voice-mail messages and Chuhi recorded them. He also copied the many text messages she had sent Mark.

Mark left Wendy's with a realization that felt like pain to his soul.

Eli had killed his wife, or found someone to do it for him.

17

The Viewing

Sun. eve. Kinner [children] in bed. Once again Eli lies
on floor, eyes closed. So often, eyes closed.
—BARBARA WEAVER, ON THE WIDENING DISTANCE
IN HER MARRIAGE TO ELI

The community's first chance to get more than a glimpse of Eli came at Barbara's viewing and funeral. Amish and Mennonite friends and neighbors were already suspicious of him. Eli's reputation for running around and being shunned by the church was well known. Samuel Miller—an Amish acquaintance of the Weavers—said that even on June 2, as word spread of the murder, many Amish had one of two reactions.

"Men asked 'Where was Eli?'" Samuel said. "Women asked 'Was it Eli?'"

A neighbor overheard Eli's bishop question him about the murder. "What happened, Eli? Who did this?"

Eli replied defiantly, "I'm telling you sincerely from my heart that I don't know!"

Despite the horrific nature of her death, funeral services for Barbara Weaver adhered to Amish customs as much as possible. Burial is usually within three days of death, the time needed for one man to build a coffin and four men to dig a grave.

The autopsy was conducted at 8:30 a.m. on June 3, the day after she was murdered. Because Wayne County didn't have a forensic pathologist, the autopsy was performed in Akron by Summit County's chief medical examiner, Lisa Kohler. It was observed, as usual, by police, in this case Detective Chuhi and Lieutenant Garrison, plus Dr. Kohler's investigator, Jason Grom, and Tom Uhler of the Wayne County Coroner's Office. The autopsy confirmed that Barbara Weaver died from a single gunshot wound at close range to the right chest, depositing pellets to her right lung and her heart. Also injured by the shot were her diaphragm and spine. Her unexplained injuries, including contusions on her legs, scratches on one finger, and bruising on both palms, were noted. The autopsy report did not mention the bruising on Barbara Weaver's neck, but it was visible in the photos.

After the autopsy, Barbara Weaver's body was taken to Spidell Funeral Home in Mount Eaton. Sometimes the Amish are embalmed—at a funeral home or even at home—sometimes not. Barbara Weaver was. The body is often washed and dressed by friends and family. In this case, an Amish woman who often performs the ritual for the funeral home dressed Barbara. A woman can be buried in her wedding dress, but Barbara was dressed more traditionally in her good black dress, with a starched white cape pinned over her back and chest, a white apron, and a white bonnet, or Kapp, the same clothes she might have worn to church.

An obituary in the local newspaper said only that she died "at her home."

People can view the body on three occasions: at a viewing in the home, at the funeral, and at graveside.

The Amish don't have churches—they hold services every two weeks in homes and barns. Men sit on one side and women on the other, facing each other. Because a large group was expected, the two-day viewing was held in the upper level of the barn on the Weaver property. Although the house had recently been the scene of a crime, it wasn't off-limits and friends and neighbors could enter the house to use the bathroom.

In many respects, it was a typical Amish viewing, with several hundred people attending throughout the course of the day, the majority coming in the evening. They were somberly dressed: the men in dark suits and white or pale blue shirts and the women in black or navy-blue dresses with starched white Kapps. Many arrived by horse and buggy or on foot, but there were also many taxi drivers bringing van loads of friends or relatives from a distance. A long line of mourners stretched from the barn to the road.

In certain conservative communities, a body would be laid out on a cooling board, or a viewing bed. In the summer, ice is placed beneath the perforated wooden platform to keep the body chilled. Barbara Weaver's body was displayed in its casket.

The casket was in a partitioned corner of the barn and the top was open so that friends, neighbors, and family could walk close and take one last look at the young woman. "There was more emotion than we often see," Samuel said. "Maybe not outward weeping, but a lot of emotion looking at pretty, kind, young Barbara in death and everyone suspecting her husband."

Samuel and his wife followed the line of mourners into the barn and after viewing Barbara, they threaded their way through the backless benches that had been set up for the family to sit on and greet the people attending. As the mourners made their way through the benches, they shook hands with the relatives seated there.

"I've been to hundreds of viewings, but this was the only silent one," Samuel said later. "Hundreds of people but none of the usual talking. No one knew what to say."

Eli didn't either, and he didn't seem to try. "Eli looked very pale, sweaty, and unlike [the bereaved at] all other Amish viewings I've been to, he was not looking up or making any eye contact with everyone who spoke to him.

"As I shook his hand, I thought, 'Oh my word, I'm shaking hands with a murderer!'" Samuel said. He thought Eli's reactions screamed "guilty."

Conversation was very subdued. "It was eerie," he said. "Eventually we saw Eli come out and head for either the Porta-John or the watercooler, leading two of his sons by the hands. An Amish man standing in the crowd whispered, "Now *there* is something that has not been seen often before—Eli showing attention to his children."

A Mennonite neighbor, Pearl Wyse, said that at one point Eli was helped to his feet and wailed as he walked past the coffin. "But there were no tears and it was very obvious he was faking," she said. "He kept his head down the rest of the time I was there. The next day, the second day of the viewing, he was sitting in the yard on a bench with the visitors and his manner was very casual. He was drinking coffee and had his shirt unbuttoned." She found his behavior inappropriate.

Eli's parents were protective of him at the viewing.

Steve Chupp and Mark Weaver went to the viewing and spoke briefly to Eli. By then they were convinced Eli had been involved with the murder. Both decided to keep their distance from him.

The funeral, on Saturday, June 6, was also held in Eli's barn. The two-hour service was led by Bishop Leroy Keim in Pennsylvania Dutch and attended by hundreds of black-clad friends and relatives. There are no eulogies at Amish funerals. The focus is on giving thanks and praising God, not on speaking of the deceased. A meal prepared by the women of the community was served after the funeral.

There were no special prayers for Barbara. The Amish belief is that once a person has died, no amount of prayer will change how she met her Maker. Between themselves, Barbara's Andy Weaver community discussed how she'd handled her heartbreak. Her friends and neighbors said she'd "never lost her faith" and "kept wanting what was right."

Four men who were friends of the family carried the casket from the house to a black horse-drawn hearse, and took it to the graveyard. Barbara Weaver was buried in a small Amish cemetery in Salt Creek Township.

There were no flowers at the viewing or at the cemetery. Cemetery plots are usually left untended—no flowers, no landscaping, just a simple cement or concrete headstone made by an Amish man with the name, birth date, and death date carved into it.

Family members wear black for a period of mourning. Grief is private. The Amish do not usually show their emotions.

Scott Spidell, a second-generation undertaker, took charge of the funeral. He knew Barbara's family because he had overseen her mother's funeral in 2008. The sadness surrounding the murder stunned everyone.

"It was shocking," Spidell said. "Everyone was speculating" about who might have killed Barbara Weaver. Since Eli was the surviving spouse, Spidell worked with him on funeral details.

Samuel Miller and his wife heard a story making the rounds after the funeral. Eli had reportedly said to his widowed father-in-law, "Now I know how you feel." Barbara's father replied with great emotion, "*No!* You do *not* know how I feel!"

It was the first murder among the Andy Weaver Amish in the area, although Spidell's father, Waid Spidell, had handled funeral services for Ida Stutzman, victim of an alleged murder that was never prosecuted. She and her husband, Eli Stutzman, were Swartzentruber Amish, the most well known subgroup of Old Order Amish. Ida died from what her husband claimed was "a weak heart" during a suspicious barn fire in 1977. She was eight months pregnant. After her death, Eli Stutzman took to the road with his young son, Daniel, and began a series of affairs with gay men. He was later convicted of leaving his nine-year-old son's body in a Nebraska ditch in 1985 and concealing his death. He served time in a Texas prison for an unrelated 1989 murder, was paroled in 2005, and remains a person of interest in the murders of two Colorado men. Stutzman committed suicide in 2007.

Detective Chuhi and Lieutenant Garrison attended Barbara Weaver's funeral—to show the Amish community that the sheriff's department cared and was serious about solving the crime, and to observe Barbara Weaver's family and friends. The murder looked personal.

Lieutenant Garrison was contacted after the service by an Amish man who wanted to remain anonymous. There was something strange, he said. Eli's good friends of many years, Barb and Ed Raber, hadn't been at the funeral. The man said he'd been told the Rabers had chosen to drive to Illinois that day to drop off some equipment—something to do with Ed's job. After speaking with him, Lieutenant Garrison wrote the following in his report:

> *He thought it was odd that they chose to be out of the area and miss the funeral. It was also strange that Barbara went with Ed when normally she would*

*much rather remain in the area hauling Amish or
just men in general talking dirty.*

Eli and Barb Raber saw each other at the viewing, but
there wasn't time to talk. They texted and met up in Eli's
barn the day after the funeral.

They had to discuss cleanup.

18

Eli and Barb

I asked him, "If I'd die, would you actually cry?" He answered, "Oh yes." I don't believe he would because I'm so far from what he wants.
—BARBARA WEAVER, IN A LETTER FORESHADOWING HER
OWN DEATH

Barb Raber was frazzled. She'd come undone. When she met Eli at the barn, she was a shell of what she had been, a broken dish, a cracked mirror. She shook as she stood there, fighting for composure. Eli later told investigators that the reason for the meeting was that he needed some feed delivered.

Just another one of his lies.

Those close to the case would wonder if he'd asked her there to calm her. Placate her. Ensure that she didn't fall completely apart.

"Look," said one person close to the case, "Raber was in love with Eli. She'd do anything for him. Sex when he wanted. Murder when he asked her to. I wonder how long she would have lasted once he saw that she was about to fall apart?"

Barb loved her .410 gauge shotguns. No one who knew her would deny that. She loved the light weight of the .410s. She loved the way there was almost no kickback when they were fired. She loved that they were ideal for close-distance shooting, anything under forty yards—even better, fifteen to twenty. It was the smallest-gauge shotgun made, perfect for a youth learning to shoot, or for a woman, even if she was an experienced hunter.

In the barn the day after the funeral, she teared up. Eli put his hands on her, stopping her from collapsing.

"Can you clean a shotgun so it looks like it hasn't been fired?" Barb asked.

Eli offered his advice. But the moment wasn't about offering tips to clean a shotgun. It was about keeping the secret. Barb had to get control of herself.

Despite the rumors that neither directly acknowledged, the pair had managed to keep their destructive sexual relationship quiet.

She performed oral sex on Eli in her Ford Explorer; they'd had intercourse at a motel the few times she drove him out of town for an overnight stay. The barn had been their main place for their illicit affair. She'd drop to her knees at his bidding and make sure he'd have the "happy ending" he'd begged her for.

It wasn't about sex that day, or about Eli's needs at all. Instead, she begged for help.

"I'm scared," she said.

Barb probably knew guns as well as Eli. Yes, he said, it was possible to clean a shotgun so it would appear not to have been fired recently. Eli reminded her of the process. Get rid of gunpowder residue by cleaning the barrel with acetone and don't forget to clean the trigger and hammer, too. Use a brush, an old toothbrush, steel wool, or a cleaning-polishing rod. Finish it off with a good wipe with a dry cloth."What do I tell Ed if he notices the shotgun is missing?" she asked.

Eli knew they didn't have to worry about Ed. He was blind to what had been going on with his wife. She'd been with Eli and other men. She'd lied to him time and again. And he fell for it.

Ed Raber was clueless. He'd been the perfect dupe.

BARB RABER WASN'T the only one having anxious days and nights.

Linda and Firman Yoder—who lived in one-half of Eli's store, where Linda occasionally worked—called the sheriff's office to say someone had broken into their home.

They thought it was Eli.

Detective Maxwell met them at a nearby Amish residence. They didn't want Eli to see the detective at their house.

The day before, Linda had returned home on her bike from visiting a friend and found that someone had been in their side of the building. A door leading from the shop into the Yoders' home, which Linda had left shut and locked, was open. Her windows had been unlocked.

Nothing appeared to have been taken, but it was as if the perpetrator were planning a return visit.

They were afraid of Eli and thought he might harm them. They knew about his relationship with Barb Raber. They knew about his having a cell phone. They knew all of Eli's problems and faults. They even thought they knew what he had done with the murder weapon.

Three weeks before the murder, Linda had gone along on a fishing trip to Lake Erie with a group that included

Eli. She overheard a man telling Eli how he had disposed of a rifle in the lake. Maybe that had given Eli the idea of how to get rid of the shotgun?

Detective Maxwell put a tap on the shanty phone and reassured them they were safe. An arrest was imminent.

19

Warrants

Why do I cringe every time I need to ask him for money? Am I not being submissive? I grew up with what was Dad's was Mom's, and what was Mom's was Dad's.

—BARBARA WEAVER, LAMENTING THAT HER MARRIAGE TO ELI
WAS NOTHING LIKE SHE'D HOPED IT WOULD BE

Edna Boyle studied the affidavit for a search warrant that was on her desk. As the assistant district attorney assigned to prosecute the case, she was looking through police reports and preparing a warrant to seize computers, phones, and guns from Barb Raber's house, garage, and outbuildings. The thing about a search warrant is that you have to have a pretty good idea of what you'll find *before* you find it and convince a judge of it.

Thanks to text messaging—still somewhat in its infancy when Eli discovered how easy it was for him to hook up with women—Boyle knew what she was looking for.

She was forty-three years old, married, and the mother of two young children. It didn't escape trial watchers that there was an interesting equation about to play out: a woman with young children was prosecuting a woman with young children for the murder of a woman with young children.

As a feature story about her in a local newspaper stated, she'd leave you in the dust if you tried to catch her. Boyle was competitive, smart, and no-nonsense. By the time she came on to the Weaver case the day after the murder, she had been an attorney in private practice, a municipal judge in Akron Municipal Court, a certified fitness coach, and a marathon runner.

As an African-American, she was a bit of an anomaly in Amish country. She was an experienced attorney, but she knew little about the Amish. Just days before the murder, Boyle was working on a trial involving a case of felonious assault. She happened to be driving through Amish country with a detective on their way back from prison.

"He said, 'Do you know how to tell an Amish house?' I said, 'No.'"

"'No power lines.'"

Although she had spent most of her adult life in Akron, northeast of Wooster, she had had very little contact with the Amish. She saw Amish people occasionally as they passed through the juvenile court system—usually young people drinking. She said the Amish often confess, and don't understand why they need an attorney.

"I tell them, 'You need an attorney.'"

Boyle prepared for a trial the way she trained for a race. All out.

The affidavit she prepared cited the facts of the case to date, plus information gleaned from Cherie, Tabitha, and others who had heard Eli openly discussing wanting to be rid of his wife and knew of his close relationship with Barb Raber.

In order to justify the warrant, she included some of the

text messages exchanged between her two best suspects recovered from Verizon after Mark Weaver supplied Eli's and Barb's phone numbers. From May 30 to June 2, Eli and Barb exchanged messages about methods of murder. Poison? Insecticide or nitrogen? Maybe an explosion? They even considered killing the children.

There were dozens of texts between 330-473-0453 (Barb) and 330-473-0392 (Eli) on Barb's Verizon Friends & Family plan. Perhaps ironically, while there were hundreds of texts, phone records would show that Eli and Barb had used their phones for *talking* fewer than ten times in six months.

As a result, everything was there in their text messages: means, motive, and opportunity. And proof.

Evening, May 30:

Eli: Do you think 3 cc's of that tempo would do it?
Barb: How would that ant stuff work?

Morning, May 31:

Eli: Morning. Any ideas how we could do it Tuesday morning?
Barb: I was thinking.
Eli: Thinking of what.
Barb: I was thinking of diff. ways.
Eli: Tell me!

Afternoon, May 31:

Eli: was just curious. What are you thinking of for Tuesday?
Barb: Don't know? Be kind of hard with the kids in there!

Eli: Yeah, it would but we know they would go straight to heaven if it would happen that way.

Barb: I know!

Evening, May 31:

Eli: Just blow up the house or something Tuesday morning! Or come do her tonight.

Barb: I heard ya!

Eli: Okay. Thought you might be ignoring me. I don't care at all how it's done, just do it.

Late evening, May 31:

Eli: She's going to wash again at 5 in the morn and I want you to do something in the morn, Barb, plz.

Barb: I'll see what I can come up with.

Eli: 2 maro morning, babe, okay!!

Barb: What if I get caught?

Late evening, June 1:

Barb: Ed's off tomorrow! So now what?

Eli: Why the fuck is he off? Tell him you have to haul somebody, please.

Eli: Please Barb.

Barb: What time are you leaving?

Eli: Three in the morning.

Barb: Is he picking you up first or Dave? I am so scared. What if I get caught? What if someone blames me?

Eli: Who would see you? Who would blame you?

Barb: Don't know? David Weaver.

Eli: Not if we do it this way he won't know. Don't

tell Ed you're leaving, maybe you can sneak out
and back in.

Barb: Do you want me to be there before you leave?

Early morning, June 2:

Barb: I shud just do it now. How am I supposed 2
see in the dark? Damn Eli I don't kno if I can. Its
2 scary!

Eli: Morning! The bottom door is open.

Barb: You have no idea how I feel?

Eli: Take a light with you hon. M-w-h-a!

Barb: I'm so scared. Where are you?

Eli: We're in Wooster . . . just don't loose *[sic]*
anything.

Barb: Do you think I can drive in behind the pines.

Eli: Yes.

Afternoon, June 2:

Barb: Whatever you do don't give them your phone!!
Please.

Barb: If someone gives the cops your number they
can trace it down. The only way they can't is if
the number is changed.

And that's what Barb did later that day. She got them
new phone numbers.

Barb: I just feel so bad about everything. I just want
to hold you! Do you think it would lead to this? I
just don't want to lose you or my boys.

Eli didn't thank her or ask how she was—he was fixated on getting a different phone.

*   *   *

GETTING THE TEXTS was critical to solving the Weaver murder. It nearly didn't happen. In fact, the texts were the only proof that Barb Raber was anywhere near the house the night of the murder.

"If we hadn't requested the text messages right away, we would have lost the case," Boyle said later. In 2009, phone companies, like Verizon, could retrieve only the five most recent days of text messages. Then they were gone. Police had gotten the phone numbers just in time.

In addition to contacting Verizon, the Wayne County Sheriff's Office requested records of Eli's online meetups from MocoSpace. They also wanted a look at phone records between Barb and her friend David Weaver, and those between David and Eli.

David, father of five, had once worked for Barb Raber's father-in-law. As with Eli, Barb had been his driver and they had been lovers. He left his Amish community in 2007 and married and drove trucks between Ohio and Pennsylvania. On the day of Barbara Weaver's murder, his old friend Barb asked him to make a phone call.

Eli's neighbor Firman Yoder—who had been the first to call Eli the morning of June 2 and tell him to come home—heard a suspicious phone message left on the shanty telephone's answering machine the next day and told police. Fortunately, he did not erase it.

"Eli, we got the wrong person. You can run but not hide," a man's voice said. It was left at 7:36 a.m. on June 3.

It was a ruse, Barb or Eli's idea to make it appear that Barbara Weaver's murder was a "mistake" committed by some unknown men gunning for Eli. Verizon phone records confirmed that the call had come from David Weaver's number. Detectives also learned from David that he had loaned Barb a .410 gauge shotgun a few years before the murder and never got it back.

It wasn't just his women friends whom Eli tried to recruit to kill his wife. Eli had reportedly suggested that Weaver take Barbara on a long truck haul to California—and not bring her back.

The next time Barb Raber contacted David, she seemed anxious, but not about any supposed calls made to the shanty. Barb was worried about possible evidence left at the scene.

"My tire tracks are probably all over there," she told David. "I was there the night before."

He told Barb not to worry. She had nothing to do with what had happened to Eli's wife. Right? Neither of them did.

Boyle finished the search warrant to search the Raber house. Now it would go to a judge. Then it would be time to make some arrests.

20

Arrests

She was his driver, mailed out his catalogs, and that's all I can think of.
—ED RABER, ON WHAT HE KNEW OF HIS WIFE'S
FRIENDSHIP WITH ELI

It was so bad it was worth mentioning in court—twice.

When he testified about the search of Barb Raber's home, Wayne County Sheriff's Office deputy Alex Abel was asked if photographs taken inside the house on the afternoon of June 10—pictures of a cluttered kitchen, a cluttered home office, cluttered bedrooms, and a cluttered living room—adequately reflected the house he'd helped search. He said they did. Then he added a clarification.

"The house was a mess."

Later in the trial, Barb's defense attorney John Leonard acknowledged the state of the Raber house. "I think we all agree this house was kind of a mess, huh? Things strewn all over the place?"

The hours spent with search warrant in hand were challenging ones. Deputies looking for evidence that Barb

Raber had played a part in a murder had to slog through the usual belongings of a family of five—but in a disarray that made the job harder.

The search of the home wasn't the only reason the law was knocking at Barb's door.

Just after 4:15 p.m., Abel and Detectives Chuhi and Maxwell arrived at the Raber house in Millersburg. Since the town is in neighboring Holmes County, their colleagues from the sheriff's office there accompanied them. It had been eight days since Barbara Weaver's murder.

Holmes County sheriff Timothy Zimmerly knocked for several minutes before Barb answered.

Abel and Zimmerly presented Barb with the search warrant. Then Abel said Chuhi would like to speak with her outside. As she walked out, Abel, Zimmerly, and the deputies stepped into the house and found the children. They made arrangements for them to be picked up by relatives or friends.

Chuhi asked if Barb remembered him from several days before—in fact, the day after the murder—when they sat in his car and talked. She said she did. He introduced Detective Maxwell who told her she was under arrest for the aggravated murder of Barbara Weaver. She was read her Miranda rights.

Barb became "very emotional" as they walked her toward Maxwell's car. She collapsed on the tire of a boat trailer parked in the driveway. "Can I have an attorney?" she asked.

As Chuhi helped her stand and walk to the car, she became more emotional, cried, and asked about her children. Chuhi said they would be taken care of, put her in the backseat, and slid in beside her. Maxwell drove. Chuhi gave her several minutes to compose herself.

"You asked me if you can have an attorney," he said. "Yes, you can have an attorney if you wish." He then asked her if she understood this, and she said she did. She felt a brief moment of relief. She would have an attorney beside her, protecting her. Everything would work out. She knew enough to ask for an attorney, and the police had promised her one.

Chuhi also asked if she understood the Miranda rights read to her and she said she did. Would she speak with the detectives? Yes. They asked her to tell them about June 2.

BARB TRIED TO remember back to that morning. It was dark. As dark as dark can be. Barb slipped past her sleeping husband on the couch and made her way through her messy living room to the door. It was early. She knew that Eli would be leaving soon on his fishing trip. She also knew what he wanted her to do. Inside her was the kind of turmoil that comes from thinking about something so very terrible and fighting the compulsion to please someone. She slid behind the wheel of her Explorer. If Barb had taken the time to look at herself in the rearview mirror as she backed out of the driveway to head to Apple Creek, she might have caught a glimpse of what she was becoming.

A shell. A hollow remnant of a woman. An imposter among her friends and family. The things that circled through her mind were so dark that she could scarcely understand them.

Eli Weaver. He had the answers. He was the one that made her feel loved. Valued. He was the object of the desire of so many younger—prettier—women and yet he chose her. Her life was grim and Eli was one part of her life that breathed in color.

She buckled up. She could prove her worth. It would be hard to do, but he had asked only one thing.

She worked the keys on her phone as she texted him saying she was scared and wondering how to see in the

dark. He said she should take a flashlight. Between 2:21
a.m. and 4:47 a.m., Barb and Eli texted several times.
There's no proof of exactly what time Eli left the house
and what time Barb arrived. But by 3:37 a.m. he was having breakfast in Wooster and at 3:39 a.m. she was asking
where she should park. Eli texted back that he had left the
basement door unlocked.

She looked at the message. She could barely make sense
of what was on the screen. Her heart pounded. She was
looking for something else right then. Maybe an out? A
message that said he loved her and didn't want her to take
this risk? But oblivious to the impact his plan was having
on his lover, Eli was practical, telling her to take a flashlight. Ever the charmer, he typed the letters MWHA—the
sound of a kiss.

He didn't tell her to turn back. He didn't tell her how to
shoot his wife. It was possible that she didn't have to do
any of that. Maybe he'd taken care of everything himself?
Maybe he only needed her to be there so she could take
the fall?

Something delayed Barb. Her conscience? It doesn't
take 90 minutes to drive from her home in Millersburg to
the Weaver house in Apple Creek.

At 4:47 a.m. Eli texted one last time, telling Barb she
could park behind the pine trees. The next time they com-
municated, it would be about disposing of their phones.

WHILE MAXWELL AND Chuhi drove Barb to the Wayne
County Justice Center, the search of the house, garage, and
outbuildings began.

The rental home of Ed and Barb Raber and their three
children on TR 310—or Township Road 310—was a two-
story, four-bedroom, three-and-a-half-bath brown brick
house of about 2,500 square feet. It had an attached two-car

garage, a wood deck off the second story, and two white outbuildings, all on one acre. It would sell the next year for nearly $200,000.

Outside, the house was neatly maintained, with a mowed yard, trimmed shrubs, firewood neatly stacked, lawn chairs folded up, and a powerboat in the driveway.

Inside was another story. There was nowhere to walk, stand, or sit. Piles of stuff filled every room to overflowing. It was hard to see where anyone slept, since clothes—the ones not on the floor—covered mattresses, tables, and bureaus. Things were topsy-turvy. It was June, but Christmas odds and ends were still displayed. A television set with rabbit ears sat at one end of the living room, while a ceramic snowman balanced on top of a sofa nearby.

A curio cabinet in one corner was a clue to a collector in the family, most likely Barb—there seemed to be dozens of bells and porcelain figurines, all of perfect children.

Every surface in every room—chairs, couches, beds, a kitchen table, counters, floors, even the desk in the home office—was covered in stuff. Even the floor and counters of the bathroom, with worn-looking purple flowered wallpaper and window curtains, were overflowing. One room was chin-high with empty boxes, luggage, and Christmas wreaths.

What may have been the master bedroom seemed uninhabitable. From photos the detectives took, it was difficult to tell where Barb's three sons slept; maybe in one of the bedrooms that had several small boys' jackets hanging in a closet, one of the only spaces that was nearly empty.

The only show of organization was a clothes drying rack with men's shirts neatly hung. It had claimed a corner of the kitchen.

The boat was in the driveway because every inch of the double garage was filled with more stuff, plus ATVs and toolboxes. Their landlord's son told a local reporter that the family "got a little behind in the rent" but always made it up. He remembers Barb Raber as "nice," but said, "She came across as a little extreme at times, and I figured that's just her personality . . . but there was nothing crazy, nothing off the wall."

At the house, Deputy Abel called Barb's husband, Ed. He said he was away on business and it would take a couple of hours for him to get home. Abel told him that they had served a search warrant. Raber protested, claiming they couldn't search his property without him there. Abel explained that they could, and were searching. Raber asked to speak to his wife. That's when Abel told him that Barb had been arrested for aggravated murder and was on her way to the Wayne County Justice Center. Abel said a copy of the search warrant and a receipt for any items taken would be left on the kitchen counter. Ed should call them.

It was an interesting list of items taken into evidence—from key pieces that would substantiate a murder charge to the seemingly mundane.

Verizon cell phone
A second cell phone
Two Toshiba satellite laptops
One HP Pavilion laptop
Composition notebook
Pink notebook
.22 caliber Ruger rifle
Mossberg .20 gauge shotgun
Remington model 870 .20 gauge
Federal .22 caliber birdshot rifle
CCI. 22 long rifle bullet or shell
Boxes of various cartridges, shells, magazines, and
    bullets
A brown purse containing:

Miscellaneous papers
Miscellaneous receipts
A Nintendo DS Blue game player with charger
Inhaler
Cigarettes
Body care items
LED light
Pens
Coins
$282 in bills
Hunting license
Driver's license
Social Security card
Store-issued credit cards

One of the phones was one Barb Raber handed them. The other was found behind a TV set in the living room. The purse and one laptop were on a messy kitchen counter. Other computers were upstairs, in the office and in a closet. The flashlight was in her purse. Notebooks were on the kitchen counter. One rifle was in a closet and one was in a corner.

Conspicuous by its absence was a .410 gauge shotgun, believed to have been the weapon that killed Barbara Weaver.

As BARB RABER was being arrested, so was Eli.

Lieutenant Kurt Garrison and Captain Doug Hunter pulled up to Maysville Outfitters simultaneously. No one was at Eli's store, but they saw him walking from the house toward them. They advised him that he was under arrest on complicity to commit aggravated murder. Hunter hand-cuffed Eli's hands behind his back. Garrison frisked him for weapons. Eli became so emotional, his knees buckled

RIGHT: Eli Weaver called himself "Amish Stud" on dating sites. He met many women and told all of them that they were his "best friend." *Courtesy Wayne County Sheriff's Department*

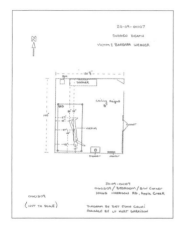

LEFT: A police sketch of the master bedroom the morning Barbara Weaver, 30, was found shot at close range. It was only the third time an Amish man was suspected of killing his wife in more than two hundred years in America. *Courtesy Wayne County Sheriff's Department*

RIGHT: The first floor of the Weaver home. Six young children were in the house at the time of the murder—four upstairs, a toddler in a nursery, and a boy in the living room. *Courtesy Wayne County Sheriff's Department*

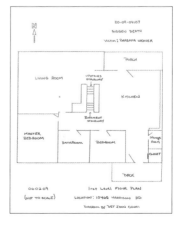

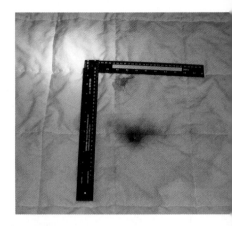

RIGHT: The comforter that covered Barbara Weaver the morning of the murder. In addition to the shotgun wound, her body had unexplained injuries, including contusions, scratches, and bruising on her neck, raising the possibility that she was dead before she was shot. *Photo Courtesy Wayne County Sheriff's Department*

RIGHT: The upstairs bedroom, painted pink, used by the young Weaver daughters, on the morning their mother was murdered. *Courtesy Wayne County Sheriff's Department*

RIGHT: Wayne County Sheriff's Dept. detectives sit on the back deck of the Weaver house, discussing what they found at the murder scene the morning of June 2, 2009. *Courtesy Wayne County Sheriff's Department*

LEFT: Among the buildings searched on the property was Eli's store, Maysville Outfitter. *Courtesy Wayne County Sheriff's Department*

RIGHT: Eli had sex with at least one of his girlfriends in his store, on the floor beneath a wall of guns, fishing rods, and dog trophies. The murder weapon was never found. *Courtesy Wayne County Sheriff's Department*

LEFT: The two-story barn was the scene of sexual trysts. Barbara Weaver's viewing and funeral were also held there. *Courtesy of a community member, used with permission*

LEFT: Detectives arrested Mennonite taxi driver Barb Raber at her home. Within minutes she asked for an attorney, but then got emotional and proceeded to talk voluntarily. It would be two days before she asked again and was permitted to see one. *All photos on this page courtesy Wayne County Sheriff's Department*

ABOVE: Sheriff's deputies immediately began a search of her cluttered home. Adopted and raised Amish, her childhood was shaped by multiple tragedies.
BELOW: They were looking for shotguns, computers, and cell phones.

LEFT: Just a few miles away, Eli Weaver was simultaneously arrested at his house. Two of his children looked on as he was handcuffed.

ABOVE LEFT: The peacefulness of the Amish in Wayne County was shattered when one of their own was arrested for murdering his wife. *Courtesy of a community member, used with permission* ABOVE RIGHT: An iconic image in Amish country— a horse and buggy and a car. *Courtesy of a community member, used with permission*

Barb Raber and Eli Weaver, being arraigned on first-degree murder charges, June 23, 2009. *Joel Troyer,* Wooster Daily Record

ABOVE: Both were incarcerated in the Wayne County Justice Center while they awaited their murder trials. One of them would make a deal. *Courtesy of a community member, used with permission*

ABOVE: The room was so crowded with the curious and the Amish that Barb Raber's trial had to be moved to a larger courtroom inside the Wayne County Court of Common Pleas. *Courtesy of a community member, used with permission.* RIGHT: An Amish family shops at Maysville Grocery, where Barbara Weaver and her sister Fannie Troyer often stopped for staples. *Courtesy of a community member, used with permission*

ABOVE: The Amish sell farm produce, flowers, fresh baked goods, and preserves at roadside stands. Many have left farming to work in factories owned by the non-Amish. *Courtesy of a community member, used with permission*

ABOVE: Prosecutor Edna Boyle questioning Eli Weaver at Barb Raber's murder trial. *Joel Troyer,* Wooster Daily Record

RIGHT: Wayne County Sheriff's Detective John Chuhi, testifying how text messages incriminated both Barb Raber and Eli Weaver in murder. *Michael Schenk,* Wooster Daily Record

ABOVE LEFT: Eli Weaver with his attorney Andy Hyde. Judge Robert Brown chastised Eli, reminding him that instead of plotting a murder, he could have left his family, as he had done before. ABOVE RIGHT: Barb Raber with attorney John Leonard, hearing her sentence. She continues to say she is innocent. There was no physical evidence that she was ever in the Weaver house. Leonard believed that Eli framed her. *Both photos courtesy of Joel Troyer,* Wooster Daily Record

Barbara Weaver is buried in an Amish cemetery in Salt Creek Township, Ohio. Amish graveyards have no flowers or landscaping. Some Amish say bishops pressure them to keep domestic violence and other crimes hidden. *Courtesy of a community member, used with permission*

and—just as Barb had had to rest on a boat trailer—he had to lean against the patrol car for support.

Eli's two older sons, Harley and Jacob, were at the house. Garrison called Fannie Troyer to come pick up the children. Wayne County sheriff Thomas Maurer and Captain Charles Hardman arrived and took Eli to the Justice Center, too—in the same building but a different wing than where his friend the taxi lady was being interrogated.

Detectives continued to question Barb Raber. They could proceed because she had asked "Can I have an attorney?" rather than said "I want an attorney" or "I will not speak without an attorney present." The difference was lost on Barb. Later, many would concede they might have made the error.

The police would later claim her question was ambiguous.

Barb knew none of this. She thought there would be an attorney waiting for her at the Justice Center. Or that one would arrive soon.

Barb told the detectives she had no knowledge of and no involvement in the murder of Barbara Weaver. Chuhi and Maxwell told her they had text messages between her and Eli talking about possible methods of murder—poison, gas, a shooting.

That brought her up short. She explained that she had wondered how far Eli intended to take his plan. "I guess it looks bad for me," she said.

They got her a can of pop and sat down with a printout of texts and read them to her.

Her texts implicated her in the planning of the murder.

As Detectives Chuhi and Maxwell read more texts to her, Barb broke down and started crying. "It was an accident," she sobbed, then proceeded to tell them details—some true, some not.

She said she'd taken a gun from her husband's gun

cabinet. She was a frequent hunter but claimed she didn't know what type or size of gun it was or what kind of shell it used, and said she didn't remember loading it. She thought she'd arrived at the Weaver house at about 4:30 a.m. She'd parked her Ford Explorer behind the barn, walked through the field, and entered the house through an unlocked basement door. It was dark. She didn't remember if she'd had a flashlight. She'd gone into the bedroom and seen Barbara lying in bed. Barb had stood in the doorway. She said she'd planned just to scare her—but the gun went off.

"I was scared half to death," she said. "I never intended for anything to happen, but when it did it was, like, 'Oh, crap.'"

She'd driven to her house and put the gun back in the cabinet.

She told confusing versions of the story. It was all Eli's idea. She had shown up with a shotgun and it went off accidentally. She hadn't killed his wife, Eli had. She had never told Eli that she had shot his wife, but she had told him she was sorry. Eli had said it was his fault and he would help her get "through this." Eli had made a statement to her that "whoever did this [had] to turn themselves in because he [Eli] didn't want to go to prison."

Where was the attorney she had requested, she wondered. The detectives didn't mention one, but she was certain she had been clear—she wanted an attorney.

But they kept drilling her with questions, and she was incapable of being quiet.

When detectives asked her why she'd committed the murder, she said Eli had kept begging her to. If something should go wrong—for example, if she was arrested—he'd promised to get her out of jail. He'd offered her $10,000 (it was unclear if it was for the shooting itself or for bail money), but she'd told him, "I can't do this. I need my husband and kids." Then again, Eli was Eli and was persistent.

Why, the detectives wanted to know, had Eli hated his wife? Barb said Eli had complained of the nagging and yelling. She claimed she had seen Barbara punch him in the ribs a couple of times.

They asked Barb whom else Eli had talked to about killing his wife. There was Tabitha, and their mutual friend David Weaver. Eli had asked David if he knew someone who would do it. David said they would want a lot of money.

Among other outlandish ideas, Eli had told Barb he wanted her to send someone over to his home to make it look like someone was after him. They could pound on the side of the house and yell something threatening. She'd told Eli she would send someone but never did. This was a part of the pitiful attempt at a cover-up that included David Weaver's fake threatening phone message: "Eli, we got the wrong person. You can run but not hide."

One of the more curious details Barb shared with the detectives was her claim that Eli had told her he had killed two other women, or, as he phrased it, had "put two other women down."

She said she'd carried out the crime because she had become afraid of Eli and felt threatened by him. "I was threatened and scared for my family if I didn't cooperate with him."

The interrogation lasted just two hours. Maxwell and Chuhi offered her another can of soda pop, a meal, and a bathroom break, and believed they had their confession: "It was an accident."

At the end of the interview, the detectives asked Barb if she had anything more to say. She said she was sorry. She refused to write out a statement. The interview was not taped, because the sheriff's office didn't make an audio or video recording of an interrogation unless the person being questioned could not read or write. Barb was taken to a jail cell.

Where was the attorney she'd later insist she'd requested?

DETECTIVES CHUHI AND Maxwell met with her the next day in a jail interview room. Once again they advised her of her rights. Now they had the results of the search of her house. They had learned that there was no gun in her husband's gun cabinet that had been fired and was the right gauge. They asked her if perhaps someone had given her the gun. She couldn't remember getting the gun—and now she wasn't sure she had fired the shot. She had admitted the shooting because she'd felt "cornered" and because it would make things "better." She felt that if she cooperated, she would be able to go home.

By then they knew she was lying about standing in the doorway and the shotgun "accidentally" going off. Barbara Weaver had been shot at close range.

This time, Barb stated she wanted a lawyer. That ended the interview.

The evening they were arrested, both Barb and Eli posed for their mug shots. She looked weary and frightened. As for Eli, this time the Amish Stud didn't flash his biceps.

On June 23, Eli and Barb stood side by side—for the last time. Eli was in an orange jail jumpsuit and Barb was garbed in baby blue. Both wore handcuffs as they were arraigned on murder charges. Both pleaded not guilty to aggravated murder. Eli's attorney Andy Hyde, and Dave Knowlton, who was representing Barb, asked for a reduction in bail so their clients could care for "their respective children." Judge Robert Brown turned down the request and kept bail at a million dollars each. Knowlton wouldn't be on the case for long—Ed Raber couldn't raise the money to retain him. Eventually, Barb would be assigned John Leonard, an assistant public defender.

He would learn that the sheriff's office had its version of what happened on June 2, but Leonard didn't think it fit the facts. He was sure Eli was more than a mere puppet master. He had blood on his hands, too.

MARK WEAVER FELT a sick feeling deep in his gut. The idea that his buddy had either killed his wife or orchestrated her murder was beyond any real comprehension. Just how had Eli gone through the motions of fishing that day, laughing, joking, and acting as though nothing at all had happened at home?

When he knew that something had.

Mark had known of Eli's culpability since Detective Chuhi had laid out the evidence during their talk at Wendy's.

Eli's fishing pal hadn't seen the wayward Amish man since the viewing of his wife's body—which was just fine with him. Eli Weaver had brought nothing but pain to his family and friends. Indeed, the wretched tentacles of his crime reached across the entire community. Mark's wife, Elsie, had lost a good friend. His children were afraid. If the mother of their friends could be killed in her own bed, couldn't it happen to them?

Mark had been cautioned by the detective that it could take weeks or even months before there was an arrest. So when it came with such speed on June 10, it stunned him.

Mark was at a social gathering with fellow metalworkers from Ohio, Pennsylvania, and Indiana. Most of the men were Amish, but a few were Conservative Mennonite. They were just finishing lunch and having their coffee when a neighbor called.

"What's up?" Mark asked.

The voice at on the other end of the line blurted out what he'd just observed.

"Eli was just arrested," he said.

Despite having known that the noose was tightening around Eli's neck, Mark was taken by surprise.

"Eli was outside, walking from the house to his store, when the sheriff's car pulled up," the neighbor went on. "They frisked him and handcuffed him."

Mark asked about Eli's reaction to the arrest.

"Well, his legs kind of gave way, and he had to lean against the car, like he was catching his breath," the neighbor said.

Mark was worried about Eli's children seeing their father arrested. Were some of the kids there at the time of the arrest?

The man sighed. "Yeah, two of the boys were there. I think the cops called someone to come get them."

Mark shook his head at the image. No one could have brought a greater disaster onto his family than Eli Weaver. He'd moved between Amish and English life with a kind of selfishness that few had ever seen. Amish friends heard of his conquests with English girls. They put up with his complaints that his wife wouldn't submit to his every desire. And now this.

When Mark got off the phone, he felt a little relieved, which surprised him. He would have to tell Elsie and others in the family, and he dreaded that. But his kids would sleep more soundly.

Still, Mark was conflicted. Even though he had no doubt that Eli was guilty and that his dead wife deserved justice, it was unsettling, too. For years to come there wasn't a day when Mark didn't want to ask Eli, "Why did you do this?"

Eli's arrest became a sort of "Where were you when you heard the news?" moment for the Amish of Wayne and Holmes counties. Mark was at work. Steve was driving between his jobs as an auctioneer.

The Amish gossip line didn't reach the city in northeastern Ohio where Cherie Lindstrom and her daughter made their home.

She learned of Eli's arrest by reading the *Wooster Daily Record* the next day. She was shocked but not really surprised. When she'd first heard about the murder, a dozen red flags had gone up. She knew that whatever had happened, Eli had been behind it. A couple of days after she read the news, he called. He was matter-of-fact—someone had killed his wife.

Like Steve and Mark, Cherie would be subpoenaed by the prosecution. She did not attend the trial but had to phone in every morning to see if she was to report to court. It was fine by her that she wasn't called to testify. She'd been sleeping with a monster in Amish clothes. As the trial worked its way to a conclusion, Cherie learned there was much about her lover that she hadn't known. She'd been played by a master manipulator.

She hadn't known of his long affair with Barb Raber.

Or that he had many other English girlfriends.

Or that he had even fathered a baby with one.

Or that he had left his family twice, been shunned, and returned.

Cherie sunk into a depression, feeling like the fool. The Amish romance novel she'd thought she was living with Eli was a fraud. Her idea of their love bridging two different worlds was a schoolgirl fantasy.

"Most people wouldn't understand," she later said about her affair with the man who'd begged her to take him away from the Amish. "There were real feelings there. He swept me off my feet," she said. "I always swore I wouldn't be 'the other woman.'"

21

Barb in Jail

*He became emotional and at times his eyes teared up
in disbelief at his wife's involvement.*
—FROM A WAYNE COUNTY SHERIFF'S OFFICE INTERVIEW
WITH ED RABER

Barb didn't like jail. The food. The isolation. The nosy
woman in the next cell.

She thought that if she just said she was sorry, if she
could just explain that the gun went off accidentally, she
could go home.

Even house arrest wouldn't be so bad.

"I just want to get out so I can spend time with my
little children," she told her husband in one of their many
phone conversations from jail. She was worried that the
local newspapers were writing about the murder. "People
can treat me how they want. I already got treated like shit.
They can keep treating me like shit. I just want to go home
to my kids."

On June 11, the day after his wife was arrested, Ed Raber
sat at his kitchen table with Lieutenant Kurt Garrison.

Ed's brother, Daniel Raber, and his brother-in-law Roy Miller were present. During their conversation, the father of three cried and seemed in disbelief that his wife could be involved in the murder.

Garrison asked him what he knew about the last few days.

Ed remembered that Barb had left early Monday evening to pick up Eli and a couple of other men who had been fishing at Berlin Reservoir. She was home by 11:00 p.m. He saw her then, and a few hours later. At about 5:30 a.m. Tuesday he stuck his head into the bedroom to say goodbye. He said it was possible she'd left and returned during the several hours he slept.

Ed explained that he traveled all over Ohio and Pennsylvania for his employer, Miller's Storage Barns, which manufactures garden sheds, two-story barns, A-frame cabins, tack rooms, and storage sheds.

Between 9:00 a.m. and 9:30 a.m. Barb called him, crying, and told him Eli's wife had been found dead in her bed. Barb kept him updated during the day, calling later to say that someone had gone into the Weaver house and shot Barbara.

Ed told the detectives that after the news of the murder, Barb had no appetite and cried often. She admitted to her husband that she was worried about texts she had sent Eli. When Eli had texted her about his frustrations with his wife, and said he felt like shooting her, Barb had in jest responded, "What shall I use?" She was relieved when a friend told her that the police would never be able to arrest her just because she had written some questionable texts.

Barb told Ed that if she went to prison—falsely accused, of course—she would kill herself. Ed tried to talk a little sense into her, pointing out that then she wouldn't see her children or him again.

Ed told detectives that the four firearms found in the house during the search were the only guns they owned. He offered that Barb had borrowed a .410 shotgun from David Weaver to hunt with. He thought Barb had returned the gun, but he wasn't sure.

Ed asked for one computer to be returned and some things from Barb's wallet—the children's health insurance cards, credit cards, and some cash. Lieutenant Garrison agreed.

Then Lieutenant Garrison had the unenviable task of asking Barb's husband what everyone else knew—except Ed.

What about a sexual relationship between Barb and Eli? Was there one? He said no.

The husband sitting across the kitchen table from Lieutenant Garrison didn't try to defend his wife, or claim she was framed, or speak in her defense. He seemed resigned.

"I didn't want to believe it," he told Garrison. "We're all human, you know. I still can't see how she could do it—have the heart to kill someone."

The next day his wife was indicted by a grand jury on one count of aggravated murder.

THE TWO-HUNDRED-MEMBER CONGREGATION of Sharon Conservative Mennonite Church, which sits between Walnut Creek and Sugarcreek, was "mortified" and "dumbfounded," according to one longtime member and friend of the Rabers. One of their own had been arrested for murder. Yes, she was a strange woman whom you would keep your distance from once you met her, but still.

Murder.

"You could tell she was different," one woman said. "She made up stories, and kind of lied and twisted things. She exaggerated."

One of her favorite topics to brag about was her girlhood, when, according to Barb, she had more gentleman
callers than Blanche DuBois.

"She wanted attention," the friend said. "People would
back off when they got to know her."

Some family members backed away from Barb, too.
They had never visited the house. One relative by marriage
said she had no idea the Raber home had become the house
of a hoarder.

Immediately after her arrest, the church looked for ways
to help Ed and his sons. They provided child care and
meals. Prayers were offered.

As for why the formerly Amish, now Conservative
Mennonite, woman would commit murder, many in the
congregation saw a simple answer.

"They wanted to be together," the family member said.
"Barbara and that man wanted to be together."

That might have surprised Eli, who never for one minute was planning a future with Barb. He wanted to be free
of everyone.

DURING A JAILHOUSE phone conversation, Barb's sister
Susan Miller asked if their calls were being recorded. They
were, Barb told her—that's why she was speaking Dutch.
The calls wouldn't be understood. "We have them that
way," she said.

Barb didn't know about Joe Mullet.

Mullet had been a deputy in the Holmes County Sheriff's
Office for twelve years. As the community policing officer for the county, he talked at schools—both Amish and
English—and to groups about everything from gun safety
to child car seats. Wayne County borrowed him to translate
recorded jailhouse phone calls between Barb, her husband,
and her sister.

Mullet was raised Amish and his first language is Pennsylvania Dutch. He left home when he was sixteen, during the Rumspringa years. His wife is a schoolteacher in Berlin, the oldest existing village in Holmes County, where the Amish established a community in 1820. Berlin is just a few miles east of Millersburg.

Most of Mullet's family is Amish. His sisters are married to Amish preachers. Both his and his wife's family speak Pennsylvania Dutch. He had done translations for other criminal cases.

Wayne County gave Mullet CDs with the audio of phone calls. He played them on his computer and translated the calls into English. A secretary took his handwritten notes and typed them up. Barb's defense attorney argued that Mullet didn't translate everything, just what he thought was "relevant." He admitted that, as a rule, he left out conversations about the couple's children and some of their arguments about money.

During the calls, Barb offered to perform community service. Maybe her penance would be to warn others of the dangers of texting.

The calls were made and recorded the first few weeks Barb Raber was in jail, after she was indicted, as the case against her continued to be built, and as she awaited trial.

22

Jailhouse Talk

I wish they would come in here, take my cuffs off, and
say I am innocent, you can go home.
—BARB RABER, COMPLAINING ABOUT HER NEW HOME

Barb Raber and telecommunications were a bad fit.
While she knew full well that her sexting and texting with
Eli Weaver had been the subject of keen interest among
the detectives working the case, she didn't think about the
fallout that might occur from the jailhouse phone calls she
made to her husband, Ed. All were recorded and shared
with the prosecution as she awaited trial.

And poor Ed Raber. It was easy to hold a measure of
sympathy for what he was enduring as the result of his
wife's affair. He tested her a few times during the calls,
but he always circled back to her point of view.

She was innocent.

As soon as she'd calm him, placate him, she'd drop a
mini bomb and move on.

Ed: Everyone is saying you did it.

Barb: I did not; that is why I need an attorney. Do
  they have my computer?
Ed: Huh?
Barb: Do they have my computer?
Ed: Yeah, they got everyone's.
Barb: Yours too?
Ed: Yeah.

He didn't ask why she was asking, and his jailed wife
didn't leave him any room to do so.

Barb: I got to get out of here, Ed.
Ed: I know, but I ain't got a million dollars.

He kept pressing her for answers and she kept denying
everything.

Ed: So what is Eli accusing you of?
Barb: I have no idea what he's doing. I don't know if
  David [Weaver] is involved. They are going on all
  the text messages. Did they take all the phones?
Ed: They did not get the boys'.
Barb Did they get the other phone?
Ed: Yeah.
Barb: Shit.

Another call showed how Barb didn't understand that
she was in the kettle and the heat was on high. When she
called Ed, he told her he was at a friend's house.

Barb: Do they think it was me?
Ed: Yeah, oh, no, no, nope.

Ed pointed out that the Amish gossip line was on fire
and he was trying to figure out what was happening and

who knew what. He told his wife there was a lot of talk about a man Eli had asked to murder his wife.

"Well, someone has to report that stuff so I can leave," she said. "He also asked David Weaver to do it."

Ed was incredulous and Barb went on with what she knew.

"David Weaver said he had someone to do it, but they wanted $5,000 now and $5,000 when it is done," she said.

Ed couldn't believe what he was hearing. He was so far out of the loop on what his wife had been doing—and whom she'd done it with.

"No way," he said.

Barb went on. Her husband was still in her corner and she couldn't lose him.

"But they are giving me all the blame because of the text messages. They are sticking text messages together that don't have anything to do with it," she said.

Next, she gave him specific instructions, telling him to cancel Eli's cell phone, and cancel hers too. She had already changed their phone numbers, but now she wanted everything gone yesterday.

"Because if I get out of here," she said, "I don't want a cell phone, then we will go from there. If I do want a cell phone, I don't want any text."

Ed agreed.

Barb told him to raise some money by selling the Explorer. When she got home—which she said she expected to sometime soon—she'd want to stay home with her children anyway.

ED RABER RECEIVED a lot of desperate calls from the county jail. Barb needed some TLC and she wasn't going to get it anywhere but from him. There was an enormous irony to that. Those listening to the calls thought that Ed was a fool to listen to his wife.

Barb: I'm starting to get scared again.
Ed: You are afraid or what?
Barb: I'm scared.
Ed: Why?
Barb: That paper they gave me.
Ed: What papers?
Barb: Indictment for aggravated murder on the bottom. It says subject to life in prison.
Ed: Oh yeah. Don't worry about that.
Barb: What are you gonna do if they put me in prison for life?

Ed tried to calm her. He reminded Barb that the state didn't have any evidence against her. She hadn't even been away from the house. He'd swear to that on the witness stand if asked to. She was home. He was home. She couldn't have left to kill Barbara Weaver, could she?

BARB RABER WAS rattled. She had thought that Eli loved her, but she'd been duped. She knew a few days into her jail time that Eli had turned on her. She dialed her husband to discuss the importance of her alibi.

"If you talk to the lawyer, make sure you tell him you were home all night. I don't care what it takes, I just want out."

Ed listened. He was standing by her because he didn't know what else to do. She was so insistent that she hadn't done anything wrong. She assured him that there would be some good to come out of all of this. She'd be willing to go on the road to discuss the dangers of sexting.

"I will gladly stand in front of crowds of people and warn people of sending text messages that they don't want people to see," she said. "They can delete them, but they are still there."

"He used you," Ed said.

"Definitely."

"You got framed."

Barb, who'd had sex with any number of men, who had lied to her husband, lied to her children, and was accused of colluding with a man to kill his wife, told her husband she had had it up to *there* with the way the other women in the jail talked. They were so trashy and it was completely insulting.

"I am gonna go nuts," she said.

"Why?"

"Because they cuss unbelievably bad," she said.

"Huh?"

"They cuss so bad," she repeated.

"Oh yeah, just be an example and don't," he said. "You don't need to say nothing to no one."

"I know," she said. "They knew when I got up here that I was a murderer."

THE TIMELINE was crucial. Barb Raber saw her only chance out of the mess as having a stalwart and believable alibi. That was Ed Raber's job and Barb made no bones about the fact that her life hung in the balance and he was the only one who could save her. She also needed Ed as a source of news.

"Did you tell him you were home all night and stuff?" she asked during a call, aware that detectives had been talking with Ed.

"Yeah," he said.

"Somebody was talking up here that their mom saw on the news that they had not found the murder weapon yet," she said.

Ed tried to put the brakes on.

"You're not supposed to talk about it," he said.

"I did not say anything, nothing at all. I just let them talk. They were talking about the Amish man. I did not say a word. I did not say anything, Eddie. I just let them talk."

FINALLY IT WAS Ed Raber's turn to talk. He'd listened to his wife spout off all sorts of reasons why she hadn't been involved in the murder. How she couldn't possibly have done any of the things the detectives and media were reporting. They had it all wrong. People in the community felt sorry for Ed. Many considered him a complete dupe. He just couldn't take it anymore. He summoned the courage to ask her what was so very heavy on his mind.

"I don't know how I want to ask this, uh, now I am only going to ask you once," he said, stumbling through his words on a phone call with Barb in jail. "Now, uh, I will accept the answer, whatever you give me, okay?"

"Uh-huh," Barb answered.

"I am still with you. Did you ever do anything, you know, do anything with him?"

Barb took a moment. She must have known that her husband would ask this.

"A long time ago, Eddie," she said.

"Before you married me?"

"Yeah."

He accepted her lie. Ed was always good at believing in her.

"I don't know what he's saying," she added. "I have no clue."

As the call wound its way to its conclusion, Barb promised she'd do her best to make things right in the eyes of the church. But there was only so much she could do.

"I am not going to sit here innocent," she said, "if you know what I mean."

"Stay by the truth," Ed told her.

Barb said she would but "they [had] to blame someone."

At least good old Ed believed that she was innocent.

"I know the Lord will get you out if you stay by the truth," he said.

Barb may or may not have known that her sister Susan Miller had met with police at their invitation about a week after her arrest.

Susan sat in an unmarked patrol car with Lieutenant Kurt Garrison. She told him that she used to be close to her sister, but that had changed when Susan and her family moved to Wooster the year before. She knew Barb was close to Eli and suspected they had a sexual relationship.

Garrison asked if Barb and Ed had argued about her driving Eli everywhere. "Yes," she said. "He did not like that she drove Eli. Ed wanted her to stay at home and take care of the house."

Barb had phoned her just before noon the day of the murder, crying, and told her Eli's wife was dead. In the days that followed, Barb threatened to end her life, and was upset about deputies coming to her home. Susan didn't know her sister had been arrested until she read it in the newspaper.

In a phone conversation, Barb told Susan that the detectives who arrested her yelled at her in the car. When they got to jail, she asked what they wanted of her. They wrote down that she confessed.

On the phone with Susan, Barb said she didn't know if there was any evidence other than the text messages. She told her sister she needed her support now more than ever.

"I got to have all the alibis and good alibis so I can get out of here," Barb said.

Her sister was speechless, and could only acknowledge she was listening.

"Um-hum."

Barb pinned all her hopes on her husband.

"At least Eddie can say I was home all night."

"Um-hum."

23

Eli in Jail

He can be very charming if he wants something.
—Barbara Weaver, on her husband's ability
to manipulate

Eli made far fewer phone calls than Barb did. No one seemed to want to talk to him. He'd leave messages, but his calls weren't returned. By luck he trapped a few people into talking to him.

His most peculiar call was to Ed Raber.

Ed must have been in shock when he heard the voice on the other end of the phone.

"Ed?"

"Yeah."

"How are you?"

How did Eli *think* he was?

"Not too good."

"Not too good, huh? Yeah, hey what is the deal? I seen your wife in here the other day. Are they—can you hear me?"

"Yeah."

"It is kinda hard. I almost can't hear you."

Eli was acting as if this were a business call. As though he needed a new shed. Or wanted to know whether Ed was interested in a sale on fishing poles he had at the shop.

Ed brought Eli down to earth but still was bizarrely patient with him.

"They are blaming her for doing it."

"Yeah. What is, what is the deal? I mean, they are blaming your wife."

"Yeah. They are blaming my wife for killing her."

Eli decided he should warn Ed that the calls were probably being recorded.

"Yeah, but come on, you realize this is all being recorded, you know that, right?"

"Yeah, I know."

Another segue, this time back to the issue at hand.

"Okay, but I mean you were at home, right?" Eli asked Ed.

"Yeah, I was at home with her. I told them that."

"Well then, what is the deal? I mean wow, wow."

Eli was ignoring the elephant in the room, so Ed pointed to it.

"But you know they got text messages."

"You said they got what?"

"They do have texts."

Eli continued to pretend he was surprised.

"Texts. That is what they are going by?"

"Yep."

"Yeah, but if your wife was home and you can prove she was at home, I mean what is the deal?"

"I don't know. I don't know what their problem is."

Eli said how surprised he had been to see Barb at their arraignment, although he had to have known she had been arrested, too. Eli had been smoothing the way with Ed because he wanted something.

"I did not know if you would talk to me or not if I called you or not. I mean, oh my goodness. Could you call someone for me?"

"Who?"

"My neighbor. I have to talk to my preachers. I think they can get us out of here. Then we can get this worked out. If you would do that for me, her name is—."

Ed's response to Eli wasn't translated. Maybe he said yes. Maybe he said no. Maybe he finally told Eli what he thought of him.

If that wasn't shocking enough, Eli called Ed a second time—to try to borrow money for his bail and to pay an attorney. Ed refused. He couldn't even afford to hire an attorney for his wife.

It was lonely behind bars and Eli didn't do lonely. The disgraced Amish man thrived only when the attention of others was heaped on him—online or in person. In the dour confines of the Wayne County jail, he was isolated. Friendless. No one would return his calls. His girlfriends didn't want anything to do with him. The woman he could count on for sex whenever he wanted it was not available—she was in a cell on the other side of the building.

And yet his belief that he could control his situation was unbreakable. Despite all that he'd done, he had the nerve to write to his father-in-law, David Miller.

Please write back to me. I long to hear from you. I wrote two letters prior to this one and no answer.

It shouldn't have been surprising that David Miller rebuffed those missives. Eli could not have found a more inappropriate person to pour out his heart to.

I long to sit and talk with some lady that feels the pain I do, to cry together and just let tears flow together, but I can't so I cry alone.

And then he suddenly remembered his wife. *She* had felt his pain and cried with him.

How I long to sit down and talk again with her, to look into her eyes, to hear her laugh, see her smile, feel her touch. It's more than I can bear at times. She loved me, and I loved her, but I don't think I know [sic] how much she loved me.

He asked his father-in-law to "have mercy on a poor sinner."

Keep me in your prayers that I can keep a strong mind and faith. And pray that I can come home (Lord willing) and be with my children who I love so much and are all I have left or would you all rather I stay locked up and away?

He always stopped short of telling the truth.

I want you to know that I didn't know what was going to happen, and that's the truth no matter what happens here in the courtroom or what somebody says. And I could never let my kids find their mom like they did. I know I'm a bad person, but that's something I couldn't do.

Eli mailed the letter along with one to his children to his father-in-law, who in turn gave them to Fannie Troyer, who took them to the police.

In the letter to his children—the children who were in the house when their mother was murdered, and who might have died had he followed through with one of his plans, to blow up the house—he sounded as if he were gone on business for a few days but would be home soon.

IT WOULD BE hard to imagine a more cruel father than one who would plot the murder of his children's mother, then adorn his letters to them with smiley faces and hearts—which is exactly what Eli Weaver did from the confines of his cell.

Eli never seemed to grasp the utter evil of his actions. He never seemed to own up to the truth, which was that he'd set Barb Raber up to be a kind of suicide bomber on his old life.

In every sense, his children were collateral damage.

He invoked the name of Jesus in his salutation; he asked the children if they'd been to church, if they'd been eating corn on the cob yet, if fresh peas had been picked from the garden.

Was wishing I could be home and go to church with you, but I can't right now.

Children I miss you so much and how I wish I could see you and talk to you.

He begged them to write. He wanted them to visit. He told them how he missed them. He never once said he was sorry. That what happened to their mother had been a terrible mistake.

But it hadn't. It had been exactly what he wanted.

I cry every day to see you and your mom. My heart hurts very bad for you all. Children pray for me so I can come home again. It would make me sooo happy.

Eli thought his heart hurt, but the hearts of his children were broken.

THE CHILDREN WEREN'T doing so great. They all knew their mother was gone. The older ones knew why. Smiley faces on letters weren't helping.

Natasha Siebert, of Wayne County Children Services, who had first interviewed the Weaver children and their cousins the day of the murder, met with Harley Weaver and Susie Troyer again.

Siebert went to the Troyers' and saw all eight children, as well as Fannie and her husband, Cristy. In front of the group, Fannie told her the children were doing well. Privately, she was more candid.

The Troyers had hoped to have the three youngest

children live with an aunt and uncle of Fannie's—but a judge denied the request. There was to be a hearing, though.

Fannie told Siebert that Harley was troubled. He got angry easily and said people wanted to know about "the blood and guts" of the murder. They encouraged him to grieve, and talked to him daily about the event. One night six-year-old Sarah was nearly hysterical when she woke and couldn't find her aunt, who was downstairs rocking the baby, Lizzie. As for Susie, Fannie said her older daughter felt guilty about what had happened and about not having heard a disturbance during the night. Siebert made arrangements for Harley and Susie to have therapy.

Siebert talked to the younger children. Jacob and Sarah told her that they enjoyed playing outside and helping care for rabbits. Joseph hid from the social worker, but he smiled when she tried to draw him out. Lizzie, the youngest, seemed healthy and happy. Early on, when Fannie told Lizzie she was going to bathe her, she said, "No, Mama do it." But now she was calling Fannie mama.

Siebert next spoke to Susie alone. The girl remembered speaking with her the day of the shooting. Susie told her she was sad that her Aunt Barbara was gone and that her cousins didn't have a mother. She said Harley got upset, missed his mom, and wished that his dad were not in prison.

It was Susie who had told Siebert that Harley had heard a bang that night. Siebert wondered if it was thunder or a shot.

Then Siebert met with Harley privately.

"How are things here, Harley?" she asked.

"They're good."

"Do you know where your father is?" Siebert was curious as to how Harley would answer.

"He's in jail. Aunt Fannie said he did not have Jesus in his heart."

"Why do you think he's in jail?"

The boy was stoic, and had difficulty looking the social worker in the eye.

"He helped get Barb Raber to shoot my mom."

"What do you think should happen to your father?"

"He should be punished, but I miss my dad and my mom."

Siebert thought the boy looked incredibly sad. She wanted him to know that whatever he was feeling or thinking, it was normal.

"It is okay to miss your parents, to cry for them, to cry for yourself, to be angry and upset."

As if all he needed was reassurance that it was okay to be sad, Harley started to cry.

"Does it help to talk about it?"

Harley nodded.

Siebert talked about going to see a therapist with him. Harley said that would be okay. Then he blurted out a question that all the adults around him were having trouble answering.

"Why did my dad do it?"

Siebert didn't have an answer, but she continued to reassure him that he and his brothers and sisters would be loved and cared for.

"Can I go see my dad?"

"Not right now. Your father needs some time to think about things, but maybe one day you can see him."

She encouraged the boy to write a letter to his father, and to ask his aunt or uncle for help with the letter. Harley nodded.

Siebert asked if he had known Barb Raber. Harley nodded again, and said that Barb sometimes drove them places.

She had taken him, Sarah, and Joseph to his grandparents' once and he knew she drove Eli when he went fishing. Siebert asked if Harley had ever been to the Raber house. He said no.

"Tell me again about the night your mom passed away, Harley."

"There was a storm, and we went downstairs to sleep. But I didn't hear anything."

"Susie says that you told her you heard a bang. Remember the sketch you drew for me, Harley? You were sleeping very close to your mother's bedroom wall. I think you might have heard something."

It was too much for Harley.

"Harley became nervous," she wrote in her report, "not able to look at this worker and fidgety. Harley stated that he heard a loud thunder bang, but when he heard this his mother was still sitting in the living room."

Siebert encouraged Fannie and Cristy to talk with Harley. He seemed fearful. Maybe he remembered more than he was saying.

24

Evidence

He makes remarks about himself, "I'm just a stupid,
stupid man." I've tried to assure him he's not . . .
though I imagine he feels so, if he's not living
"by the truth."
—BARBARA WEAVER, ONCE MORE DOCUMENTING
ELI'S CLEVER MANIPULATIONS

While Eli and Barb were phoning family, writing letters, and planning how they would spend their time once they were freed from jail, Edna Boyle and investigators were building the case against them. It wasn't hard, though it was tedious.

A computer forensic specialist spent months analyzing three laptop computers, one desktop computer, and two cell phones. It wasn't just text messages that proved that Eli and Barb had spent weeks plotting murder. There were computer searches. Lots of them. Barb and Eli had discussed carbon monoxide poisoning, insecticides, and sleeping pills.

There seems to be no record of one fateful conversation

between Eli and Barb—the one where they decided a shotgun was preferable to poison.

Which was the biggest obstacle to making a case. Where was the murder weapon?

It wasn't found during searches of the Weaver house, Eli's business, or the Raber home.

Eli had two .410 shotguns in his store, and a shell was missing from a box of slugs, but the guns were brand-new and had not been fired. Of course, Eli knew how to clean a gun so it would appear not to have been fired.

Detectives knew that Barb was partial to the lighter, smaller .410 shotgun. She and Ed had other rifles in their home, but she had borrowed a .410 from David Weaver a few years before and no one seemed to remember if she had returned it or not. Now detectives found that she had also purchased a .410 from Miller's Gun & Supply in Sugarcreek on November 15, 2008. She may have bought it at Eli's request so it could only be traced to her.

Detectives and the coroner had concluded that Barbara Weaver died of a single shot to her right chest from a .410 gauge shotgun. Barb had access to two. And both were missing. Detectives contacted a national tracing center with the serial number of the gun purchased in 2008.

David Weaver's name kept popping up in the investigation. He was a friend of Eli's, had once had an affair with Barb, had worked for Barb's father-in-law, and said Eli had asked him to poison Barbara. David had "jumped the fence"—left the Amish—and said he was no relation to Eli, not that he knew of anyway. He seemed beholden to both Barb and Eli.

Detectives Chuhi and Maxwell went to his house in Fresno, Ohio, to talk to the father of five and long-distance truck driver. He admitted that Barb had asked him to make the fake harassment phone call to the shanty the day after the murder. He said he hadn't found the request unusual and didn't think the two were involved in the murder. He had heard Eli spout off about killing his wife.

And David told them a wild story about a hit man. Just before the murder, a woman had contacted David—she knew somebody who knew somebody who would commit murder for money. He passed on the information to Eli, who turned down the offer, saying there would be "too many people involved."

David told them that a woman named Cora had suggested the hit man.

ON JULY 7, Cora Anderson, a bottle blonde with a ready smile and a tanned complexion, took a seat across from Detective John Chuhi and Lieutenant Kurt Garrison at a McDonald's near her home in a rural area of Tuscarawas County.

Cora told the investigators that she used to be a driver for David Weaver when he was Amish. She'd met Barb Raber once or twice. And she was absolutely adamant that she hadn't met Eli Weaver.

"Never," she said.

The detectives let her talk, occasionally pressing for details on the reason that she'd been mentioned in the case.

As the story unfolded, it seemed like a cross between an Amish *Peyton Place* and an episode of *Law & Order*. Cora's daughter-in-law had, in fact, been having an affair with David Weaver. (Who *wasn't* sleeping with someone else's wife or husband?) She talked about how David had told her that Eli wanted to kill his wife.

"David told me that Eli had made comments to him about getting rid of his wife. He said that Eli suggested that David take his wife to California on a long-haul trip and never bring her back."

According to Cora, Eli called the whole thing off with

a text message to David. And throughout that conversation and subsequent ones with law enforcement and the defense, Cora emphasized one thing over and over. "I never said I knew a hit man," she said.

That seemed to be that. The detectives didn't seem interested in following up on the hit man theory. Or on the theory that Eli had killed his wife but set up Barb to take the fall. Or on any possibility other than that Barb Raber acted alone.

There was pressure on the sheriff's department to make a case as quickly and as quietly as possible. Murder wasn't good for the economy or tourism. Amish businesses wanted to sell quilts, baked goods, jams, and cheese to visitors hopping off tour buses, not have them distracted by news of a lurid murder. That doesn't mean the Amish didn't talk about the crime—they did, but only with one another.

ED RABER HAD struck the detectives as being benign and clueless. He didn't know his wife had snuck out in the early-morning hours of June 2. He didn't know she had a long sexual history with Eli. He didn't know there were texts putting Barb at the murder scene. He didn't know Barb had "confessed" to the murder—until he read it in the papers.

But did Ed know more than he let on? Joe Mullet transcribed a phone call between Barb and her husband that seemed to be about hiding a gun.

Barb: If that guy comes out Monday night, mention nothing about that thing that was in the camper.
Ed: I know.
Barb: You know why.
Ed: Yeah, I know why, you don't have to say more.

Barb: Okay. If he says something, just tell him [it's]
the one I bought.
Ed: Yeah.

They continued the conversation in a second call.

Barb: Do they have fingerprints?
Ed: I have no idea. I touched it last when I put it in
the case and put it in the other place.

Detectives concluded that "that thing" was the missing
murder weapon and "the other place" was code for wherever the murder weapon had been stashed.

Barb: Both our prints are probably on there. They
got to have that to prove it.

Even Ed was confused about which shotgun was the
murder weapon.

Ed: Well, do you know it was the one?
Barb: Well, well, well that is what I say. They must
[indecipherable] like something like that to prove
it and fingerprints.
Ed: Yeah.

It seemed that the shotgun had first been hidden in a
camper, then moved. Lieutenant Garrison and Detective
Chuhi paid another visit to Ed Raber, this time at his place
of employment. Raber stood outside and talked with them.
They informed him that they'd been taping Barb's
phone calls and were interested in two calls that mentioned
a firearm and a camper. Ed told them he used to have a
camper, but it was scrap now. It had been registered to
Barb but owned by Eli, who used it on his hunting trips.

Eli had given Ed permission to "dismantle" the camper. Ed thought the .410 had been kept in the camper but had been returned to David Weaver. Ed said he'd gutted the camper and sold it to Kidron Auction, supposedly back in 2008, long before the murder.

Ed admitted that he'd mentioned fingerprints on a gun to his wife in a phone call, but he denied any conversation about moving the gun to another location. And he had an answer to the confusion over the recorded call. Maybe, he suggested helpfully, it was a problem with the English translation of the Dutch?

Garrison and Chuhi made something clear to Ed—if they learned in the future that he had hidden or disposed of the murder weapon, he could be charged with complicity or tampering with evidence.

WHEN ANDY HYDE agreed to represent Eli Weaver, the attorney who would become known for representing errant Amish didn't know about the only other adjudicated murders committed by members of the religious sect.

Hyde had been finishing law school and starting his career when they occurred.

In 1993, Edward Gingerich, of Rockdale Township, Pennsylvania, was convicted of killing his wife, Katie. He beat her to death, then removed all her internal organs and piled them next to her body. He was found guilty of involuntary manslaughter and mentally ill. He served five years in prison, was released, and committed suicide in 2011.

In 1995 near Mechanicsville, Maryland, a sixteen-year-old farmworker, Thomas Ballard, known for his hot temper, shot and killed twenty-eight-year-old Hannah Stoltzfus, beat her three children, then killed himself. All were Amish.

Now there was Barb Raber, raised Amish, now Conservative Mennonite, and Eli Weaver, Andy Weaver Amish, charged with killing Barbara Weaver.

During their first conversation outside his father's house, Eli had said he could afford Andy. Now he went before a judge to say he couldn't.

It was a small community, and probably not coincidental that the court assigned Hyde to represent Eli as a public defender rather than bring in someone else. He had, after all, already done some prep work. The defense lawyer still wonders how the court arrived at its decision— it never looked at Eli's business and finances, just took Eli's word for it that he needed free representation.

"He had a business; he had a house," Hyde said. "The court never even looked at his finances; they just appointed me as public defender."

Eli's lawyer also met briefly with Barb Raber before she was assigned a public defender. Barb told Hyde she was innocent.

25

A Husband's Questions

There is nothing I can do. I will leave it up to the Lord.
—ED RABER, WHO COULD NOT UNDERSTAND HIS WIFE'S ACTIONS
BUT WAS CONVINCED SHE WAS INNOCENT

The Amish are famously forgiving. When a gunman shot ten girls ages six to thirteen at an Amish one-room school-house in Nickel Mines, a village in Lancaster County, Pennsylvania, on October 2, 2006, killing five, before committing suicide, the reaction from the Amish community stunned other Americans.

The Amish told their young people not to hate the gunman. Some Amish went to the home of the gunman's parents' to comfort them, and to his widow, and to offer forgiveness. About thirty Amish went to the man's funeral.

The Amish might appear to be quick to forgive, but that doesn't mean forgiveness comes easily or automatically. Even after forgiveness, the memory and the hurt are still alive, said Eli's friend Samuel Miller.

Ed Raber had received his own show of kindness from

Barbara Weaver's father. He told Barb about it in a jail-house phone call. It seemed to have left her uncharacteristically speechless.

Ed: Did you have a good night?

Barb: Nope.

Ed: [indecipherable]

Barb: It is alright. I don't deserve to have a good night.

Ed: Uh, Barb, her dad called me.

Barb: Oh yeah? Why?

Ed: He just said they were thinking about us, praying for us.

Barb: [Barbara's] dad?

Ed: Yeah.

Barb: The one who died.

Ed: Yeah.

Barb: Her dad.

Ed: Uh-huh.

Barb: Oh.

Ed: Why?

Barb: What else did he say?

Ed: He was really nice.

Barb: What else did he say?

Ed: He just said that he wanted to say that you had been up at Eli's way too much and that he should have called me earlier and uh, they too feel Eli knows what happened but [inaudible].

Barb: I was not up there that often the whole last year, Eddie.

Ed: Yeah.

Barb: Does he feel it was me?

Ed: I don't think so . . .

Barb: Alright, whatever. What else did he say about me?

Ed: Nothing that I know, just up there too often.

Barb: Did you tell him I was not up there that much the last whole year?

Ed: Yeah, I told him; he knew.

Not unexpectedly, Barb's moods ranged from confident, to defiant, to fearful. Her husband was more matter-of-fact because he thought she was innocent. He also had a faith that was greater than hers.

Barb: I don't know what I am, Eddie.

Ed: Why?

Barb: You have no clue how I feel.

Ed: Why?

Barb: You don't have the fear of sitting in here for the rest of your life.

Ed: Well, if you did not do anything wrong, then . . .

Barb: Well, sorry I called you.

Ed: No, it is fine. I am glad you called. I have committed it to the Lord and He will do the right thing. There are enough people praying that I feel it will turn good. I mean, if they don't have more than them texts, then I don't think they can do anything unless you did it.

Barb: [crying]

Ed: But I can't see you did it. You were home all the time.

Barb: [crying] Okay.

Ed: I love you; we believe you, okay?

Barb: Okay.

Ed: Go sleep. Get a good night of sleep, that's an order, okay? I have to get up at 2:30 to go to work so I am going to bed.

Over the course of his wife's incarceration, Ed began

to wise up. A lot of what she was saying didn't match what the detectives were telling him.

Ed: Honey, they just said what kind of gun was used. They did not say what or whose.
Barb: Did they put it on me?
Ed: No.
Barb: That I did the shooting.
Ed: Yes, they said you did, but did not say where the gun is at.
Barb: Alright.

The more Ed heard from friends and family, or read in the news, the more questions he had. Like why hadn't Barb gone to the police when Eli began planning his wife's murder? He asked her in a phone call.

Barb: Because David called me about it.
Ed: Huh?
Barb: David called me about it and I said hey, I don't want to be bothered about it. I said I can't do anything and I'm tired of this shit.
Ed: But you should have gone right away to the authorities.
Barb: I know. I was going for help, but it was not through them.
Ed: But you should have called the cops.
Barb: I know, I know.
Ed: Then this would have never happened.

Ed was developing a spine, but he could still be shocked by how little he knew about his wife.

Barb: I just want out to be with my kids before school starts and stuff.

Ed: Yeah, maybe you can just talk to your attorney Monday morning.

Barb: They better not let him out before me or I am going to get mad. So much stuff he has against him.

Ed: I hope he don't get out, period.

Barb: I don't know.

Ed: Now listen, if you both get out, just don't go behind [my back] and have contact.

Barb: I won't.

Ed: Does he still owe you money?

Barb: Yeah.

Ed: How much?

Barb: About $5,000.

Ed: What?

Barb: About $5,000.

Ed: Why so much?

Barb: Telephone bill [to] way back who knows when.

Ed: I thought he was paying.

Barb: Yeah, a little at a time. He would tell me he has no money. He would just give me 50 bucks or so.

Ed: My goodness.

Barb: He was giving over $1,500 a month to the one woman for the baby.

Ed: Well, where do you have your figures?

Barb: I got them all written down.

Ed: Where at?

Barb: Somewhere in the desk, I think. No, it might be in one of the storage tubs. I don't know. I would have to look when I get home. There is nothing I can do now, Eddie.

Ed: Yeah, I know, but we will go to his preachers or something.

Barb: Just relax and get me out of here. Did you bor-

row money or what or don't you know what is
going on?

Ed: I don't know what is going on. They will find
out tonight or Sunday. I am going to call the
attorney Sunday.

Ed hoped members of their church might help with attorney fees. In one conversation he told Barb he had to
raise $35,000 in a couple of days in order to hire an attor-
ney. He couldn't get the money, and an assistant public
defender was assigned to represent her.

26

Too Much Information

I am going to be pissed off if I sat in here for nothing.
They are gonna make up for what I lost, trust me.
—BARB RABER, CONFIDENT THAT SHE WOULD
NOT GO TO TRIAL

Even before his wife's arrest, Ed's Conservative Mennonite congregation was trying to help the family. The church did not try to help with Barb's bail or attorney costs, or to make up for that huge phone bill of Eli's. Rather, a member of the church, George, was asked to befriend Ed and look out for him. George helped Ed get his family's finances in order.

George had known Barb for many years, since her Amish childhood. Like other family friends, he didn't have much good to say about her. Her reputation for lying went way back.

"Her mother talked a lot about how Barb lied as a child," George said. When she lied as an adult, it hurt her marriage to Ed. "Their relationship was not the best. Ed believed her, including what was not true. She'd be ever so nice, then change. And she left those boys alone all the time." Her lies would do her in.

Barb's admission to sheriff's deputies that she had shot Barbara was catching up with her. She'd never admitted to her husband that she'd "confessed." It's not in writing or recorded, only in detective's notes from when they first questioned her at the justice center the day of her arrest.

But now it had made the news. Ed was trying desperately to understand how Barb could have confessed to detectives yet worked hard to convince him she was innocent.

Barb: Eddie, I never said it was me.

Ed: I know, but you said about the texts.

Barb: Eddie, they already had them.

Ed: Huh?

Barb: They already had them.

Ed: Yeah, but where [did they get it] that you admitted it?

Barb: That is where they are just hanging these text messages together. That is how they do. They ask other questions that has [*sic*] absolutely nothing to do with it and make a story from it.

Barb made excuses, trying to explain her theory, but she may have been right—the detectives had stumbled on an easy scenario. Barb had pulled the trigger.

Barb: Once I spend 15 to 18 days here, then I can request with Rev. Anderson for family counseling. Then my whole family can come. We can spend two hours with each other.

Ed: Oh, yeah.

Barb: If I am here for that long. It pissed me off that they went and said I admitted it, to put it in the newspaper like that.

Ed: Yeah.

Barb: Someone told me if you want to deal with the Wayne County cops or the detectives never ask for the two I had.

Some days Ed was the positive one, although Barb had a way of defeating his temporary upbeat outlook.

Ed: I don't think I have to worry.

Barb: You don't have to worry what?

Ed: You don't have to worry then that they got a case.

Barb: Well, I don't know, Eddie.

Ed: Honey, they have nothing. The attorney said they can't do anything with them texts; they have to have evidence.

Barb: I am gonna get pissed off if I sat here 15 days.

Ed: Yeah, like I said, let the Lord repay.

Barb: I finally told them here I am, what do you want from me if I say I did it, if I say yes, I did it, I would be lying to myself and God and they . . .

Ed: We are not even supposed to say anything like that.

Barb: Yeah, Eddie, and they took the yes I did it.

Ed: What?

Barb: I told them if I would say yes, I did it, I would be lying to myself and God and they just took the yes, I did it.

Ed: Aah. Did they record that?

Barb: No.

Ed: Huh?

Barb: Not that I know of, no. And even a couple times I text him and said uh, I am scared, I am so scared.

For Ed, anything Barb had to say about Eli was TMI—too much information.

Barb: It is like I told him, you can't kill someone and get away with it. It is not going to work. I had told him that. Then they said, well, I am the only one he talked to about that and I am the only one that he ever text so much and blah, blah, blah. Then I said I am not the only one. I said I knew he texted other people and I know he talked on the phone with some others, either on the phone or he went to their house. I am not the only one.

Ed: You should have recorded him.

Barb: But I am the only one that text him last before this happened. Well, how was I supposed to know this was going to happen?

The more conversations they had, the more nuggets of information Barb revealed.

Barb: Do you know why he wanted it done right away?

Ed: Why?

Barb: Because communion was coming up and one of his boys caught him in the shop with one of his English girlfriends.

Ed: Doing what?

Barb: His little boys caught him in the shop screwing one of his girlfriends.

Ed: Are you serious?

Barb: And they ran and told her [Barbara] and she was going to go to the preachers.

Ed: Oh, are you serious?

Barb: Uh-huh.

Ed: How did you find that out?

Barb: He told me the night before that is why. He said the bitch must go down.

Ed: Uh-huh.

Barb: Now it's here on one of his papers that [a woman] was there. Three English women said they met him on the Internet then came to his shop. All three of them say they did it in his shop.

Ed: Oh, yeah?

Some days Barb's mood swung to delusional. One day she had it in for a mental health counselor and told Ed about it.

Barb: She said there is someone up here on this floor that told one of the employees that I pulled the trigger. And I looked at her and said you are lying to my face and I don't like it because I have not talked up here, so why would they go say something like that? Then she was done pretty quickly. Whatever. I would like to know tomorrow if they got more evidence or what he thinks if they are going to sentence me, which I don't figure they will. Is he positively sure he can get me out of here? Ask him [her attorney] that and then ask him if he thinks I can't get dismissed between now and my trial. Then I want house arrest.

The truth—Ed kept reminding Barb—would set her free. And it would console him. As Ed spoke to Barb's friends, he began to have doubts about his wife. One friend in particular, a woman named Heidi, lit a fire under Ed. It took everything he had to confront his wife about it.

Ed: May I ask you something?

Barb: Yeah.

Ed: What did you ever tell Heidi about me?

Barb: Heidi?

Ed: Yeah, did you tell her I slept on the couch?

Barb: I don't know. Why? I can't really remember.

Ed: Well, she just, there [are] some things that came out that you were saying about Eli that he was frisky and things. You talked more about Eli than me.

Barb: Eddie, I did not.

Ed: I just want the truth, honey.

But Barb wasn't capable of telling it to him. Her conversation circled over to Heidi's love life and problems she might have had in her marriage.

Ed gave up and questioned her about an income tax refund check that he couldn't find, and why she was reluctant to pay family members back money they owed them.

And yet their conversations always came back to one subject.

Ed: I just want the truth.

Barb: I am telling you the truth, Eddie.

Ed: I mean the truth will come out.

Barb: I know that, Eddie, I know that.

Ed: The truth is going to come out, and if you did not do it, then that will come out.

Barb: So now you're coming against me now?

Ed: No, I am not coming against you, absolutely not.

Barb: Do they have fingerprints on the gun or what?

Ed: I don't even know if that was the gun that was used.

Barb: I don't know either.

Through the grapevine Ed had been told there was enough evidence to convict her.

Ed: Somebody up in Wooster, the chief, just said, "We have more than enough."

Barb: Yeah, but what does the attorney say?

Ed: I don't know, but we had that gun before that. If you are innocent, we want to welcome you home with open arms.

He finally suggested that she take some responsibility.

Barb: What is the use to come home, Eddie, if they are blaming me for all this stuff?

Ed: Now, honey, [no reason] to get all upset right away, okay? That is not wise. You know in your heart the truth.

Barb: I know that, I know that, but I have [said] that I did not do it and here I sit.

Ed: Okay, look at it this way, why are you in there? What, okay, were you living right? There is a reason you are in there. They got something on you.

Barb: Eddie, were me and you living right?

Ed: I was trying. Were you not living right?

Barb: Well, I tried to.

Ed: Yeah, I want to know just for my sake. I mean, why are you sitting in there?

Barb: I don't know, Eddie. That is what I don't know.

Ed: I mean, the Lord won't let you sit in prison for something you did not do, okay.

Barb: I did text that stuff.

Ed: Why?

Barb: I was not always totally alright. I mean, not like I should have. I admit that, whatever, Eddie.

Ed: I am not going against you.

Barb: Well, it sounds so.

Ed: No, I am not coming against you. I like you, you are still my wife, and I want to believe you.

Barb: I know I have had problems with not being truthful and stuff, but I was trying to do better, Eddie. I was trying. Like I said yesterday, I want a clean slate, [to] start all over with my life and marriage, but if nobody wants me around that is fine.

27

Defense

I didn't try to charm her.
—ELI WEAVER, WHO HAD A COMPLICATED HOLD OVER
BARB RABER

Even in jail, Eli was full of surprises.

On August 27, just a few weeks before his trial was to begin, Eli agreed to plead guilty to complicity to commit murder. In return for a lighter sentence, he would testify against Barb Raber. Andy Hyde was good at getting his clients to know when it was time to cry uncle.

In an office at the sheriff's department, Edna Boyle sat with Hyde, Detective Chuhi, Detective Maxwell, Lieutenant Garrison, and Eli Weaver.

They got the truth—or Eli's version of it—on the record. Finally. His troubled marriage. His affairs. His discussions with Barb Raber about killing his wife. How Barb had set out one night a couple of weeks before the murder to kill Barbara but had called it off. How his fishing buddies had had trouble waking him.

"Eli was very matter-of-fact," Boyle said later. Then the

interview turned Kafkaesque. They asked him every detail about the early-morning hours when he struggled to get up and dress and answer his friends pounding on the door.

She never forgot how he answered one question.

"What struck me the most was when we asked him, 'And that was the last time you saw your wife alive?' and he said very coldly, 'Yes.'

"It was chilling."

Hyde saw the same coldness from Eli. "There was no remorse. There was some emotion, but it was all about how it was affecting him," he said. "He was focused on 'me—take *me* out of this mess.'"

It was a bit of a race between Eli and Barb, although they may not have known it at the time. The one who accepted a plea deal first would serve less time because testimony from an accomplice makes for a stronger case.

Eli agreed to the deal.

"It was a better deal than he deserved," Hyde said.

He was sickened by Eli's crimes. He still chokes up when he talks about reading Barbara Weaver's diary and letters, the stories of "a father not there for his children."

"In most cases, you do your job and move on," he said later. "But there was something about reading those letters." He is emotional about Barb Raber's children, too. "Theirs was a house with an absent mother."

There were times Hyde wanted to grab Eli and shake him. "Eli was very selfish. The story of his life was looking out for himself."

AFTER THEIR ARRESTS, Eli and Barb went their separate ways. Of course, Eli wasn't going anywhere. He would sit in jail until he testified against Barb.

Edna Boyle offered Barb deals, too—the first offer was

twenty-three years to life, and the second was fifteen years
to life plus three years for using a gun. Barb turned both
down and the offers were taken off the table, for good. She
wanted a trial.

John Leonard, Barb's public defender, planned to argue
that Barb was afraid of Eli because she believed he killed
his wife and then tried to make it appear she was involved.
There were texts that could be interpreted as Barb trying
to back out of the murder.

He could say that Barb thought his plans to kill his wife
were "jokes." He could argue that Barb had been manipulated by Eli, who'd "charmed" her into giving him a cell
phone and a laptop and helping plan the murder.

The defense could oppose testimony about the telephone conversations that were recorded in Pennsylvania
Dutch and then translated into English on the grounds that
the investigators were selective in what was transcribed.

Working in Barb Raber's favor was the fact that the
murder weapon had not been found and her fingerprints
weren't in the Weaver house. In fact, there was nothing to
place her at the crime scene except a text about where to
park her car.

And Leonard could put Eli on trial. Eli *wasn't* on trial,
because he had made the plea deal. But Leonard planned
to convince the jury that the timing of Barbara Weaver's
death led to one conclusion—that Eli murdered his wife
at the early end of the coroner's time frame, about 2:00
a.m.

John Leonard had been an assistant public defender
since 1998. He'd handled a few cases involving the Amish
over the years, but most of the time they had been minor.
Sometimes Amish young people get into trouble with
alcohol during Rumspringa and there's a fender bender
involving a buggy and a car. The Amish are much more
likely to be the victim of a crime than to commit one. And

when it is serious, they try to keep matters "in-house" with their council of bishops.

This murder among the Amish was the biggest case he'd ever had.

Leonard was forty years old. He had dark, thinning hair, and wore wire-rimmed glasses. His face told the story of the seriousness of his client's case. This was no laughing matter, and he often looked grim as the trial unfolded.

Two days after Eli pleaded guilty, Leonard and Barb Raber were in court for a pretrial hearing before Judge Brown. Barb waived her right to a speedy trial. Because Leonard was appointed to represent Barb late in the game, he needed more time to prepare a case. By the time a case is assigned to a public defender, the prosecution has had months to prepare and is nearly ready to go to trial.

That was the case here. Within a day of the murder, the sheriff and the district attorney had decided that Barb Raber and Eli were responsible for Barbara Weaver's murder.

Barb Raber had not been able to raise the money needed to post bond, not even a fraction of her million-dollar bail. Leonard told the court that he had some "catching up" to do. Judge Brown approved Leonard's request to hire a computer expert to review the phone and computer records Edna Boyle planned to introduce during the trial. He also approved the hiring of an investigator to help Leonard.

Leonard had to explain to Barb that she would remain in custody for now and that this wasn't the type of case they would "rush into."

He would have to scramble, though. He would have only a few weeks to plan her defense.

A key point in her trial—and later—would be that after Detective Maxwell placed her under arrest and read Barb her Miranda rights, she had asked Detective Chuhi, "Can I have an attorney?"

She had then become emotional and asked about her

children. After a few moments, Chuhi asked if she understood her rights and asked if she would be willing to speak with the detectives. She said yes to both. It wasn't until the next day that she clearly stated, "Give me a lawyer."

Leonard hoped to prove that it was during that extremely emotional time when Barb was arrested that she had requested an attorney and was not provided with one.

There was no question that Barb's "confession" to the police was incriminating. She had admitted that she was at the Weaver home the morning of the murder, went through an unlocked basement door, and only intended to scare Barbara, but "the gun went off" when she was standing in the bedroom doorway. But she also told the police, "I don't even know if I done this."

On August 21, Leonard filed a motion to suppress her statement made to police at the time of her arrest. It was denied, and the trial went forward.

What looked really bad were the texts to Eli, sent just days before the murder, showing that Barb had helped *plan* the murder. It didn't prove she had committed the murder.

Barb: If we could get something in her to make her sleep hard and then get a can or two of nitrogen or CO2 gas, let it leak out under the bed, it would look like carbon monoxide poisoning.

And:

Barb: I thought if we could get that fly stuff in a spice cupcake she might not detect it.

Leonard wanted to prove that by this time Eli was impatient and desperate and that Barb became frightened of him.

Eli: I don't care at all how it's done, just do it.

By the morning of June 2, Barb's fears were evident.

Barb: It's too scary, Eli. Damn, Eli, I don't know if I can do it. It's too scary.

When she advised Eli not to give investigators his cell phone, Leonard would argue it was because she was convinced he had killed his wife. She was still protecting him.

Leonard thought her confession could be used to create reasonable doubt. She said she was standing at the bedroom door, but the shot had been fired at close range; she said she had taken a shotgun from her husband's cabinet and returned it, but it wasn't there. If her story didn't match the facts, maybe her admission of guilt wasn't true either.

John Leonard would try to paint a picture for the jury of a thirty-nine-year-old woman, mother of three, married for twelve years, with steady employment, who had never been in trouble with the law. She had become entangled in Eli's schemes to murder his wife. Barb Raber would not take the stand. Leonard would speak for her. Despite depictions of defendants dramatically testifying on television or in movies, it's risky and not often done.

Leonard could pull out all the stops—showing that Barb had been denied an attorney when she first requested one, that she was fearful of Eli, that her texts and statements were confusing enough to throw doubt on her confession.

There was no way Leonard could counter other aspects of the trial still to come. What was there to say about photographs of a dead Barbara Weaver, murdered in her bed with her children nearby?

28

Prosecution

You're not supposed to be talking about that stuff.
—ED RABER, REMINDING HIS WIFE NOT TO TALK TO
OTHER INMATES

When it came to Eli, Barb Raber never did think clearly. His other girlfriends and even the men he fished with or who cleaned his shop's Porta-Potty laughed off his questions about how to kill his wife. Barb didn't. Through hell and high water, during his other affairs and comings and goings from his home, she was loyal to him, in her own misguided way.

It had landed her in jail.

Barb thought it was smart to insist on a trial. "She thought Eli wouldn't testify; she thought witnesses wouldn't show up," Edna Boyle said. Eli *would* testify and witnesses *would* show up. Boyle would see to that.

After meeting with Eli and the detectives, Boyle plotted the trial. The evidence, to be given by Eli, and detectives Chuhi and Maxwell, was solid. Text messages proved that Eli and Barb had planned the murder. Barb had researched various poisons and finally, without much discussion, settled on a shotgun as the murder weapon. Texts placed Barb at the murder scene. After the murder, Barb had asked Eli how to clean a shotgun and told him to stop using his cell phone until she changed the number.

The detectives would testify that there was no sign of a break-in, that burglary wasn't the motive, and then there were all those texts.

Boyle would call David Weaver, Barb's friend and one-time lover, to testify that she'd asked him to make the fake threatening call to the shanty phone. And she had another surprise for Barb.

No one could argue that desperation and tragedy hadn't enveloped Jamie Wood for most of her young adult life. They were a dark cloud that hung over her, following her, taking control. It was too bad. The young woman wasn't stupid. She was quick on her feet. Spoke a good line. She was strikingly beautiful with thick, dark hair and lively green eyes. Yet at every fork in the road, trouble beckoned her to turn in its direction. By the time she was in her early twenties, Jamie had marked up her body with tattoos that told her sad story.

On her right shoulder an artist had inked a pair of angel wings and the name of her fiancé, a twenty-two-year-old landscaper who'd died in a car accident in Wadsworth, Ohio. Jamie hadn't made perfect choices up to then, but her life spiraled downward afterward. At twenty-five, she found herself in the Wayne County jail, facing a charge of corruption of a minor for a sexual encounter that she insisted had been consensual.

A sex offender. It was the lowest of the low. Now she sat in jail with nothing but time to think.

How am I going to get out of this?

The answer came to her in the form of a mousy little woman who barely made eye contact with anyone.

For all of Barb's promises to her husband that she wouldn't gossip in jail, she had. Jamie had chatted up Barb. They had confided in each other. Barb—who wasn't much of a mother to her own three children—became a maternal figure to Jamie.

Just in case, Jamie kept notes.

While TV and films paint an ugly picture of a jailhouse snitch and what other prisoners think of those who kiss and tell to get a reduced sentence, in reality any con that has the opportunity to get out will go for it. Jamie Wood's criminal record had stacked up on her. Petty theft. Corruption of a minor. Parole violations. She'd been in jail before and the endless hours of waiting were wearing on her. She wanted out to see her daughter, and her release date seemed so far off.

Barb Raber was her way out.

While her cellmate opened up about her miserable life, the lightbulb glowed over Jamie's head. When Barb was out of the cell, Jamie wrote a letter to Judge Bill Rickett, who had sentenced Jamie to jail. She told him she knew things about the Amish murder case that had grabbed headlines all summer. She wondered in her letter whether if she shared her information with the detectives and prosecutor, her sentence could be reduced.

And she waited.

Not long after she sent the letter, Detective Chuhi came calling.

Later, Jamie would insist that what she knew was offered freely without the promise of anything by the authorities.

Still, she hoped to get a sentence modification in return for the details of her conversations with Barb. Detective

Chuhi said he couldn't promise anything, but he promised to send her letter along to her probation officer and to Edna Boyle.

Jamie had organized her notes into a list.

Barb Raber asked how long fingerprints remain on a gun.

Eli gave Barb the money to buy a gun for him.

Eli asked her to blow up his house. He was confident his children would go to heaven.

They had slept together.

She bought rat poison for him to give his wife.

She said they won't find the gun so they won't be able to charge her.

Eli hid the gun in a case outside. She thinks her prints are all over it.

Eli claimed he sold the gun.

He knew the cops were coming and hid the gun in shrubbery.

The gun is a .410 and it was bought at a gun store Barb's cousin owns.

She talked about committing suicide by putting her blanket through holes in the top bunk and tossing it over the side and hanging herself.

She didn't shoot Barbara Weaver. Eli asked four different people to shoot her.

He left the basement door open for her because he left his wallet in her car. She opened the door and threw it on the floor but didn't enter the house the night of the murder. She said it was storming badly.

He told her to have two guys go to his house the night of the murder with two guns and demand to see him, then shoot Barbara because they couldn't get him.

Detectives immediately told jail supervisors about the suicide threat, and they informed mental health personnel.

Barb had told Jamie a weird mishmash of truth and fiction, but Edna Boyle thought the woman had enough credibility to put her on the witness stand.

Despite the fact that detectives didn't know where the shotgun was, they'd limited their search for it to Eli's outbuildings and the Raber house.

GAINING THE JURY'S sympathy for Barbara Weaver would not be hard. She was young and she was a mother. She had been betrayed by her husband and the woman front and center in the courtroom who stood accused of her murder.

To help the jury learn more about Barbara, Boyle wanted Fannie Troyer to testify. She agreed. Boyle met with Barbara's sister to prepare her for court.

Fannie was soft-spoken and, of course, grieving. And she was busy, with her own children and caring for the five Weaver children.

Boyle told her she wanted to humanize Barbara to the jury, give them a sense of who she was and of the problems in her marriage, and establish that Barb Raber was known to Fannie as someone who often had contact with Eli.

Boyle walked Fannie through the days before and after the murder. She advised Fannie that she might or might not be cross-examined by Barb's defense attorney.

Boyle also planned to question David Yoder, a member of the fishing party Eli was with both the day before the murder and the day of the murder. Barb Raber had driven the group on Monday. If she and Eli had had any time alone to discuss their plans for the next day, it would have been during a stop at McDonald's. And Boyle would call

Steve Chupp, who had taken Barb's place as driver the morning of the murder.

Barb Raber may have thought the worst thing that could happen to her would be house arrest or community service. She was naïve.

29

Preparation

*It seems we can't communicate, so how is this all going
to get better? He's so on the defensive.*
—BARBARA WEAVER, ON TRYING TO FIND COMMON GROUND
TO SAVE HER MARRIAGE

Judge Robert J. Brown looked out on a virtual sea of blue, black, and white. So many wanted to attend Barb Raber's trial that it had been moved to a larger courtroom in the historical Court of Common Pleas in Wooster. The men in the gallery removed their wide-brimmed hats and set them on their laps or under their seats.

It was the most unusual thing Judge Brown had seen in his more than twenty years on the bench. A momentary urge crossed his mind.

"I wanted so badly to take a photograph looking out," he said years later. "But it would not have been appropriate."

Although Amish men and women are segregated at worship services, couples may sit together at funerals and other public events, which is what they did in Judge Brown's courtroom on September 17. The defendant's husband, Ed Raber, attended every day. Sometimes his friend George from church sat with him. The wait for the trial had taken its toll on Ed. He looked a little lost. Tired. He tried to keep his expression stoic, but there were cracks in the veneer. He not only had to endure being the spouse of a potential murderer, he had to listen to revelations of the sexual exploits of his wife and her lover. Some might have felt he was foolish for sticking with her, considering what she'd done. But Ed Raber loved her. She'd had a lifetime of people abandoning her and he didn't have the heart to be one of them. No matter what she had done.

Barb wore a simple skirt and striped blouse. Her shoulders slumped and when she wasn't turning to look at her husband, she stared at the table where she sat.

After the jury, sheriff's deputies, judge, and Edna Boyle returned from the visit to the scene of the crime, opening statements got under way.

Assistant Public Defender John Leonard's plan was to put Eli Weaver on trial in absentia. With all the secrecy and collusion in the case, muddying the waters about who had done what wasn't a terrible plan. He told the jury that the timing of Barbara Weaver's death pointed to the fact that Eli had murdered his wife.

"It's sad and it's tragic, but these are the facts," he said.

The defense lawyer said his client was scared and worried after her arrest. Her statements that she had shot Barbara Weaver accidentally were made in a state of fear and confusion.

"She's able to put two and two together. She figures out Eli Weaver killed his wife," Leonard said. "But she's afraid. Because now she's afraid of the trouble she can be in, the *appearance* that it looks like she may be involved."

Leonard said Barb was the victim of Eli Weaver's manipulation, and like all the others Eli had blabbed to, she'd believed that his pleas for help in ending his marriage were nothing but jokes.

"He's the kind of person that is a charmer," Leonard said. "He's the kind of person, for whatever reason, he seemed to have an effect on people . . . for whatever reason he could make the ladies like him."

And Barb Raber would do anything for Eli Weaver, supplying him with a cell phone and a computer.

"She pretty much did anything he wanted because he was a charming person," her attorney said.

Leonard explained that he would prove that text messages between Barb Raber and Eli Weaver showed a timeline that didn't match with Eli's story of leaving for a fishing trip at 3:00 a.m. Eli had killed his wife earlier, at about 2:00 a.m., then left when his ride showed up.

Eli Weaver was making Barb Raber take the fall for what he'd done. There were two victims in the case—the two main women in Eli Weaver's life.

For her part, Boyle portrayed Eli Weaver as a husband who was increasingly unhappy in his marriage. He was a man who talked about ways to get rid of his wife, Boyle said, and the defendant was the one who listened.

Barb Raber had researched poisons, gases, and other ways to "get rid of someone." She was the one who called David Weaver asking for a favor, that he leave the warning on the answering machine of the shanty telephone outside Eli's shop.

Eli Weaver might have wanted his wife dead, but it was Barb Raber who pulled the trigger.

BARB RABER'S AFFECT could be peculiar. At times when people saw her—as she waited for her day in court—the woman who'd thought she'd be freed and sent on a tour to talk about the evils of texting seemed bewildered at the events that swirled around her. Her eyes, amplified by the lenses of her almost always smudged glasses, often appeared vacant, as though none of what was happening to her was really registering. Her stringy hair hung down in a way that suggested she didn't have a clue about how she was perceived or what she might do to defend herself.

And while some might have looked at her with hate and disgust for what she'd been accused of doing, Barb Raber didn't seem to notice any of that. It was as though she were a common garden snail, pulled into her shell, hiding from whatever it was that someone was trying to do for her or to her. She was intent on having a trial, and proving her innocence.

The Amish gossip hotline percolated with comments about her potential fate should she be found guilty. But wrapped around that story line was the tragic past that had brought her family into the pages of newspapers and magazines so many years ago. Everyone knew her parents, Katie and Menno Miller of Sugarcreek.

Four dead boys will do that kind of thing.

30

Trial

I told him, "Eli, I forgive you before you ask."
—Barbara Weaver, on forgiving her husband—no matter
what he did

Around the world, the murder made headlines. An Amish man and his girlfriend had killed his wife. In Ohio, it pushed news of county budget cuts, closed landfills, and low prices for dairy farmers off the front page.

The first person called to testify was Fannie Troyer. The jury easily sympathized with Barbara's sister. They had heard Edna Boyle and John Leonard lay out their cases, but Fannie would be the first witness to describe for them how she arrived at the murder scene just minutes after her daughter Susie had found Barbara's body. Fannie was seven months pregnant as she took the witness stand.

She described Barbara as her only sister and "a dear friend." She spoke of the last time she'd seen her, two days before Barbara's death, at the birthday party for Harley. Fannie explained how one of Barbara's children had stayed at the Troyers', and two of her own children had gone home with the Weavers.

Fannie told the story of pulling her buggy into a neighbor's place the morning of the murder because there was an ambulance at the Weaver house.

"As I turned into the driveway a neighbor lady stopped me and said they had found Barbara dead in her bed that morning and they think someone shot her. And my first thought was where are the children, and where is Eli?"

Boyle didn't ask her much about the day of the murder. Fannie was there to help the jury get to know Barbara and learn about her sister's marriage.

Which wasn't good.

"Her husband was unfaithful in many ways," Fannie said.

She knew Barb Raber slightly because Eli had once worked with Barb's husband, Ed. But she also knew her because Barb hung around Eli's business.

Leonard chose not to cross-examine the victim's sister. Pressing her on any details would only serve to antagonize the jury.

Next, Boyle called Linda Yoder, the Weavers' neighbor, who recounted the story of Harley knocking on her door and saying his mother was dead. Linda was the first adult to see Barbara's body. Her first words to another neighbor were that she wished she hadn't seen her lovely friend dead.

KEY TO PROSECUTING Barb Raber was the forensics investigation of her and Eli's cell phones and computers. Not only did Eli and Barb talk about ways to kill Eli's wife, they left an electronic trail of their planning that led only to them.

It was the most damaging evidence of their conspiracy and Edna Boyle vowed to make the most of it.

Allan Buxton, a computer forensic specialist with the Ohio Bureau of Criminal Investigation, a part of the state Attorney General's Office, spent months analyzing Barb and Eli's computers and cell phones.

The Wayne County Sheriff's Office had turned over to him three laptop computers, one desktop computer, and two cell phones.

One of the computers was Ed Raber's. It had no unusual searches on it. But on Barb's two laptops Buxton browsed forty thousand searches and found incriminating topics— not the usual ones a Conservative Mennonite, wife, and mother would Google. The searches had been conducted between April and July 2009.

After calling him to the stand, Boyle asked Buxton about how he went about searching the electronics, starting with one of Barb Raber's laptops.

"Why don't you explain to the jury what tests you run and how you conduct your testing?"

"Okay, unlike other testing, there's no sampling or disassembly required except to remove the primary storage device from a computer. In this case a hard disk. I then create a duplicate copy of that hard disk to search for data."

"And how do you do that?"

"With forensic tools. In the same way any user can search for a file through their desktop, I have tools that allow me to search entire hard disks for strings of information."

"And so did you conduct that type of testing on State's Exhibit No. 25?"

"I did."

"And what did you find?"

"I recovered a series of Internet search history entries

indicating searches conducted on the World Wide Web through the browser."

Boyle asked him to summarize what types of searches had been done. A list he read made the jaws of everyone in the courtroom drop.

Where can I get strychnine poison?
Can the insecticide Tempo kill a human being?
What poisons kill humans?
How to kill yourself with poison
How much lye can kill a person?
Fastest poison to kill a person
Fastest way to kill someone
Kill yourself pills
Ten best ways to kill yourself
Effective methods poison
Rat poison suicide
How much rat poison will kill a person

"And so how did you recover these searches?"

"Again, anyone who has used Google or Yahoo knows they punch in a term and hit search. Well, there's a string of data returned to your browser. And what I did is I searched for those strings of data."

"And so there could be other terms on the computer that were searched. You were just searching for at this point poisons and those were the certain ones you were searching for?"

"No, I searched for the return entries. Instead of searching for—guessing what terms may have been searched for, I would have reviewed them all, approximately 40,000 search returns." Boyle asked if he'd reviewed the search history on another computer, Ed Raber's. Buxton said he had but there was nothing unusual on it. There was also nothing on the desktop computer.

The user names of the two laptops with the interesting stuff were "Barb" and "Barbs."

Boyle asked Buxton specifically what he had found.

Of the forty thousand searches he investigated, more than eight hundred were about poisons.

Eight hundred and forty-one, to be exact.

Boyle turned on a projector that displayed the 841 search terms on a screen. She asked Buxton to read some of them off.

" 'Pest control, strong fly killer, weed killer, Tempo, pesticide, Tempo pesticide kill people, poison that can kill a person, poisons kill humans, kill yourself poison.' "

It was devastating to the defense. Barbara Weaver had not been poisoned—she had been shot at close range—but Barb and Eli had made at least one try at poisoning her. And here was evidence they had been planning *something*.

John Leonard tried to interrupt what was now the second long discussion of search terms, but Judge Brown overruled him.

Boyle asked Buxton to read a few more.

" 'How much lye can kill a person, fastest way to kill a person, fastest poison to kill a person, methods of suicide.' "

"Thank you. And so there are 840 some entries to that effect?"

"Correct. 841."

The jury wasn't likely to forget the number.

Leonard took the only tack he could—to try to throw doubt on the investigation conducted by the sheriff's department. They had focused on Barbara Raber and no one else. Just because his client had researched poisons didn't mean she had fired the shot that killed Barbara Weaver. Like they had with the cell phone texts, the sheriff's department had known what it was looking for, and they'd told Buxton to find it.

"In any event, what you're doing is you're not giving a thorough and complete recitation of what's on the disk. You will basically come in and testify to this is what has evidentiary value. This is what fits the parameters of what I'm looking for?"

"Correct, we'd be here years if we—"

"That's exactly my point. Thank you. That's exactly what I'm trying to say. You narrowed your focus when you viewed all this computer research and evidence to what you were told to look for, what the topic was you were looking for? Because as you said we'd be here for years if it was something else?"

"Correct."

After a lengthy back-and-forth about what Buxton had and hadn't found on the four computers, Leonard got him to zero in on what he had been told to look for. In other words, what the prosecutor and detectives wanted.

"I was told to look for signs of premeditation, possible research into poisoning, possible research into shooting, any signs of contact between the suspect and the victim."

The defense attorney argued the same point he'd made about the recorded jailhouse telephone calls—who decided what was relevant?

The answer always came back to a handful of people.

The sheriff's department.

BARB RABER'S PHONE calls to her husband and her sister looked bad, just as her texts to Eli did.

The prosecution planned to introduce the worst of them. The jury would have an opportunity to read the full transcripts when they deliberated, but what they heard in court would be a tease they would have trouble forgetting.

John Leonard argued that the transcripts of the calls were inadmissible, but Judge Brown allowed them.

Edna Boyle questioned Captain James Richards, who was in charge of the jail.

"Why don't you explain for the jury if someone's incarcerated in the jail if they have access to telephones?"

"Yes. Once a person is incarcerated there's a telephone in each cell block that the prisoners have access to that they're able to make collect phone calls to friends or relatives."

"And how do they set up the ability to make collect phone calls?"

"Like I said, the phones are in each of the cell blocks and we go through a company called Securus Communications and [inmates] are able to utilize the phones from about 8:00 in the morning until about 10:00 at night to make phone calls."

"And when phone calls are made from the jail is there any recording at the beginning of each of those phone calls?"

"Yes, there is."

"And what is that recording?"

"At the beginning of each phone call, after the individual dials the number, the called party picks up and they have the option to either accept the phone call or not accept the phone call. If the person accepts the phone call then at that point there's a recording that says that these phone conversations are monitored and recorded."

Captain Richards had been asked by Detective Maxwell to retrieve every phone call Barb Raber made while she was a guest of the Wayne County jail.

When Detective Maxwell provided him with a phone number that had either placed or received a call from Barb Raber, Richards could search and retrieve audio of the calls from a computer. He then put the audio on CDs.

Leonard asked Captain Richards to clarify that inmates knew they were being recorded. If Barb Raber knew she was being recorded, naturally she wouldn't say anything incriminating. It might *sound* incriminating, but it wouldn't be. Would it?

"And you've testified that there's a message at the beginning of the phone call saying that your phone calls are going to be recorded?"

"That is correct."

"Right, it's only on these particular cell block phones. And where are these phones located specifically?"

"On each one of the cell blocks."

Captain Richards explained that every cell block was different. Some had phones in a dayroom area, some had phone booths with a door that closed. Maximum security had one phone booth and one in a dayroom.

Barb Raber's cell block—3A—had two phones in the dayroom and one in a booth. Richards didn't know which phone or phones Barb used for her calls.

Barb knew her calls were being recorded, but she thought she was safe speaking Pennsylvania Dutch. That's what she told her sister during a call.

"We have them that way."

The tapes wouldn't be played in court because they were in a language the English jury didn't know. So the prosecution called the man who had transcribed them, Holmes County Sheriff's Office deputy Joe Mullet. Leonard objected, questioning Mullet's competence to transcribe the language.

But Mullet's expertise was as good as it gets—he had been raised Amish and most of his family was still Amish. Pennsylvania Dutch was his first language.

Mullet had been a deputy with Holmes County Sheriff's Office for twelve years. He was a patrol officer and a school resource officer in Amish schools and English elementary schools.

Boyle asked him to explain the Dutch language.

"It's the Amish language. It's our primary language. It's not German, it's Dutch. German and Dutch are two different languages." He said there are some English words mixed in.

"And so when you do go to visit relatives Amish or Dutch is spoken when you visit? Even today you still speak Dutch?"

"Right, even on my wife's side, still Dutch."

Deputy Mullet explained that Detective Maxwell had given him computer disks to translate the calls on them.

"I took them back to our office. In our office I've got a computer that has two speakers. Some of the tapes were hard to hear so I had to plug headsets into the speakers."

He knew the calls were between the defendant and her husband. Most of the calls lasted six to ten or more minutes. He handwrote his notes, then turned them over to Maxwell to have a secretary type them up. Mullet had a chance after they were typed to compare them to his original notes.

John Leonard was not nearly as accepting of this translation business as Edna Boyle was.

"I want to ask you some questions because I want to make sure that there's a full understanding of the amount of information you're looking at here. On CD A, if I understand correctly, there are seven phone calls, is that correct?"

"That is correct."

"And on the notes that I have here I don't have anything listed for call number one? I could be mistaken about what I have."

Mullet explained that there was no information pertinent to the case on that call.

The defense pointed out the inconsistencies—some calls were transcribed, some were not, some partially.

"I'm only trying to point out that the length of these calls and that there are a couple of comments. You know, this is a ten-minute conversation and there's ten *lines* of dialogue that's considered important to the State. And I'm trying to make sure that the jury understands that in a ten-minute conversation this is what came out of it."

To the jury, it may have sounded as if the defense attorney didn't know what had been translated. He did. He didn't like the editing, and he made sure he mentioned more than once that Barb could be heard on the calls denying that she had been involved in the murder—even if those parts weren't deemed most important.

Judge Brown was adamant that the defense attorney could not imply that the prosecution had held back some calls.

"My point is not that there's something missing," Leonard said, "not that they're keeping something from us. My point is that in a ten-minute conversation, this gentleman who I'm not in any way disparaging, doesn't think that there's anything related to the case until two minutes and twenty-three seconds in."

The prosecution explained that conversations about Barb and Ed's children, for example, were not considered relevant and were not translated.

What the prosecution thought was relevant obviously painted Barb Raber in a bad light.

The state of the Raber marriage, for example.

Ed had asked Barb if it was true that she'd had sex with Eli.

"Did you ever do anything, you know, do anything with him?"

"A long time ago, Eddie," she said.

"Before you married me?"

"Yeah."

Her defiance about finding herself in jail.

"I am not going to sit here innocent," she said, *"if you know what I mean."*

"Stay by the truth," Ed told her. *"I know the Lord will get you out if you stay by the truth,"* he said.

Her appearing cold and calculating in a call to her sister.

"I got to have all the alibis and good alibis so I can get out of here."

And her not having a good answer when her husband asked why she hadn't gone to the police when she heard Eli talking about killing his wife.

"But you should have gone right away to the authorities . . . you should have called the cops."

"I know, I know."

"Then this would have never happened."

Her own husband wasn't sure he could trust her.

"Now listen, if you both get out, just don't go behind [my back] and have contact."

"I won't."

John Leonard wanted the jury to understand that the transcriptions were missing context, the day-to-day things a husband and wife would discuss.

If that was missing, then statements that could prove her innocence might be missing, too.

Again, Judge Brown admonished him to not suggest that the prosecution was withholding something.

"You can't just stand there and say, 'We're missing ten minutes of the conversation here.'"

"With all due respect, why can't I? If they're presenting evidence and they're saying we only got transcribed what we thought was relevant, how can we then not argue that they only described what they thought was relevant?"

After a back-and-forth, Leonard muttered loudly enough to be heard, "Who the heck knows what else is on there."

31

The Shot

State firearms expert John Gardner explained to the jury that there were two pairs of holes in the comforter—meaning that it was folded over when Barbara was shot. Based on forensic evidence of shotgun pellets found in her body and the size of the holes through the comforter—four-tenths of an inch—Gardner said they were consistent with No. 6 shot, used in a variety of guns, including a .410 gauge shotgun. Because skin is elastic, the size of a hole in a blanket is a more accurate test of shell size than the size of a wound.

Unlike rifles that fire bullets, shotguns don't leave markings on pellets. Even if the prosecution had found what they thought was the murder weapon, it would have been impossible to say if it had fired the deadly shot.

The quilted comforter with satin edging told a story that literally didn't line up with Barb Raber's account. It was scientifically impossible for her to have stood in the doorway in the darkness of an Amish home in the blackest hours of the morning and fire the lethal shot. She would had to have been either very lucky or the best sharpshooter since Annie Oakley. Those who knew her never thought she was either. But there, that night, the evidence suggested that she had to have walked across the room and pressed the barrel of her shotgun into Eli's wife's chest and fired. The examination of the comforter by the forensics team indicated as much.

Gardner concluded that the shot that killed Barbara Weaver had been fired not only at close range but from a *distance of contact*. That meant the muzzle—the end of the shotgun's barrel—touched the fabric. The gun was "right up against that bedspread," Gardner testified.

Against Barbara's chest.

She was *not* shot from the doorway.

Barb Raber was unsure about what had happened that night. She indicated once that her gun had discharged accidentally while she stood in the doorway. A lie? A fantasy? Or somewhere in between?

John Leonard's cross-examination of Gardner implied that the expert only knew and tested what detectives Abel and Chuhi had given him. Which was true. Detectives had given Gardner only one rifle to test, Barb Raber's .22 Ruger. He test fired the semi-automatic, but there was no magazine so he borrowed one to use. The Ruger was deemed operable, but by then tests showed the holes in the comforter were most likely created by a .410. He had not been given Eli's two .410 gauge shotguns to test.

Chief medical examiner Lisa Kohler and coroner Amy

Jolliff testified about the cause of death and the difficulty in determining time of death. Barbara Weaver's death certificate said time of death was 2:00 a.m., but it could have been any time from midnight to 7:00 a.m., they said.

Dr. Kohler described the autopsy and its findings. She explained how the shot had gone through the third right rib near the chest bone, damaging the right lung, the heart sac, and the upper chambers of the heart. The diaphragm, liver, and spine were also injured. Autopsy photos and X-rays of the wounds were shown.

Just as disturbing were the photos taken by Detective Maxwell at the murder scene. Both the defense and the prosecution wanted the time they were displayed in court to be brief. The jury would see them again during deliberations.

The photos showed a beautiful young woman lying on her right side who could have been asleep except that her porcelain skin was slightly blue. For those who had never seen the damage one shell from a shotgun could do, it looked minor—just a half-inch round hole through the blanket that covered Barbara. It had left a black ring and traces of gunpowder residue on the blanket and a small hole near her right breast. Most of the blood was on her nightgown, from the waist up, and on the bottom sheet.

Dr. Kohler mentioned "healing bruises" on Barbara's leg which pre-dated the murder. She also stated that Barbara had fresh bruises on a palm, a scratch on an index finger, and "other minor injuries" but she was not questioned about those wounds, or the bruising on Barbara's neck.

After the photos the focus turned to Barb Raber's "confession" to detectives and exactly when she had invoked her right to an attorney. Detective Maxwell stayed on the stand and testified how the defendant was read her Miranda rights twice—as she was arrested and the next day—and how he asked her both times if she understood them. She said she did. She had vaguely mentioned talking to an attorney as she was driven to the Justice Center but did not make a clear statement. Maxwell believed they were on solid ground and continued to question her.

It was after her arrest, when they talked to her at the Justice Center, that they read her some of the texts she had exchanged with Eli. "She began crying and told myself and Detective Chuhi that it was an accident," he said. This conversation with the detectives, as Barb told them details about taking a shotgun from her house, driving to the Weavers', and entering through the basement door, and the gun going off, was not taped. The detectives asked if she wanted to make a written statement. She did not. The next day they met with her again, and asked specifically about the gun. Now she said she didn't remember, and didn't know if she had even fired it. That day she specifically asked for an attorney and the questioning stopped.

Leonard confronted Maxwell about the fact that the murder weapon had never been found. It was one more detail, he thought, that made the case against Barb Raber shaky.

If Eli had killed his wife even as he was texting Barb Raber—setting her up to take the fall for the crime—wasn't it possible that he still had the shotgun or had disposed of it? Barb said she'd returned the gun to her husband's gun cabinet, except it wasn't there. Couldn't Eli have the shotgun?

Maxwell tried any number of ways to say no, then finally conceded it was possible Eli had the shotgun.

It could be anywhere, hidden in a field near Apple Creek, or at the bottom of Lake Erie.

* * *

THE MOST DAMAGING evidence were the texts between the lovers. John Leonard strenuously objected to the messages being introduced as evidence, but Judge Brown allowed them.

Edna Boyle had Detective Maxwell read some of the text messages to the stunned courtroom. It was the first time Ed Raber, Mark Weaver, Steve Chupp, the Amish community, and the jury had heard them.

Most were from May 30 to June 2, the weekend leading up to the day of the murder. As their spouses went about their usual weekend chores, carrying the load of parenting and everything necessary to keep a family together, Eli and Barb were preoccupied with researching how to kill a person. Detective Maxwell read:

If we could get something in her to make her sleep hard then get a can or two of nitrogen or CO2 gas, let it leak out under the bed it would look like carbon monoxide poisoning, Barb had suggested to Eli on May 30.

Later the same day, Eli texted Barb about how much insecticide might be lethal:

Do you think three CC's of that Tempo would do it?

Her response was:

Don't know, it should.

That evening Barb texted Eli:

How would that ant stuff work?

The next two days the texts showed they still hadn't settled on a manner of death.

Eli messaged Barb:

I was just curious what you were thinking of for Tuesday.

Nothing, really was just having diff ideas?

From Barb to Eli:

I thought if we could get that fly stuff in a spice cupcake she might not detect it.

Eli was beginning to lose patience:

*Just blow up the house or something Tuesday morning!
Or come do her tonight.*

I don't care at all how it's done, just do it.

But Barb was reluctant, and asked what to do about the
children—Eli's children—who would likely be in the
house. Eli answered that the children would go straight to
heaven if it happened that way.

Later on May 31, Eli texted Barb: *She's going to wash
again at 5 in the morn and I want you to do something in
the morn, Barb, plz.*

All John Leonard could do in his cross was look for
holes. The texts, after all, did not prove that his client had
killed Barbara Weaver. It was clear that Eli had intimi-
dated Barb. She became scared. She didn't think she could
go through with it.

"She didn't think he was serious. She's playing, going
along with him," Leonard asked Maxwell, "and then she
became scared?"

"Oh yeah, that's what she said."

"And you agree with me when you were interpreting
these messages that certainly gives the impression that Eli
Weaver really, really, really wants something done right
away doesn't he?"

"Sure, it sounds—"

"Shows impatience, desperation, whatever term you
want to use. He wants it done?"

"It appears that way, yes."

Even on the morning of the murder, Barb's messages
showed that she was not convinced she could go through
with it: *It's too scary, Eli. Damn, Eli, I don't know if I can
do it. It's too scary, she texted.*

Detective Maxwell read texts that showed Eli was in-
structing Barb. He may have already killed his wife, he
may have been on his way to Lake Erie, but he had Barb
quaking in her tennies.

* * *

IT WAS A question that didn't surprise the Amish in the courtroom. Their names were a reflection of a closed society.

"For clarification, you're not related to Eli Weaver?" John Leonard asked the witness.

"No, not that I'm aware of."

David Weaver had agreed to testify in exchange for immunity. He could have been charged with obstruction of justice, for making the fake phone call, the one warning Eli that someone was out to get him. But Weaver wouldn't be charged. He was too important to the prosecution's case against Barb.

He said he'd never second-guessed her request to make the call. They were friends, and isn't that what friends do for each other? Do favors and not ask questions?

Edna Boyle asked him what his relationship was with Barb Raber. She had been a driver for him when he was still living as Amish. But did they have any other relationship?

"Not really. Basically we're just friends."

Neither Boyle nor Leonard pressed him to explain in court what it meant to be a "friend" of Barb Raber. Like Eli, David Weaver had a sexual history with her. He had admitted that to detectives. Once a friend of Barb, always a friend of Barb.

"After the death of Barbara Weaver did you have contact with Barbara Raber?"

"Yes. I got a phone call about 9:00 in the morning the next day or something like that telling me that Barbara Weaver was killed."

It was Barb asking him for one of those favors old lovers can ask of each other.

"She asked me to make a phone call to the phone booth

and leave a message for whoever, you know, saying something about 'Eli, you can run but not hide.'"

Two days after he made the call to the shanty, Weaver heard directly from Eli. He had a new scheme. "He told me he wanted guys to come up to his door, whoever done it. For what reason he called me I don't know."

This was the plot Eli mentioned to Barb—to have some people pound on the walls. That way Eli could tell sheriff's deputies that "they" were still out there.

Another favor David had performed was loaning Barb his .410 gauge shotgun four or five years before. He didn't seem curious about where his gun was or what use it had been put to.

John Leonard got David Weaver to admit that although he *said* he hardly knew Eli, David had been one of the people Eli had confided in. In the weeks prior to the murder, Eli had told or texted David a couple of times that he wanted to get rid of his wife.

And, muddying the waters, Cora Anderson had contacted David before the murder saying she could probably find a hit man Eli could hire. When Eli heard this, David said, he dismissed it as too risky, involving too many people in his plot.

Leonard was intent on proving that Eli had manipulated Barb, David Weaver, and many others, when planning the murder. And if he'd planned it, he could have executed it.

John Leonard and Edna Boyle laid out the case for and against Barb Raber. The star of the show, the man everyone wanted to hear from, would soon take the stand.

WHILE HIS LOVER'S trial was under way, Eli stuck to his story, playing the victim card like a Vegas dealer. He continued to tell people that Barb Raber was some kind of evil seductress, bewitching him to do the unthinkable. It was as though mousy, dowdy Barb were some kind of sexual siren.

He might have been the Amish Stud, but he was no match for cunning female wiles.

He wrote to a family member from jail:

I was feeling down one day and Barb texted me and wanted to have sex with me and I told her no (but I must say I did give in sometimes) that day and she was upset and told me she wished she could do away with my wife so she could have me whenever she wanted me.

Poor Eli was hoping to find someone sympathetic to him. There was no one left in Amish country who cared.

32

Best Friends

*Should I think differently when he still acts as he did
then—ignoring me in bed (and out) and making
me feel so dumb. I know I'm not smart but I'm
not stupid.*

—BARBARA WEAVER, ON TRYING TO WALK THE LINE BETWEEN
SUBMISSION AND INDEPENDENCE

As Ed Raber had feared, Barb had, in fact, made friends
in jail. Unbeknownst to either of the Rabers until the betrayal had been set into motion, Jamie Wood had been
pressed into service by the prosecution. While the cellmate's credibility teetered like a busted pair of heels on a
gravel road, she had a story to tell.

It was all about Barb. The murder. And the details
shared during the long days and nights of their incarceration in the Wayne County jail. Jamie had done exactly
what the prosecution had asked her to do since she first
came to them—and maybe more. She'd kept notes. She'd
asked questions. She prepped herself for her opportunity
to do the right thing. It was her chance at a lighter sentence.

Edna Boyle led off the questioning, having Jamie explain how she and Barb had shared a jail cell for several weeks.

"And did there come a point in time when you started talking about why she was there?"

"Probably a week or two after she had been incarcerated."

"And what did she say?"

"She had told me about the gun. She purchased a .412 I do believe is what it was from Miller Gun Supplies."

Edna had Jamie correct herself. It was a .410 gauge shotgun Barb had discussed, not a .412.

"Did you take some notes as she's telling you things about the case?"

"Yes, ma'am."

"And did you have the opportunity to speak to detectives in this case?"

"Yes, ma'am."

"And did you turn over those notes that you took to the detectives?"

"Yes, ma'am."

Boyle presented two sheets of paper to Jamie and she acknowledged it was her handwriting.

"And did she make any statements about her knowledge of guns?"

"She said she was pretty familiar with them. She had been hunting and so on."

"And did she make any statement about fingerprints?"

John Leonard objected to the leading question, and Boyle began again.

"Did the defendant make any statements about Eli Weaver?"

"Yes."

"And what did she say?"

"She said that he had asked her to catch the house on

fire, blow the house up with his kids in it and he said they would go to heaven because they're innocent."

"Did she make any other statements about Eli Weaver?"

"Yeah, that he hid the gun in the shrubs around his house. And he asked her to find two to four people to put on a show, more or less go to the house and act like they were looking for him with an unloaded gun." It was just one of several schemes Eli considered and rejected.

"Why did you write these notes down?"

"Because I felt that somebody should know about it."

"And did you speak to a detective about this?"

"Yes, ma'am."

"And who did you speak to?"

"The guy to the left of you."

She nodded toward John Chuhi.

"And did he make any promises to you for you to come in here and testify today?"

"No, ma'am."

"Has anyone made any promises to you?"

"No, ma'am."

Detective Chuhi may not have made any promises, but he had said he would pass on her notes to Judge Rickett, and he did. Jamie had nothing to lose. Her cooperation just might make a difference in the length of her stay in jail.

"Why are you testifying?"

"Because I feel sorry for the family."

Boyle had to bring up Jamie's criminal record because Leonard was sure going to. Better to get it out now.

"You have prior criminal convictions?"

"Yes, ma'am."

"And what are they for?"

"Corruption of a minor and petty theft."

"And what are you currently incarcerated for?"

"Petty theft, probation violation."

"And what is your release date?"

"January 2nd."

"How long were you incarcerated with the defendant Barbara Raber?"

"I was in there June 2nd. She came in probably a week or two after me so until probably about a month ago [when] she got moved."

"And how did this information become known to the police?"

"I contacted them."

"And how did you contact law enforcement?"

"I wrote a letter to the judge, actually, and then they furthered it."

"And you wrote a letter to which judge?"

"Judge Rickett."

"Did you ask for anything in that letter?"

She said she asked if she would receive a shorter sentence if she testified against her friend Barb Raber.

"And the judge didn't promise you that?"

"No."

"And no one else has promised you anything?"

"Correct."

"Were there any other conversations that you had with Barbara Raber?"

"We talked about our kids going and doing things after we both got out of jail and stuff like that."

"And did she make any other statements about her case?"

"Not that I'm remembering at the moment."

But there was more, and Boyle wanted to get it entered as evidence. There was another legal tussle with Leonard about the witness looking at her notes to prompt her memory. She was allowed to.

"She did ask me about fingerprints on a gun, how long they would stay on there. She told me that Eli had—"

Leonard interrupted, objecting that she was reading from her statement, something the judge had prohibited.

Judge Brown said that she could use it to refresh her memory, then give it back to Boyle. But Boyle was done questioning Jamie.

In his cross-examination, Leonard focused on Jamie's motivation for sending the letter to Judge Rickett on July 29, 2009. Hadn't she contacted him because he had sent her to jail for petty theft and probation violation?

"Yes."

"Because you stole something?"

"Yes, sir."

"So your motive in doing all this information was because you wanted to get out early?"

"Originally, yes."

"But that's not what you just testified to. You testified your motive was because you wanted to do the right thing and felt bad and that kind of stuff. But really that's not your actual motive for coming in here today is it?"

"No, sir. Actually it was for the family."

Leonard was determined to show Jamie's lack of credibility.

"Okay, but that's not what you wrote in your letter to Judge Rickett, right? You're writing a letter to the judge on your case that's incarcerated you and can let you out early if he so desires, correct?"

"Correct."

"He's the one that can do it, Judge Rickett?"

"Correct."

"And you wrote him a letter addressed to Judge Rickett saying for example I was incarcerated, sentenced to ninety days. I was wondering about getting an early release, correct?"

"Correct."

"Not 'I care about the children and the terrible tragedy,' right?"

"Correct."

Leonard read excerpts from the letter to the judge.

"And you said . . . 'I have an eight-month-old daughter that has a brain malformation and has specialists in Cleveland. Her visits are critical. My mother is fifty-three years old and has a problem with getting her back and forth to appointments,' right?"

"Correct."

"Not to mention 'I have a six-year-old who also has to be put in the first grade. They need me,' right?"

"Correct."

"Not, 'Oh my gosh, this is a terrible tragedy,' right?"

"Correct."

Leonard hammered home the point that Jamie's motivation was a selfish one.

"Right, you talked about the information you claimed to have about a murder case. Let's just say—this is your words. Let's just say 'I've gotten really close to Barb Raber and I think I may know some information she hasn't told.' You got real close to her?"

"Correct."

"Again, nothing in this letter about the tragedy and doing the right thing?"

"That's correct."

" 'If it will get me home with my children I'm more than willing to let you know what I know,' right?"

"Correct."

Leonard suggested Jamie had "made up" the stories about Barb Raber. And there was more that Boyle had not brought out—Jamie had also written what seemed to be heartfelt letters to the woman she considered a mother figure.

"You wrote a couple letters to Barb Raber, correct?"

"Two of them, yes."

"One of them was done July 22nd, right?"

"Yep."

"And this would have been before you wrote the letter on July 27th to the judge, right?"

"That's correct."

"Okay, so while you're gathering information about her case you call her my dearest Barb, right?"

"Yep."

He asked Jamie to read the letter.

My dearest Barb. Hey, I just wanted to tell you that I appreciate everything you've done for me. I'm so glad to have met you. You are not only like a mom to me, you are like my best friend. Thank you. I hope we can hang out on the outside. I have faith that good things will come to you. Yours truly, Jamie.

Leonard pointed out that Jamie had written the letter to her BFF just five days before she wrote to Judge Rickett.

Jamie read a second letter she had written Barb.

Barb. Hey, you're an awesome friend and I honestly love you. You helped me through my hard times and you'll always have a shoulder for me to cry on. For that I thank you. As for me getting in trouble, if it happens I'll deal with it. I just hope my answers don't hurt you in the long run. Regardless I'm always going to be here if you need me. I'm sorry things happened the way they did. I wish they would just let you go.

"What about how did you sign that?"

"Love always, Jamie."

Leonard pressed how Jamie could treat her good friend so badly.

"When you told her you would always have a shoulder for me to cry on and I thank you, you didn't really mean that?"

"Yes, I did."

"And 'I honestly love you,' you meant that too?"

"Yes, sir, and I still do."

Barb continued to grimace and shake her head in disbelief as she listened to the testimony.

"And when you said 'you're like my best friend,' you meant that too?"

"Yes, sir."

"And this is how you treat your best friend. You then write letters to the judge saying 'I can give you information to get myself out of jail early'?"

"Correct."

"Right, that's how you treat your friends. And you make up stories and you twist the words around and make them sound incriminating."

"No, sir."

The defense attorney finally used Jamie's criminal record against her.

"Your conviction that you're incarcerated for is what?"

"Petty theft."

"And that's stealing, right?"

"Yes."

"And you also indicated your other conviction was?"

"Corruption of a minor."

In redirect, Edna Boyle asked Jamie about her knowledge of the murder before she became friendly with Barb, hoping to show that what she knew could only have come from their one-on-one conversations.

"Did you have any independent knowledge of this case?"

"Beforehand, no."

"And where did you get all the information from?"

"Barbara Raber."

"Did you read anything about this in the newspaper?"

"No, ma'am. We're not allowed to have them."

"Did you hear anything about this on the news?"

"No, ma'am."

"Did anyone promise you anything?"

"No, ma'am."

"Did Judge Rickett promise you anything?"

"No, ma'am."

"Did Detective Chuhi or anyone else from the Wayne County Sheriff's Department promise you anything?"

"No, ma'am."

"When I met with you did I promise you anything to get you to testify here today?"

"No, ma'am."

John Leonard had one last question for her on re-cross-examination that probed her real intentions.

"And if they let you out early before your January out date you're going to say 'No, I'm going to stay in custody?'"

"No, sir."

WHEN TABITHA MILTON sat in the witness stand and finally laid eyes on the defendant, her jaw dropped. Eli had scrolled though photos of his loves before, showing attractive girls that he wanted to date—or who wanted to date him. He was a nice-looking guy and the girls were pretty.

But Barb Raber?

That woman's completely ugly, Tabitha thought. *Why was Eli with her?*

For her part, Barb never once looked up at Tabitha. She kept her eyes focused on what appeared to be a blank note-pad on the table in front of her. Every once in a while she'd glance around the courtroom, but her eyes never landed in any particular place.

Tabitha didn't hold back. She couldn't. By then she felt hurt, betrayed, and angry. She thought of all the circumstances that had brought her face-to-face with Barb Raber in that courtroom.

Fuck you, Eli! You lied to me! she thought.

Edna Boyle needed to ask the obvious. How had Tabitha met Eli?

"In a chat room, on Lavalife," she said.

"Did you have a sexual relationship with him?" Boyle asked.

"No."

Boyle first questioned the witness about the cell phone that Eli and Barb had given her.

"So this family share plan, I'm not quite sure how that works. Can you explain that?"

"I think it was her original phone and then she added him and then he added me."

"And so then who actually paid for the phone?"

"Eli."

Actually, Barb Raber was paying for Tabitha's cell phone service. It was among the many bills Barb paid for Eli that, according to Barb, amounted—to date—to some $5,000. In return, Tabitha had helped Eli with his business.

"He told me he wanted to put his business on the website and didn't really know how to go about it. Asked me if I knew anything and I said yes, sort of. I would definitely help him."

"And so what were you going to do to help with the website?"

"Actually build it."

"And so how were you going to build it?"

"Um—"

"Did he provide anything to you to build it?"

"Oh, a laptop. He gave me a laptop to use."

"And do you recall when you were provided with the laptop computer?"

"Sometime in January."

"January of what year?"

"09."

"And about how many conversations have you had with the defendant Barb Raber?"

"Not many."

"And you never met in person?"

"No."

"Did there come a point in time after June 2nd that you learned of the death of Barbara Weaver?"

"Yeah, I seen it on the news."

"And did you also get it from other—did you get a phone call from anyone after you learned of Barbara Weaver's death?"

"Yes."

"And who called you?"

"Barbara."

"And when you say Barbara . . . ?"

"Raber."

"So when she called you did she say anything to you?"

"I texted her and asked her if all of this was true, if this was really Eli and she didn't respond. I went tanning. I came out of the tanning bed, she had called me. I had to call her back because I missed it and that is when she spoke to me about everything."

"And what did she say?"

"She said that she (Barbara Weaver) was found dead in her bedroom shot in the chest."

"And do you recall what day you talked to her?"

"I don't know what day, no. I don't remember now."

"And when the defendant Barbara Raber contacted you . . . how did you know it was her calling?"

"Eli gave me her number so if I ever needed to talk to her about help on the computer. There was some things I didn't understand like Word Office, how to get to all that in there."

"And so you actually got her phone number from Eli Weaver?"

"Yes."

"And when she called you what would come up on your screen?"

"Barb."

John Leonard took over questioning and asked Tabitha about the nature of the texts she and Barb Raber had exchanged.

Tabitha said they had discussed what they had in common—Eli had talked to them both before the murder about killing his wife.

"And . . . she also texted you," Leonard asked, "and said 'I don't know what to say. He said remarks and so did I but nothing serious,' right? Do you remember that?"

"Yeah."

"And you said, 'Same here, we joked but now I think he was serious.' And not to be flippant but obviously it's a good reason to believe he was serious at this point, right?"

"Yes."

"And in fact, he'd made comments like that to you before?"

"Yes."

"And there's been testimony he made these comments to other people as well. You didn't—and I'm not saying you did anything wrong. You didn't think that these were serious enough that you need to call the police or anything?"

"No."

"I mean, had Mr. Weaver been making comments that

you did take seriously you would have contacted the police ahead of time, right?"

"Right."

"And, in fact, you did contact the police when you heard about what happened, right?"

"Yes."

Actually, Tabitha had not contacted the police to volunteer that she was a friend of Eli's with possible information. Her former boyfriend had.

"And you did the right thing. I respect that. So Eli had made comments, you didn't think anything of it and you got a message from Ms. Raber saying that she was also aware of these comments and had made some, but really didn't think it was serious?"

"Uh-huh."

"Does that sound like pretty much the crux and the full amount of your conversation about that? Just surprise, couldn't believe he really did it?"

"Right, yeah, we just were both in disbelief."

The defense attorney wanted to show that Barb Raber was just like Tabitha—not a killer, just someone the killer had joked with.

No one thought to ask Tabitha if Barb had mentioned a shotgun.

33

It Was Lust

*He looks at me and lies. Sometimes I already know
the truth, other times I find out the truth later.*
—BARBARA WEAVER, IN A LETTER TO HER COUNSELOR

Every member of the courtroom had been waiting for the
big moment, when Eli Weaver would take the stand to tell
his side of the story. They wanted understanding of Eli and
Barb Raber's murderous affair.

Affair. The word sickened the Amish who filled the gallery. It was so trivial a word. None saw what Eli and Barb
had engaged in as anything short of an abomination, an
affront to the laws of God and the rules that governed the
Andy Weaver Amish and Conservative Mennonites. Eli
had decimated a solid chunk of the Ten Commandments
and the Amish Ordnung. Thou shalt not covet thy neighbor's wife; thou shalt not commit adultery; thou shalt
not kill.

The Amish who made up almost the entire gallery
barely looked Eli in the eye. It was doubtful that many

would truly forgive him for what he had done, though they said they would.

"They say they forgive, but they never really forget. He brought shame and attention to an entire community in a way that just doesn't wash well," said an observer of the trial. "Forgive? That's a tall order even for the Amish."

There would be a volley of questions, thrown first by prosecutor Edna Boyle and then by defense attorney John Leonard.

Leonard would put Eli on trial. He *wasn't* on trial because he had copped a plea. But Leonard wanted to hold Eli responsible for manipulating Barb Raber and maybe, just maybe, convince the jury that there was some doubt about who actually committed the murder.

Mark Weaver, Steve Chupp, and others were there because the local newspaper had said Eli would be testifying against Barb Raber. As for her side of the aisle, Barb's husband and a few of his friends were scattered on the benches.

Mark Weaver watched as Eli shuffled into the courtroom, shackled. Eli was chained at his hands and feet. Mark—his loyal friend, neighbor, and hunting and fishing companion—sat watching Eli take the small steps, dragging his chains like Marley's ghost, across a dead silent courtroom. It was awkward for Mark, who was the best Amish husband, father, son, and friend he could be. His faith and his life were important to him. Mark would learn a lot about Eli that day—things he wished he never learned.

Deputies unchained Eli's hands but left the shackles on his feet. Eli was sworn in and took the stand. Wearing an orange Wayne County jail-issued jumpsuit and slippers, Eli folded himself into the witness box in Judge Brown's courtroom. But for his bushy beard, he could have been any young offender. He looked appropriately contrite, lowering his gaze as Boyle plowed through the rudimentary questions that established his name and relationships, and the connections to the story that had led him to that place on the front pages of the local newspapers and the front of the courtroom.

"Mr. Weaver, how was your marriage?" Boyle asked.

Eli looked at her. There was no need for lying, but he did anyway.

"It wasn't the best but we always tried to work things out the best we could."

The prosecutor pressed the witness. "Did you have problems?"

"At times, yes."

"And why did you have problems in your marriage?"

He answered in a near whisper. Spectators strained to hear. "I guess I just didn't love my wife the way I should have loved her."

"And did there come a point in time where you left the Amish faith?"

"Uh-huh."

Boyle reminded him to speak up. The proceedings were being recorded in the event that Barb Raber would find some grounds for appeal in the proceedings.

Boyle asked him why he'd left the faith.

Eli paused before answering. "I just kind of wanted some more—a little bit more freedom than what I had and I wasn't happy with what I had I guess."

His answer was vague and evasive. She pushed for clarity.

"I guess I went out, you know, into the world and got myself a truck and everything. I took what I promised to God and to church and the witnesses, you know, I just kind of laid that aside." He told the court how he left his family to live with Shelley for six months before returning home to his wife and children.

As Mark listened, he thought about how he first met

Barbara and her children. Eli was living with the English woman at the time. As long as he was doing that and driving a vehicle, Barbara wouldn't permit him to be around home much. Mark and his wife, Elsie, and their children became fond of Barbara and her little ones.

"And when you went back home what happened?"

Eli hesitated. He told the court that he'd gone before the bishop, confessed his sins, and promised never to be unfaithful again. The Amish took him back. Many in the courtroom would have liked to see a do-over on that decision.

Next, Boyle questioned Eli about Amish life and how the Ordnung varied depending on which group a member had been born into. Eli danced around the particulars a little. He said he was Old Order.

To the Amish in the courtroom, it was peculiar that Eli didn't state that he was Andy Weaver Amish. The prosecutor had him explain that his home didn't have electricity but did have natural gas lights and running water. Eli didn't volunteer that he wasn't supposed to be using natural gas in the home.

"And the use of telephones, were you permitted to have telephones in your home?" she asked.

Eli shook his head. "No, not in the home."

"Okay, and how did you communicate?"

"Well, I had a phone in the shop, you know, where I had my business. You know, I could communicate that way."

"So in your order you're not permitted to have a phone in your home. What about cell phones?"

"No."

"Text messaging?"

"No."

"And access to the Internet?"

"No."

"Those are all things that are prohibited but did you have a cell phone?"

He nodded. "Yes."

"And how did you get your cell phone?"

Finally he said the defendant's name. "Through Barb Raber."

As Barb Raber sat in the courtroom and heard Eli Weaver recount their relationship, she slumped into her chair looking afraid and sad. There was something strange about how a younger man could have found her sexually appealing. She was ten years older than he but would never be confused with the kind of glamorous cougar depicted on television.

Her affairs with men, including Eli, had nothing to do with her looks. They never had.

She wasn't just a steady sexual outlet for Eli—even when he was involved with other women. He could count on her to understand him. When he was shunned by the Amish, she gave him solace. She also gave him the tools to live like the non-Amish. She was *there,* available to him when he wanted the kind of sex his wife wouldn't participate in.

She shocked people. She was Conservative Mennonite, but would "talk dirty" in the presence of Eli's friends when she drove them fishing.

Boyle wasted no time in going for the heart of the matter. "And what was your relationship with Barb Raber?"

Eli appeared uncomfortable, again refusing to meet her direct gaze. He shifted in the chair. "I mean," he stammered, searching for the words, "we were good friends but, you know, it was more than friends. You know, we had a sexual relationship."

"And when did that sexual relationship begin?"

"Approximately six years ago."

"And how long did that relationship last?"

"Till about three weeks prior to what happened."

"What happened" was his wife's murder. Throughout Eli's testimony, he tried to avoid the subject.

Mark was stunned. He had known Eli and the taxi lady had once had an affair, but he thought it had ended years ago.

Boyle moved on to the subject that was most shocking to Eli's Amish community: how Eli used forbidden technology to break his marriage vows. He'd quickly learned how to meet women on MocoSpace.

"Okay, and what is that?" she asked.

"It's for, you know, you can meet friends. You know, you can take it further if you want to take it further."

"So is it like a chat room?"

"Right."

"And so how did you access Moco—"

"With my cell phone."

"So you had Internet access on your cell phone so it was a pretty fancy cell phone you had?"

He nodded. "Yeah."

"So you would communicate online with your cell phone. Did you have any—and what was your screen name?"

"Amish Guy."

"Did you have another screen name?"

"I did at first but I changed it. You know, I didn't use that one."

Boyle let it go. She didn't make him say the name— Amish Stud—out loud. Boyle asked him about his other female companions. There was Cherie, whom he'd met in a sex chat room. There was Tabitha. There were others, too.

Including, of course, Misty.

"And how did you meet her?"

Eli looked on. "Chat line."

"And what was the nature of your relationship with her?"

Eli hesitated a little before answering.

"It started out as friends, you know," he finally said. "We got into, you know, we had a sexual relationship and she—I got her pregnant and she had a child."

Mark sat up straighter. Eli had fathered a child out of wedlock? It was the first he'd heard of it.

"How old is your child with Misty?"

"One."

"And did you pay her child support?

Eli answered quickly as though his response would put him in a favorable light—despite all that he'd done.

"Yes," he said.

"And how did you make those payments?"

"Normally by check unless she needed it right away she came down and got it in cash. It wasn't always by check."

"You had these relationships with these other women so were there times where there were—you're having relationships with multiple women at the same time?"

Again, Eli wanted to make it clear he wasn't some kind of sexual marauder.

"No."

The prosecutor wasn't buying it.

"But you had an ongoing relationship with Barb Raber while you were having a relationship with these other women?" she asked.

He finally conceded the fact. "Yes," he said.

FINALLY ELI WEAVER admitted that despite the conditions under which he was forgiven and returned to Amish life, he continued to break the rules. His bishop had warned him not to ride with taxi lady Barb Raber anymore. He did anyway. A pin dropped in that courtroom would have sounded like a knife thrown to the floor.

The betrayal was beyond belief. The Amish spectators did everything they could to remain expressionless, but that was difficult. The man in the witness box had used all of them, their faith, and their culture as a way to have sex with women. He'd used being Amish as a lure.

Barb Raber was Eli's confidante—not the only one, but the one with whom he had the longest history. She wasn't just a "friend with benefits" to Eli—her downfall was that she'd allowed herself to fall under his ruthless spell. She thought that he needed her. She believed that sex with him was merely a conduit to some kind of deeper relationship. She was using sex to make her troubled friend and lover feel better, and to escape her own messy life. It was true that Eli's other friends and sex partners might laugh off his talk of an unhappy marriage. Barb didn't. He learned that when he talked of problems in his marriage, and deadly solutions, she wasn't laughing like the others. She was listening.

Prosecutor Boyle asked Eli to explain what happened after he introduced the idea of getting rid of his wife.

"She just kind of took it and ran with it, you know. Just like she's going to take and try and find a way to help me, you know, get it accomplished."

Eli's description of how the murder was planned could have sounded juvenile if it hadn't been so deadly.

"What do you have in mind?" Eli said Barb had asked him. "And I was like well, you know, we could poison her, you know, or stuff like that and it just . . . one thing led to another."

Barb, he insisted, was really good at research. Boyle asked for a rundown of killing methods he and Barb had considered.

"There was Tempo [a bug killer]. We had the Golden

Malrin, which is a fly killer, you know. And there was some gas stuff, you know, that she did some research on it, sleeping pills."

"So she did research on gases, poisons, pills and she told you about this research?"

"Yes," he said.

"And so did you ever attempt to use any gases or poisons?"

"The gases we didn't, no. I mean, the sleeping pills I tried, you know, once for myself."

That was the night a few weeks before the murder when he had crushed sleeping pills into a glass of pop. He watched his wife sip it and spit it out.

"And where did you get the pills from?"

Without looking in her direction, he named Barb Raber.

Along with other church friends of Ed's, a woman named Helen attended the trial that day. She never went back. "I couldn't handle it," she said. "I couldn't take hearing about how they had planned the murder."

Mark had trouble stomaching the details, too. How could Eli talk so nonchalantly about poisons, sleeping pills, and murder?

Boyle continued her questioning about the sleeping pills.

"Did you tell her what you were going to do with those pills?"

"She thought it was for my wife. You know, which it was and it wasn't. You know, I mean I was going to take them myself after what all I'd been through and everything."

No one who knew Eli ever took that seriously.

"Eli kill himself?" a friend asked after the trial. "No way. That guy was all about himself. He was a complete narcissist. He thought that everyone should kowtow to his needs. It was like his wife, his girlfriends, whatever, were only there to serve him. He was too selfish to kill himself. That's why he used Barb Raber."

The prosecutor asked Eli to describe his last in-person conversation with his alleged coconspirator. It was the day before the murder when she drove Eli and his friends. By then they had a plan and had confirmed it by texting. Eli would leave the house about 3:00 a.m. to go fishing with a group of men. He had talked with her in person while the others were tying down the boat. They had gone over plans for him to leave the basement door unlocked.

This hit close to home because Mark had *been* there; he had witnessed Eli and Barb sneak private moments to discuss something that they didn't want the others on the trip to overhear. In fact, Mark had been subpoenaed to testify, but he would not be called.

Boyle asked Eli how he spent the few hours he was home before he left again and before his wife was murdered. He had carried the three children upstairs. Locked up his store. Fed his deer. Took a shower. Had a cigarette and a cup of coffee.

"And do you remember what the weather was like that night?"

"Yeah, it was raining. It was—we had a big thunderstorm rolling through."

"And did you talk to your wife at all that night about your plans for the next day or did she already know where you were going?"

"She already knew that I was going fishing."

Eli would have, at the most, two hours of sleep before he was picked up by friends to go walleye fishing at Lake Erie.

When his friends arrived to pick him up—at about 3:00 a.m.—they couldn't wake him. They pounded on his

door and after several minutes, he answered it. Eli said
Barbara had helped him get his clothes together.

"And that was the last time you saw your wife alive."

He nodded. "Yes."

Steve, who had been driving that morning, had been
subpoenaed too, but prosecutors didn't need him to describe the morning because Eli had agreed to plead guilty.
It was surreal for him to hear in Eli's own words what went
on that morning.

"Now, WERE YOU communicating with Barbara Raber in
the early morning hours of June 2?"

Edna Boyle drilled into the window of time when the
murder occurred.

"I did, you know, en route to when we were going fishing, you know. Like when we stopped at the Wooster gas
station. I didn't when we were driving because they didn't
know I had a cell phone. So I had to, you know, watch
when I used it and everything."

That's when Steve had been aware of Eli trying to hide
his cell phone from others in the car.

"And did you receive any text messages from the defendant Barbara Raber on June 2 during the early morning hours?"

"Yes."

"And do you recall the nature of those text messages?"

"The one was, you know, that she's scared and she
doesn't have—it's dark, you know. And she asked me if
she could park by the pines."

"And then do you recall sending a text message to Mrs.
Raber June 2, 2009, at 2:56, 'Morning! The bottom door
is . . . '"

John Leonard objected to the prosecutor asking Eli

questions that incriminated the defendant, Barb Raber. Leonard would protest time and again that the text messages between his client and Eli were not admissible. But the damaging texts, placing Barb at the scene, were allowed.

Boyle continued.

" 'Morning! The bottom door is open'?"

"I remember—like I said I remember I texted her that but I couldn't tell you when it was, you know, what time it was or anything like that."

"And you recall—do you recall receiving a text message June 2, 2009, 3:08, 'You have no idea how I feel?' "

"Yes."

"And that text message would have been from the defendant, Barbara Raber?"

"Yes."

"Then June 2, 2009, 3:03, 'How am I supposed to see in the dark? Damn, Eli, I don't know if I can [do it]. It's too scary.' Do you remember a message of that nature?"

Eli did.

"And then did you send a message June 2, 2009, at 3:20, 'Take a light with you hon,' and then, I don't know, 'mh—mwha' [*sic*]. Do you remember sending a text message of that nature?"

"I remember sending it, yes."

"And this mwha, what does that mean?"

Eli looked embarrassed. "Like you're blowing a kiss."

The Amish in the courtroom were sickened. A few held back a laugh. It seemed so trivial. Eli's wife is about to be murdered and he's symbolically blowing a kiss to his co-conspirator?

"Okay, June 2, 2009, 3:25 do you recall receiving a text message, 'I'm so scared . . . ' "

"Yes."

". . . from the defendant Barbara Raber. June 2, 2009,

3:26, 'Where are you?' Do you remember receiving a text message?"

"Yes."

"June 2, 2009, 3:37 do you recall sending a text message 'We're in Wooster . . . just don't lose anything.'"

"Yes."

"On June 2, 2009, 3:29 do you recall receiving a text message, 'Do you think I can drive in behind the pines?'"

"Yes."

It wasn't until 4:47 that Eli wrote, telling her to park behind the pine trees.

"Did there come a point in time where you actually arrived at Lake Erie?"

"Yes."

"Approximately what time?"

"I'd say it was probably around 6:00, 6:15, somewhere in there."

"And did you have to come back?"

"Yes."

"And why did you have to come back?"

"Because of the murder of my wife."

WITHIN A FEW hours of the murder, it occurred to Barb Raber that her and Eli's phones could tie them to the murder.

"I want to draw your attention to June 2, 2009, at about 2:46 p.m. Do you recall a text message, 'Whatever you do don't give them your cell phone, please,'" Edna Boyle asked.

Eli said he did.

"June 2, 2009, at approximately 5:55 p.m. Do you recall receiving a text message from Barbara Raber, 'If someone gives the cops your number they can trace it down. The only way they can't is if the number is changed.'"

"Yes."

Again, John Leonard objected to introducing the specific texts, since they had not been introduced into evidence yet and no foundation had been laid for them.

Judge Brown allowed Boyle to ask Eli how he and Barb had covered their tracks.

"Did you have any discussions with the defendant about your phone number after the murder?"

"She asked me if she should change the phone number, you know, so that they couldn't trace it down. And I said it's up to her because I couldn't do anything."

"And why couldn't you do anything?"

"Because the cell phone was in her name. The account and everything was in hers."

"And so after you had those discussions what happened?"

"She changed the phone number, you know, sometime during that period of time. I don't know exactly what time she changed it because I turned my phone off."

UNDER MORE OF Edna Boyle's direct examination, Eli admitted asking Barb to ask David Weaver to leave the threatening message on the shanty phone. He said he was scared, and that maybe a message would steer the detectives away from him.

"You can run but you can't hide," he had told David to say.

The phrase was prophetic in a way, but it was Barb Raber who couldn't hide. She was on trial, her lover shining the spotlight on all that she'd done.

All that he *claimed* she'd done.

34

It Was Lust II

I couldn't have what I wanted because of the rules.
—ELI WEAVER, TESTIFYING ABOUT WHY HE CONTINUED
TO LIE AND CHEAT, YEAR AFTER YEAR

If Edna Boyle's mission was to prove that Barb Raber had committed the murder, then John Leonard's was to paint Eli in the worst possible light, discrediting him as Barb's accuser. Eli was an adulterer who lied to his church, lied to the police, lied to his wife, and lied to his longtime lover. Leonard needed to create a shadow of a doubt, the possibility that Eli had killed his wife and framed Barb.

It seemed an impossible task. Eli wasn't charged with aggravated murder, as Barb was. He was charged with, and pleaded guilty to, conspiracy to commit murder. But Leonard could make him recount his sins.

"While you were trying to work things out you continued to have affairs with multiple women, is that not correct?"

"Yes."

"Okay, and, in fact, I think there's been testimony you

had affairs with maybe five or six different women during the time period that you were married?"

Eli looked almost proud of it.

"Yes," he said, "approximately."

"And you had indicated you left the Amish faith three or four years ago because you wanted more freedom and you weren't happy. And then they shunned you and you were not welcomed back in?"

"Yes."

"And I believe you were actually shunned more than once, correct, twice?"

"Twice."

"And even when you confessed your affairs you still didn't confess all of them did you?"

"No."

"So you continued to lie to the church when you were asking to be let back into the church, correct?"

"Yes."

"So you weren't even honest with them when you were attempting to ask for forgiveness of your sins and apologize? You still weren't honest with the church, were you?"

"Mostly I wasn't honest with God and the church both."

Eli admitted he'd conveniently forgotten to confess relationships he didn't want the church to know about. The pull of the English life was so tempting.

Why? Why did Eli continue year after year to cheat and lie?

Eli said it was because of all the rules. They prevented him from having what he wanted.

The defense lawyer made a face. "Sure, because you like to use electricity and you like to use cell phones . . . "

Eli looked blank eyed. "Yes," he finally said.

"And computers and all those kind of things that you weren't allowed to use?"

"Yes."

* * *

THERE WAS NO cheering section for the woman on trial, but some in the gallery began to feel sorry for Barb Raber. They saw her as a kind of fragile figure, ready to break into a million pieces.

Said one observer: "She was kind of pathetic in a way. Like she might not be all there, you know, mentally challenged. Eli was a kind of wheeler-dealer who ran circles around Barb. She was no match for him. I thought of her as a kind of sad sex slave, if you want to know the truth."

That idea doesn't seem to be far from the truth.

The lawyer pressed Eli hard on the point. "She pretty much was willing to do for you whatever you wanted done, right?"

Eli didn't bat an eye. He almost seemed proud of the hold he had over Barb.

"Yes," he said.

"You kind of strung her along a little bit there didn't you?"

"No."

"Well, did she know about the affairs you had with all the other women?"

"She knew of one, yes."

Leonard could have rolled his eyes just then, but the point was made.

"Okay, well, she didn't know about the other five or six, right? So that's kind of not being honest with her was it? She didn't know about them?"

"No," Eli said.

"Right, and you certainly didn't volunteer to her that you were seeing other women at the same time, right?"

"No."

"So you lied to her?"

"No."

In Eli's world, omission wasn't a lie. It was merely his way around the truth. He'd omitted things to his wife, his children, and his church.

Eli conceded he was supposed to pay for the use of the cell phone and laptop Barb had given him, but he'd thought they had a deal—he would trade her a musket loader. And he wanted his wife to know as little about where his money went as possible. He didn't tell his wife he was paying child support, and he wasn't about to let her know he owed the taxi lady thousands of dollars in phone bills.

"So you kind of took advantage of Barb Raber here knowing that she was willing to do it for you?"

Eli didn't see it that way. Not at all.

"Not really took advantage of her," he said, "no."

Leonard went in for the kill.

"I mean, you're kind of a charming individual to have all these different ladies and different relationships. You're not asking for anything in return?" he asked, his tone broad.

Eli leaned back in the witness box. "I don't really call it charming," he said. "I mean, it was lust."

"Well, for all these ladies to believe that you're the man of their dreams and you're the guy to be with takes a little bit of charisma, some charm, right?"

Boyle objected that Leonard was hounding Eli, but she was overruled and the debate over the extent of Eli's charm continued. Boyle had let the Amish Stud escape scrutiny, but Leonard did not.

"It takes some charisma, some charm to have all these ladies you're dating and you're a married man."

"Not really. I mean, I don't call it charm. I mean . . . "

"Just comes naturally to you?"

"No."

"Now, you indicated for example that you used the Internet. You went to a place, is it MocoSpace?"

"Yes."

"And you had a couple different names that you used on MocoSpace, is that correct?"

"Yes."

"And what was the first name you used?"

"Amish Stud."

To the Amish and Mennonite in the courtroom, including Mark Weaver and Steve Chupp, it was the worst example of what their faith feared—the temptation of technology.

"Okay, and you used that one on MocoSpace and you used that to try to meet some ladies, right? Because you don't call yourself Amish Stud to meet a buddy to go to a football game, right?"

"Actually I used that one for about two months and then I switched to Amish Guy."

In reality, the two overlapped. For part of 2008 and 2009, both Amish Stud and Amish Guy were active on MocoSpace. Eli's last visit to Amish Guy was the day before the murder.

But Eli knew that what he was doing online was not harmless—it's why he was lying and deceiving his wife.

"And your wife certainly didn't know about your Internet chats did she?"

"No."

"Because she wouldn't have approved of that, right?"

"No."

"And the church that you had continually lied to wouldn't approve of that either would they?"

"No."

CRITICAL TO BARB Raber's defense was Eli's ability to influence her.

"And you testified that she was pretty much willing to listen to you and hear you out and pretty much do what you wanted her to do, right?," Leonard asked Eli. "And, in fact, that was based upon the fact that you kind of were able to charm her, have a little bit of charisma, right?"

"I did never try to charm her."

Leonard wasn't willing to give up the topic of charm, or lying.

"You don't think—you never thought that was the case?"

"No."

"You were just straight—well, when you told her that you loved her that wasn't true, was it?"

"No."

Eli still had the power to devastate Barb. When he admitted to Leonard that he didn't love her, her face fell.

"And so that's a lie, right?"

"Yes."

Leonard handed Eli the statement he'd given to detectives and signed the day after the murder.

"And in this statement you would agree with me it pretty much is a lot of garbage isn't it? You didn't say you knew anything about your wife's death. You didn't say anything about your plot with Ms. Raber to kill your wife. None of that's in here is it?"

"No."

Barb's defense attorney kept at Eli, finally getting to the fact that it was his idea to kill his wife and he manipulated Barb into helping him.

Eli's tale that he also intended to kill himself never held much water. But Leonard used it to show that Eli continued to refine his plan to kill his wife.

"And you were going to kill yourself and your wife kind of found out about it when she took a sip and then it was a moment for both of you and your wife was obviously okay at that point?"

"Yes."

"And you still didn't feel real concern for your wife's safety and well-being at that point either, right? You had discussions with Ms. Raber under your testimony about these poisons and chemicals and then you still weren't concerned when your wife may have accidentally ingested them. Nothing stopped you at that point, right?"

"No."

"So you kind of let all your girlfriends know that you weren't happy with your wife and you wanted to get rid of her. And it was your own testimony that my client's the only person that took you up on it, right?"

"Right."

"None of these other ladies called the police or any of these other gentlemen called the police and said hey, this guy's talking about killing his wife, right?"

"No."

"In fact, Ms. Raber didn't think you were going to do it either, right?"

"No."

"So when you moved on and you decided at this point it was very clear you wanted to get rid of your wife, correct?"

"Yes."

"That you didn't want to get back with her and, in fact, you were really happy to get rid of her?"

"No, not happy.

"You were sad to get rid of her?"

"I had mixed feelings."

"And again, the feelings of getting rid of her were a whole lot stronger than the ones not?"

"Yeah, I guess I got caught up."

"Yeah, you weren't concerned about the fact that your children weren't going to have a mother anymore? You weren't concerned that if you got caught your children weren't going to have a father they could have contact with anymore? You weren't concerned about your nieces and nephews or anybody in the family that were going to be missing relatives? You were concerned about the fact that you wanted to be a womanizer. You wanted to be the Amish Stud and continue relationships with different women, correct?"

"No."

The prosecutor objected to the drill but was overruled. Leonard wanted to poke holes in Eli's version of the morning he was to be picked up to go fishing.

"Okay, and you overslept and they were knocking on the door, right?"

"Yes."

"And you didn't go to answer the door right away when you heard the knocking, right?"

"My wife woke me up."

"I understand that. That's what you tell us. But the fact of the matter is that when you heard there was a knock on the door and I believe there was also a car horn beeping you didn't go right to the door did you?"

"No."

Leonard tried to pin Eli down—people were pounding on the door and a car horn was honking but he was busy tidying the bedroom where he had just killed his wife.

Steve remembered how hard it had been for them to wake Eli. Now there was the suggestion that Eli had been busy killing Barbara? That hadn't occurred to Steve, who had sat patiently waiting for Eli that morning.

The attorney kept after Eli.

"So when you were made aware that somebody was there at your home you did not answer the door immediately did you?"

"All we did was make a light so they seen I was awake."

"I understand that. But you didn't answer the door immediately did you?"

"I never do when I oversleep."

"And I understand there's testimony it was five to eight minutes before you came to the front door? And nobody but you can testify here that your wife was alive at that point, right?"

"Yes."

"You're the only one. None of these children will come in here and say they spoke to your wife that night?"

"Not that morning."

"Nobody? The last person to see your wife alive is you?"

"That's right."

Leonard wanted to show that the timeline of the early morning of June 2 was shaky. He pointed out that some of Barb's texts to Eli overlapped with his supposedly still being asleep.

"Okay. Now we had some discussions and Ms. Boyle asked you about the timing of some of these messages. She asked you about some texts that occurred at almost 3:30. And the questions were if you recalled making these discussions. Something about being able to see in the dark and 'I don't know if I can. It's scary.' Do you remember that?"

"Yes."

"Well, what's interesting is the first time that that conversation takes place is 3:03 a.m., okay. Now, you've just testified under oath that at that point in time you had overslept. You were sleeping. You were getting up to answer the door, right?"

"Yes."

"Also let's go backtracking a little bit further. Because even before that while you're sleeping there's questions that come through at 2:20, 2:21, and all this is time when you're sleeping, right?"

"Does it say that I answered them?"

"We'll get to that. But I'm just saying that these questions, these discussions, all occurred while you were sleeping, right? Okay, let's see here. So your testimony is that Barb Raber is the one that killed your wife?"

"Yes."

"You just kind of didn't care one way or the other if it happened or not. That you gave her all these detailed instructions to do it while you were sleeping and while you were in a vehicle with other people. So let's cut to the chase here. During the time that you've indicated you were sleeping and later eating with your friends there appears to be a lengthy detailed discussion via text message about killing your wife with Ms. Raber. Your testimony is that that's accurate, right?"

"That's accurate."

Leonard continued working to show that Eli was minimizing his involvement in his wife's murder, that he knew a good offer when he heard one and had a lot to gain by avoiding a trial.

"You had the opportunity of course to take a plea deal, right?"

"Yes."

"And you know you were originally facing a legitimate possibility under Ohio law of no possibility of a parole date? You're aware of that, right?"

"Yes."

"You were originally charged with what?"

"Aggravated murder."

"And what else with the aggravated murder?"

"With gun specs."

"There's a gun specification, right?"

"Yes."

"And under the Ohio law you could have been given up to life without the possibility of parole, correct?"

"Yes."

"You didn't like that did you?"

"Nobody does."

"So you actually talked to your attorney and your attorney was able to get you a deal where what's your sentence now expected to be?"

"It's no deal. I mean, we still got to do . . . "

"It's certainly no deal for others involved. Let's talk about you. What's the sentence you've been told you're going to get?"

"Fifteen to life."

"Okay, so that's a whole lot different than never, ever, ever being able to say that you're going to get out, right?"

"Yes."

"You're how old?"

"Thirty."

"So your parole date could be about when you're about 45?"

"Could."

Neither Mark nor Steve would look forward to the day Eli was paroled. Would he be angry at them for cooperating with the police? Would they be expected to wave and say hello when they ran into him at the market or at an auction? Would he return to the Amish community at all?

"And I'm sure that you're going to be able to argue to the parole board about how cooperative you were with the police once you made the deal and how you sat down and you came in and you testified and you were able to put Barb Raber, the co-defendant, behind bars with you, right?"

"It's going to be by the grace of God when I get out."

"I'm sorry?"

"It's going to be by the grace of God when I get out."

Leonard wanted the jury to remember that Eli was the last person to see his wife alive.

"When you left the house on a stormy night there was

a child on the couch, a child on the recliner I believe, and a baby in the baby's room all on the main floor, correct?"

"Yes."

Leonard was still hammering home his theory that Eli had killed his wife, and Barb was taking the fall for it. Both Eli and Barb were focused on how his cell phone could lead police to him. If Barb was guilty of anything, it was of helping Eli cover up his involvement in his wife's murder.

"So let me get this straight," the defense lawyer said. "You said you left at 3:00. The only person who could testify that your wife was alive is you?"

Eli nodded. "Yes," he said.

"And the fact of the matter is the reason that you're the last person to see your wife alive is because you're the person that killed her?"

Eli held firm to his contention. "No," he said.

"You killed her and you knew doggone well that you could point some fingers at other people?"

"No."

"And you figured that when your wife's body was found you would be up at Lake Erie and you could pretend to be all surprised and grieving and remorseful and I can't believe this happened, but you'd be okay because you were free and nobody would find out you were involved? You figured you could—if all else fails you could put the blame on Barb Raber didn't you?"

Eli could only say one word: "No."

Leonard continued to try to crack Eli's impenetrable facade.

"You killed your wife," the defense lawyer said. "You're the last person to see her alive and you killed her and you had no problem placing the blame on her [Barb Raber]. When the heat got real tough on you, you thought 'I'm going to steer everything away from me.' Me. You're a 'me' guy aren't you?"

Eli shook his head. "No."

And with that, corrections officers shackled his hands and led him out.

The Amish in the courtroom turned their heads away.

35

Doubt

I sat there sobbing and asked, "Eli do you plan on getting a truck again? Because you are acting just like you did when you got the others. Can you just let go of her and the truck? Please don't let Satan convince you."
—BARBARA WEAVER, ON THE LURE THE OUTSIDE WORLD
HAD FOR HER HUSBAND

Eli's big moment was over. As the trial continued, some in the Amish community—and many outside it, too—wondered about the elements of the case against Barb that didn't align with the story line presented by either side of the criminal justice system. Some even went as far as blaming the Wayne County Sheriff's Office for rushing to judgment and pinning all their hopes for a swift resolution on Eli Weaver's confession.

As one local put it, "Not everything adds up. Least that's the way I see it."

John Leonard, who can't speak on the record because

of client-attorney confidentiality, said that not all the facts were presented during the trial.

Two shotguns associated with Barb and Eli were unaccounted for. The sheriff's department sent the serial number of one of them to a national registry, but it was never found.

Barb said Eli had hidden the murder weapon around his property, but sheriff's department reports never mention a thorough search for the weapon. Or had she and Ed hidden it in a camper—then gotten rid of the camper? Or had Eli taken the shotgun on his fishing trip and thrown it into Lake Erie?

Those who scoured the reports issued by the sheriff's department could find no mention of what happened to the two .410 guns—as well as assorted other shotguns and pellet guns—found at Maysville Outfitters. Only Barb Raber's .22 was tested by the state's expert.

Another omission from the reports was what, if anything, was learned from Eli's computer. Barb Raber's was sliced and diced like an onion in a late-night food-chopper commercial. What about Eli's? Was it the one he had given to Tabitha? What had been discovered from an examination of his search history?

There was no comment from the coroner or the medical examiner—or the sheriff's department—about the unexplained bruising on Barbara's body the morning of June 2. It looked like more than a scratch on a finger, as detectives had described it. Her right arm was scratched and had bled. The fingers on her left hand and palm were bruised and swollen. Her right palm was bruised. Her neck had bruising. Was all the discoloration the result of blood pooling after death? The medical examiner and coroner did not say so. Had she struggled with Eli the morning of her death? Or had she been hurt two days before when she and Eli had sex? Her sister Fannie suspected Eli was "forceful" during sex with his wife.

Barbara Weaver was shot at extremely close range. Barb Raber said her gun went off as she stood in the doorway.

Had Eli already killed her before Barb Raber showed up? Many in the Amish, Mennonite, and English communities still believe Eli killed her, then let Barb Raber fire the shot from one of the .410 gauge shotguns.

Ed Raber's friend George didn't mince words, although his opinion is at odds with the coroner's report. "I have the feeling Eli killed her, because of the marks around her neck. He strangled her before Barb arrived."

The texts don't match Eli's version of the early morning hours. He was at home—awake—when he said he was asleep.

"It seems to me that once they knew that Ms. Raber was implicated in the murder," said an observer with extensive knowledge of the case, "the authorities did everything they could to prove she had fired the deadly shot—and stopped investigating Eli."

The biggest sticking point to the case never presented in the media and in court?

"There is no direct evidence that Barb Raber was in the house. Not one shred of evidence," the observer said. "Not even fingerprints. They first interviewed her the day after the murder. They could have done tests on her person or her clothing to see if she'd fired a weapon. But they didn't."

Was Barb Raber the second victim?

36

Verdict

I am telling you the truth, Eddie.
—BARB RABER, TELLING HER HUSBAND SHE HAD NOT KILLED
BARBARA WEAVER

To the end, John Leonard insisted that Barb Raber hadn't killed Barbara Weaver.

The victim's husband had.

In his closing statement, the defense attorney argued that Eli killed Barbara at 2:00 a.m. and left an hour later on his fishing trip. The lack of a weapon as evidence and the fact that Barbara was shot at close range proved the crime was personal, he said.

Personal. That was so key to the defense. The murder was more in line with the way a husband would kill his wife. A man. *Someone who was closely connected to the victim.*

Not a girlfriend like Barb Raber.

As the defense saw it, Eli had used Barb to "facilitate" the crime, doing his dirty work, researching poisons, and giving him a computer and a cell phone.

"He suckered Barbara Raber . . . he was taking advantage" of her, Leonard told the jury.

Barb, born a foundling, had spent her life looking for someone who truly loved her. She thought Eli was that person. They were both outsiders.

But as she had with her house, which was buried in stuff, Barb had lost control of her life, all for a man who didn't care one whit about her. She was someone to be used. For a ride. For money. For sex. And finally, for murder.

In her summation, Edna Boyle told the jury that the murder was planned, and not, as Barbara Raber claimed, "an accident."

"We're talking about two selfish people here who thought they were going to get away with it," she said. The prosecutor wanted this to be very clear to those in the jury box: Eli was unhappy in his marriage, and Barb Raber wanted Eli for herself.

The jury deliberated for five hours. The only question they asked to have clarified was how time of death is determined. Observers in the courtroom wondered if the defense lawyer's push to create reasonable doubt by suggesting Eli murdered Barbara in the early morning had worked.

In the end, it hadn't.

As the jury foreman passed the verdict to the bailiff, who handed it to the judge, Barb, shaking and ravaged by sleepless nights, stood and faced judge and jury.

"In the matter of the State vs. Barbara Raber, the court has reviewed the verdict. The jury finds Ms. Raber guilty of aggravated murder. The jury further finds Ms. Raber used a firearm in the commission of the offense of aggravated murder."

As soon as it was read, the defendant collapsed in her chair. She put her hands and face on the table and started

to cry. As the judge polled the jury on what was a unani-
mous vote, she sobbed over and over, "I didn't do it, I didn't
do it."

Her anguished cries seemed so raw, so full of genuine
emotion, that few could doubt that she was in complete
agony over what had transpired.

As sheriff's deputies took her away, she continued to
cry out.

I didn't do it! I didn't do it!"

The next day Eli was sentenced for complicity to commit murder. Once again, the courtroom was packed with
members of the Amish community.

"I'm very sorry for what I did and I hope everybody can
forgive me for what I did," Eli told Judge Brown.

That didn't sit well with anyone in the courtroom. Although no one spoke up and called out to the disgraced
member of their church, the air was thick with disbelief.
They'd heard those words before. Every time Eli returned
home after carousing and partying with English women,
he'd beg for forgiveness.

This was Eli Weaver playing the part of contrition. It
was a rerun. He'd duped all of them before.

Judge Brown told Eli he could have made a different
choice, taken a different path. Eli had left the Amish faith
twice before.

"You only needed to walk away a third time," Brown
told Eli.

He sentenced Eli to serve fifteen years to life. The sentence seemed awfully short to many in the community.
After the courtroom emptied, Andy Hyde told a reporter
that although he supported Eli's plea deal, "It would have
been a tough trial to convict Mr. Weaver." Hyde pointed
out that Eli hadn't put a gun in Barb's hand, or shown her
how to shoot it. All he'd done was leave the basement door
unlocked for her. Later, the defense lawyer said, "They

made a pretty good case that he wasn't there, that he was fishing."

The jury had been faced with two liars—Eli and Barb Raber—and they didn't like either one of them. The texts before and after the shooting were the most damaging evidence against Barb, according to John Leonard.

"She wasn't believed by the jury. They decided she did it," and then tried to cover up her part, Leonard said. He remains convinced that Eli might have killed his wife.

Edna Boyle justified the plea bargain to reporters, saying Eli had provided new details to detectives, including about Barb's first attempt to kill Barbara three weeks before the June 2 murder. Barb had driven to the Weaver house but backed out because she was scared.

Boyle said Eli's cooperation did not excuse his actions.

"Five children are without a mother and father. Fannie Troyer is without a sister. Mr. Miller is without a daughter."

Eli won't be home anytime soon. According to an attorney with knowledge of the case, he almost certainly will be denied parole the first time he is eligible, in April 2024. He is incarcerated in the Marion Correctional Institution and has been formally shunned by the Amish.

A week later, Barb Raber was sentenced for aggravated murder. Members of her family, Eli's family, and spectators filled every bench in the courtroom, in addition to a series of folding chairs. Others stood at the back. Barbara Weaver's family was present but did not speak or submit a written statement.

Barb Raber was optimistic to the end. She'd wanted a trial, and she was confident that the truth—her truth—would convince the jury of her innocence. The testimony of Fannie Troyer, Jamie Wood, and Eli had been damaging, but Barb was naïve, and, far worse, she hadn't really thought clearly for years. The simplest thing could be a "sign" to her. The weather was sunny and warm every day of her trial, helping her cling to hope. It didn't matter to her that the courtroom was stuffy. Now there were threatening thunderstorms and the temperature had dropped twenty degrees. As she sat waiting to hear her sentence, she felt a chill. Just as the weather had turned, so had what little luck Barb had ever had, which wasn't much.

John Leonard asked for a lower sentencing range because Barb Raber had never been in trouble. He added that she was a good mother, although many knew different. He reminded the court that it was Eli Weaver who wanted his wife murdered and contacted people about doing it.

"If not for Mr. Weaver," the lawyer said, "we would not be here."

Boyle didn't buy that. Not at all. She responded that Barb refused to accept responsibility for her actions, the murder occurred with six young children in the house, Barb and Eli spent six months planning, and she could have backed out.

The State asked for either life without parole or thirty years to life in prison.

Saying he thought it fair that her sentence should have some "parity" with Eli's, Judge Brown sentenced her to twenty years to life, plus three years on a gun charge.

"The evidence in this case was very compelling," Judge Brown said to Barb. "You were involved in the death of Barbara Weaver. There is no evidence to contradict that.

"Without your cooperation," the judge said, "she would still be alive today."

37

Aftermath

I often think of Christ's words, "Forgive him, for he knows not what he does."
—Barbara Weaver, whose faith was with her to the end

The lives of ten children were forever changed by the murder of Barbara Weaver.

Five of the children are Barbara and Eli's. Two are their cousins, who were sleeping over on the night of the murder. The other three are Ed and Barb Raber's.

The two oldest Weaver children now live with Fannie and Cristy Troyer and their now six children. The three youngest are with another relative. For a long time all the children had bouts of crying and anxiety.

After Eli's sentencing, Fannie explained to Harley that his father wouldn't be home soon. It would be a very long time.

"Will Dad be able to attend my wedding?" Harley asked.

Like a stone tossed into the still waters of a millpond, the rings of evil that emanated from Eli Weaver continue to reverberate. It has been several seasons of quiet soul-searching in Apple Creek. Friends and family still ask themselves why they didn't take Eli seriously when he talked about killing his wife.

"It just seemed like talk," one said. "Like a joke or something. I don't know. I couldn't imagine that he really wanted to kill her. I was pretty wrong about that."

A woman who grew up with Barbara Weaver wonders if anyone ever told her friend that it's okay to leave an abusive and disrespectful husband, even if you're Amish. Maybe if today Eli Weaver wanted to come home after living with an English girlfriend, Barbara would say no.

"I'd like to think that someone would have said something [to warn Barbara to leave her husband], but even now I don't think so. The Amish want to stay separate from the world and that means keeping their own secrets," said an observer of the case.

"They should have divorced," said Barbara Weaver's girlhood friend Ruby Hofstetter, who grew up Old Order Amish. "Her church sweeps things under the rug and doesn't deal with problems." She concedes that counseling is more accepted now, and encouraged, among the Amish.

Some think the murder may have had an impact on the Amish view on staying in a marriage, no matter how troubled. Samuel Miller said that church leaders recently helped a woman in a physically abusive marriage move out of her home.

"Now there is a tendency to recognize danger," Samuel said.

Barbara's murder has had an enduring effect on the Weavers' friends and neighbors, especially the women.

Not long after Eli was arrested, Samuel's wife told him that the everyday sound of his entering the house through the basement and climbing up a stairway frightened her.

Other Amish women expressed the same fear. They asked themselves if they needed to fear their husbands.

"Who can you rely on if you can't rely on your husband?" one asked.

Gone are the days when you could trust someone "just because they are Amish," said Samuel. The Amish have learned that technology can be used for evil purposes. He said it gives pause to the Amish who want to move the line of demarcation between the old ways and the newer.

"When Eli went looking for trouble, the cell phone and Internet made it easier," Samuel said.

But Andy Hyde isn't so sure that the Amish are more likely to, as Samuel phrased it, "recognize danger." He has never heard of an Amish domestic violence case reaching the court, "because the bishop will tell them not to report it," he said. "I've seen a lot of molestation crimes in Amish families, too, but again, they are urged not to report the crime. And they could be in legal trouble because they are supposed to report it. And they will tell women they can't leave their marriage." He has represented formerly Amish women working to get custody of their children. "The Amish will not support their efforts to get custody," he said.

"It was almost the perfect murder," Hyde said. "If they hadn't found the text messages, if they had thrown their phones away, there would have been little or no evidence. Investigators would have gone after Eli's girlfriends, rivals, angry husbands and boyfriends looking for who did this."

As to that lingering question, why didn't Eli just leave his marriage, Hyde said it wasn't that Eli cared so much about being Amish—he knew which would be the easier path to the freedom he wanted.

"If he had left, he would have been shunned. If his wife is dead, they pat him on the back."

A few years after the murder, a man approached Hyde at an auction and introduced himself as Eli's brother. Not to thank him for his help. Not to deliver news about Eli.

"He wanted me to know that the rest of the family was not like Eli, that Eli was the black sheep."

BARB RABER'S CONSERVATIVE Mennonite congregation still reaches out to their most infamous member. Every week the church newsletter has a reminder to those whose turn it is to write to Barb in prison.

"We're supposed to send her cards," a longtime church member and family friend said. She has never sent a card. "I felt she needed to be punished." If the friend happens to be present when a prayer is said for Barb, she participates. But other than that, "They don't say too much in church about her."

Like Ed and Barb, the friend was raised Amish and left to become Mennonite. "We wanted a car; we wanted to get around," she said.

She sees Ed at church every Sunday, and he seems happy when he is there. "He is not over this, but it makes him happy that we send her mail. I hope she finds Christ before she dies."

Eli reportedly attends church services in prison. He rarely has visitors. A few years ago Eli's bishop came to see Steve Chupp. He had heard that Steve might visit Eli in prison and encouraged him to do so.

Steve has visited Eli three times. "He needs to know there's hope for him. All I try to do is give him hope," he said.

THE LIVES OF Barb Raber's children are oddly better. Their grades in school have improved. Their mother used to leave the three boys home alone often. Now, an aunt helps care for them and they live, by all accounts, in a better environment.

After his wife was arrested, the congregation stepped in to help Ed and his sons. A couple of members loaned him money, interest free, and also helped him get a mortgage. He bought a home for his children and himself. They left the house that was immaculate outside but a nightmare inside.

"He needed help managing things, learning to make ends meet," his friend George said. "He's improved a lot. He's a worker; he makes good money, and bought a home."

Ed visits his wife every few months. Their sons have seen their mother a couple of times.

"I don't think he'll ever divorce her," George said. "We don't believe in divorce. He's not angry. He has a forgiving attitude."

Maybe too forgiving.

After Barb was convicted, a friend of Ed's went to Hyde, asking if the attorney would meet and speak with Ed. His friends were concerned that he was still in denial about Barb's role in the murder.

Hyde agreed, and he and Ed met in a room at the courthouse. For an hour the attorney went over the evidence against Barb, including the texts. "Ed said, 'But they never found the gun, so it can't be proven that she did it,' " Hyde said later. He left the meeting knowing that Ed's belief in his wife's innocence had not been cracked.

Ed Raber's new home's telephone answering system doesn't ignore the woman who may be away for a very long time. It still tells callers they've reached the home of Barbara and Ed Raber. In 2010, Barb Raber lost an appeal of her conviction to the Court of Appeals, Ninth Judicial District, State of Ohio. An attorney for her argued four motions: That her statement to police that the murder was "an accident" should have been suppressed since it was given after she had asked for an attorney; that text messages should not have been admitted into evidence during her trial; that information from computer searches should also have been barred; and that the weight of evidence did not lead to a rightful conviction.

And the question persists—why wasn't she provided with an attorney as soon as she requested one? She was questioned for two days before detectives took her request seriously. That doesn't go down well with those who think Barb took the rap for Eli.

Her appeals now nearly exhausted, Barb Raber tells anyone who will listen that she did not commit the murder. During every weekly phone conversation with her mother, Barb says again that she did not do it.

She is incarcerated in the Ohio Reformatory for Women. Her first date with the parole board is in April 2032.

Over time, more people seem to view her with a modicum of sympathy. They wonder just how guilty she was. Had Eli Weaver already killed his wife before dispatching Barb to the scene?

A friend says Eli has not seen his children. Although he is still Banned, Eli's parents write to him. And he writes letters—a lot of them.

In the early summer of 2011, two years after the murder of his wife, Eli wrote a letter that was printed in *The Budget*, the weekly newspaper that serves the Sugarcreek, Ohio, area, as well as Amish and Mennonite communities throughout the Americas.

A Penitent Heart:
I want to apologize to my children, in-laws, family, friends, church, neighbors and entire community for all of the grief and pain I caused all of you in my involvement in the death of my wife, and loving mother, Barbara Weaver.

*I'm sorry that due to my selfishness all of you had to go
through things nobody should ever have to go through.*

*I'm sorry for all of the lies and heartache I put all of
you through, while trying to be somebody I wasn't, and
I'm sorry to everyone I misled. . . . I pray that someday
God grants me the opportunity to apologize and seek your
forgiveness face to face.*

May God bless you all.

Eli D. Weaver, Mansfield, Ohio

Eli's ministers and some family considered the missive
insincere. It was just Eli continuing to duck responsibility
for the murder of his wife. Some feel it was proof that his
manipulations continue. In 2015 Eli began writing to newly
widowed Amish women, plucking their names and ad-
dresses out of copies of *The Budget*. Was he bored—or
perhaps lining up support and a home for after he is paroled?
There had to be something in it for him. The women lived
outside of Wayne and Holmes Counties, but news of his
crimes had, of course, spread. The women were *not* happy
to have received the letters and did not respond.

ONE OF ELI's many "best friends"—all of whom were
women—was okay hearing from him. Eli Weaver was
never going to let her go, and part of that was fine with
Tabitha. She'd loved him like a friend for a very long time
and despite all the lies and deception, she could not shake
off her feelings. Whenever she heard Tim McGraw's song
"My Best Friend" on the radio, she'd think of the Amish
man who broke her heart.

When a letter arrived at her home in Massillon, Tabitha
dropped everything and tore it open. She hadn't heard from
Eli since he sent a birthday card a few months earlier. She

settled into a chair to savor his words. His salutation: *Greetings of love.*

As Tabitha read, she found herself in his world, hearing his voice. He peppered the pages with exclamation points and smiley faces. He complained about the delay in the mail. He was ecstatic that his mother still wrote to him every week.

He filled half a page with the mundane: how he missed fieldwork, how he was looking forward to softball with the other "residents," as he preferred to call the inmates.

While she was interested in all of that, Tabitha had dangled a question for her friend in her last missive. She'd wondered how Barb felt about everything that had happened. "Resentful" and "bitter" was his response.

She denies everything to everybody and gets very upset if anybody even talks about it and that's why not too many people back home have much to do with her.

He said he wrote to Barb and told her to confess what she'd done.

Yes, it's hard to admit to such a thing, but it will make her feel better and only then can healing start for her and everybody else.

Speaking of Barb, who'd once suggested that she could tour high schools and talk to kids about the dangers of texting, Eli, too, had a plan for helping young people stay on the straight and narrow. He wanted to create some kind of group home that provided shelter and guidance for those who had stumbled.

Tabitha had suggested a Facebook page to get things going in her previous letter and he loved the idea. He also indicated that a "top detective" from Holmes County had promised to help, and he was excited about a couple of Amish men coming to see him too.

He ended a letter to Tabitha with a smiley face and a

mention of the song they both loved, "My Best Friend." While she was listening to it at home, he played it over and over on the CD player/radio his aunt in Pennsylvania had sent him.

I love my music plus it drowns out most of the noise in here. My family would never approve of it.

As always, Eli Weaver blamed the Amish for keeping him away from all the things in life that he'd wanted.

Tabitha was being kept from something she wanted as well. She made multiple calls to the Wayne County Sheriff's Office asking for the return of her laptop. They refused.

"The Wayne County sheriff will protect the Amish," she said later. "They don't want to give them a bad reputation. Maybe my laptop has something on it they don't want out."

After the trial, Tabitha added another tattoo to the sixteen that already adorned her body. On the nape of her neck, concealed by her very long black hair, she has a message borne of her experiences with an Amish man that turned her life upside down: TRUST NO ONE.

SOMETHING WAS MISSING from the investigation and the Raber trial and subsequent sentencing. Why had no one spoken for the victim?

Barbara Weaver was all but absent from the proceedings. The only time Eli Weaver's wife was mentioned during the trial was when her sister described her as "a dear friend."

Americans are used to victims and families giving tearful television interviews and facing down murderers in court to speak bitterly about how the crime has changed their lives forever. They pour out memories of their dead loved ones—their kindnesses, how well-loved they were, the children left behind.

Except for a brief exchange between Eli and his father-in-law at Barbara's funeral, no one confronted the two people convicted of her death.

One reason there wasn't more from her family and friends was that this had never happened before in Wayne County.

"Facing one of our own on trial for the murder of one of our own was an event unprecedented in this community," said an Amish friend and neighbor of Eli.

"For the family to have remained silent at Barb Raber's trial, and at sentencing for both Eli and Barb, screams volumes. I can see how it looks 'cold' to a non-Amish person. There's a deep feeling of horror and shame that this happened."

If the Amish talked about Barbara, it would force them to face the outside world and they would have to give up their separateness from that world. And being isolated is central to the Amish. They keep their grief and pain private from a world they do not understand.

Barbara Weaver's parents may have found themselves struggling with their beliefs on forgiveness as they watched her husband on trial for the murder of their daughter, his wife. The Amish teach and believe in the necessity of forgiveness. But even for the Amish, forgiving murder is difficult, and much more so when the murderer is one of their own.

There were no pleas for clemency or statements of forgiveness as there have been when other crimes have been committed against the Amish. Just silence.

She *is* still discussed in the privacy of the Amish community. The neighbor believes Barbara would want them to forgive Eli.

It speaks volumes about the kind of person Barbara was—nice, maybe to a fault.

Human nature being what it is, the Amish, former Amish, and non-Amish talk about Eli more than they do about Barbara. Eli continues to provide plenty of fodder for conversation.

For hundreds of years there were few murders perpetrated by an Amish man, and only two before Barbara Weaver's that were widely known or even reported to English authorities. The Amish have a history of settling things themselves. But Eli Weaver was not the first Amish man to commit ungodly acts and he won't be the last.

As one Amish leader said, the Amish have their good ones and bad ones, just like the rest of the world.

Afterword

by Karen M. Johnson-Weiner

THE STORY OF Eli and Barbara Weaver is, unfortunately, a human story, not a particularly Amish one.

In America, ten million men and women suffer physical violence at the hands of their intimate partners each year.

While partner abuse is less well documented in the Amish world, it certainly exists. After all, the Amish are human. Yet Barbara Weaver's death at the hands of her husband is unique in the Amish world, for unlike the two other murders of Amish individuals—Katie Gingerich and Hannah Stolzfus—Barbara died at the hands of her all-too-sane husband and his formerly Amish, now Mennonite, lover.

Perhaps what makes the story of Barbara and Eli so compelling is that Eli brought the world into a church community ill-equipped to deal with it. Had Eli just left the Amish (as he had done before), Barbara would have been expected to remain single, but she would have had the support of family and church. The church community, like Barbara, was unable to handle the selfishness of the man who wanted it all, had no desire to yield to the teachings of the church, and was willing to manipulate those around him for his own ends.

Much is made of the wife's role in Amish church culture. The man is the head of the household and the woman is responsible for housekeeping and mothering. She is the helpmeet, a "keeper at home," a role that is biblically defined. Titus 2 instructs women to "be discreet, chaste, keepers at home, good, obedient to their own husbands, that the word of God be not blasphemed" (Titus 2:5).

The Amish would deny that women are less than men. Indeed, many have told me that men and women are equal according to scripture, for, as it says in Galatians, "There is neither male nor female; for you are all one in Christ Jesus" (Galatians 3:28).

Nevertheless, referring to the creation of Adam and "his mate," Eve, and their subsequent expulsion from the Garden of Eden, Amish historian Joseph Stoll argues that "scripture very clearly places the man in a position of responsibility as the head of the household, and his wife in a position of subjection." Amish magazines and stories often cite the fifth chapter of Paul's letter to the Ephesians, "Wives, submit yourselves unto your own husbands, as unto the Lord. For the husband is the head of the wife, even as Christ also is the head of the church . . . Therefore as the church is subject unto Christ, so let the wives be to their own husbands in everything." (Ephesians 5:22-24).

Yet this verse also commands men to follow Christ's example. An article titled "The Husband's Role" in the Amish magazine *Family Life* begins by stating, "The role of the Christian husband is summarized in the verse 'Husbands, love your wives, even as Christ also loved the church, and gave himself for it' (Ephesians 5:25)."[1] As another Amish publication put it, "When a man vows before God to take a woman as his wife, he is accepting responsibility for her physical and spiritual well-being until death parts them."[2]

---

[1] "The Husband's Role." *Family Life*, May 2004, pp. 9–11.

[2] *A God-Centered Marriage, The Husband's Role*. Pathway Reprint Series, #1. Aylmer, Ontario: Pathway Publishers, 2008, pp. 7–9.

Barbara Weaver attempted to be a good wife, but Eli Weaver was a horrible husband. A church community in which members trust one another to act in good faith and give themselves up to the teachings of the church and Christ's example was no match for Eli's selfish and pathological manipulation of family, friends, and lovers.

It's not unusual for the Amish to talk to a counselor. Eli had refused to see the one Barbara was in touch with. Given that he had repeatedly left the church, it's likely that the ministry would have wanted to be involved. But no one in the church could have told Barbara to leave her husband, for that would go against Biblical teaching. As it says in Matthew 19:6, "What therefore God hath joined together let not man put asunder." Encouraged by scripture to give the offender the benefit of the doubt, they probably trusted Eli when he returned home and made his confession, and they would have encouraged Barbara to give Eli another chance, forgive him, and remain committed to him.

In the popular imagination, the Amish are isolated from the world and its technology and live a simple life. In reality, there is great diversity in the Amish world, and while some Amish groups have held cell phones, computers, and other twenty-first-century technologies at bay, others have accepted them while modifying them or limiting their use. All Amish want to keep their distance from "the world"— how they do so is dictated by tradition and the Ordnung, or discipline of the church community.[3]

Eli and Barbara Weaver were members of an Andy Weaver Amish church community. The group differs from

---

[3] For a good (and very accessible) discussion of the Amish and technology, see chapter 17 of *The Amish*, by D. B. Kraybill, K. M. Johnson-Weiner, and S. M. Nolt. (Baltimore: Johns Hopkins University Press, 2013)

the Old Order in its stronger view of shunning, and it has remained more conservative technologically.[4] Yet while the Andy Weaver churches in Ohio do not fellowship with their Old Order neighbors—meaning they don't worship together or intermarry—they do fellowship with the technologically more progressive Amish in Lancaster County, Pennsylvania, leading some younger folks to question church leaders. One Andy Weaver Amish man commented that the behavior of the young folk was a factor in the decision by several families, his own included, to leave and start a new settlement. Too often, he noted, the young folk "just followed their own desires."[5]

Certainly this was true of Eli. He was neither isolated from mainstream society nor naïve about what it offered him. He simply followed his own desires.

Karen M. Johnson-Weiner is Distinguished Service Professor, Department of Anthropology, State University of New York, Potsdam. With Donald B. Kraybill and Steven M. Nolt, Johnson-Weiner is the author of *The Amish,* the companion to the PBS series of the same name. She is also the author of *Train Up a Child: Old Order Amish and Mennonite Schools*; and *New York Amish: Life in the Plain Communities of the Empire State.*

---

[4] Weaver is a very common Amish surname. For a good discussion of the Andy Weaver Amish, see C. E. Hurst and D. L. McConnell, *An Amish Paradox. Diversity and Change in the World's Largest Amish Community.* (Baltimore: Johns Hopkins University Press, 2010).

[5] This is discussed in more depth in K. M. Johnson-Weiner, *New York Amish. Life in the Plain Communities of the Empire State.* (Ithaca, NY: Cornell University Press, 2010).

Acknowledgments

MORE THAN TWENTY-FIVE years ago I visited Wayne County while researching a book about the murders of an Amish wife and her little boy. I talked with dozens of Amish people close to the victims—friends, family members, neighbors. In fact, I formed a close bond with many of them. Most were Swartzentruber Amish, which casual readers may or may not know are considered among the most conservative subgroups of Old Order Amish that make their home in that part of Ohio.

The Amish people I got to know were devastated over the loss not only of Ida and Danny Stutzman, but of the man who'd caused the unspeakable hurt. Eli Stutzman was his name, and although he had brought great hurt to them, there was still a measure of compassion mixed with their anger, and disappointment in the justice system that had failed them.

Just as I was interested in learning about what had happened to Ida, Danny, and Eli, those I met were equally interested in me. My day-to-day life was a mystery of sorts. Back then the Amish didn't watch TV.

Close family friends of Ida's took the train cross-country to the Seattle suburbs where my wife and twin girls and I lived. I drove Elmer and Erma Miller of Fredericksburg to see the Pacific Ocean. I took them to Bellevue Square, a high-end shopping mall near our home. As we strode past shops selling things they'd never seen—and never wanted—shoppers gawked in their direction.

Elmer looked over at me with a sly smile. "They don't see many like us, do they?" he said.

No, they didn't.

My wife worked and brought home Kentucky Fried Chicken one night while the Millers stayed at our house. Both Elmer and Erma felt sorry for her—that she wasn't able to make a home-cooked meal.

In the quarter of a century since I wrote *Abandoned Prayers*, the Amish have been integrated into our culture in ways that we could not have predicted when Elmer and Erma and I walked into that suburban mall. Today a visit to KFC or McDonald's in Wayne County would surely include an encounter with Amish people. They don't have time to make a home-cooked meal either. When Barbara Weaver needed a birthday cake for her son, she bought one at Walmart. Crime scene photos show it half eaten, still in its plastic package, sitting on the kitchen counter.

Amish Mafia, *Breaking Amish*, and other TV shows have made the Amish more than the subject of curiosity. Today, they've been transformed into a kind of inescapable sideshow. Twenty-five years ago, Lancaster County, Pennsylvania, was the primary Amish tourism mecca. Wayne and Holmes counties were just getting started. Now they're catching up. Many Amish profit from the attention and interest, but on the days they're bombarded by tourists, they surely must feel like creatures in a zoo.

I write all of this with a somewhat heavy heart. The Amish life that I glimpsed when I wrote *Abandoned Prayers* doesn't exist in Ohio anymore except in my memory.

That brings me to the book you're holding in your hands now. When law enforcement and many of the Amish that my coauthor, Rebecca Morris, hoped to interview declined, the excuse was that they didn't want to "hurt the Amish" or "damage the reputation of the Amish." What remained unspoken was that the hurt they wanted to avoid likely had less to do with the feelings of the Amish people than with the commerce that attracts people with their cameras and fat wallets, hoping to bring home something of the simple life to put on the foot of a bed, hang on a wall, or post on Facebook.

Rebecca and I persevered. If no one would speak for Barbara Weaver—if no one will look into how it was that a Mennonite woman like Barb Raber would find herself behind bars at the instigation of her lover, Barbara's husband, Eli Weaver—then we would. Thousands of pages of information provided by the courts and the sheriff's department, including heartbreaking witness statements, helped us tell this story. While not a single member of the Wayne County Sheriff's Office would provide any context or perspective, some outside the department did.

Rebecca and I are immensely grateful for those who broke ranks on both sides of the Weaver murder case. While many of the Amish, former Amish, and Mennonites who spoke with us did not want to be identified by name, they helped with the kind of courage and love that fueled the truth that was so important to Ida Gingerich's family twenty-five years ago. They have our admiration, respect, and profound appreciation.

Two of them deserve special appreciation. We called them "our Amish and Mennonite detectives"—they provided materials, surreptitiously took photographs, and trusted us as we asked questions about the personal lives of the Amish. Both knew Barbara and Eli Weaver.

In addition, we could not have written this book without the cooperation of the brave women who'd been ensnared in Eli Weaver's lie-filled quest for sex. We talked with them not out of some prurient interest in their affairs, but to better understand the man who billed himself as "Amish Stud." They saw the need to alert other women that meeting men online can be dangerous, even if they cloak themselves in the garb of the Plain People.

We also wish to acknowledge Andy Hyde; John Leonard; Edna Boyle; Scott Spidell; Mark Weaver; Steve Chupp; Ella Kay Mast; Ruby Hofstetter; *The Budget*; *The Wooster Daily-Record*; *Family Life*; Ted Cook; Dr. Margaret Adam, Seattle Children's Hospital geneticist and pediatrician, who helped us understand the deaths that colored Barbara Raber's childhood; and the many people who asked to remain anonymous, or were given pseudonyms, who witnessed this terrible tragedy, one compounded by the sudden death of Ed Raber of an apparent heart attack at age thirty-nine on January 6, 2016.

Gregg Olsen
Olalla, Washington

Rebecca Morris
Seattle, Washington
January 2016